SOCIAL PERSPECTIVES
in the History of
ECONOMIC THEORY

SOCIAL PERSPECTIVES

in the History of

ECONOMIC THEORY

by Everett Johnson Burtt, Jr.

St. Martin's Press, New York

Acknowledgments

Chapter ii   Table adapted from Almarin Phillips, *"The Tableau Economique* as a Leontief Model," *Quarterly Journal of Economics,* 69 (1955), 141. Reprinted by permission of the *Quarterly Journal of Economics.*

Chapter v   Excerpts from *Principles of Political Economy* by John Stuart Mill, text edited by J. M. Robson (Collected Works of John Stuart Mill, General Editor: F. E. L. Priestley), © University of Toronto Press 1965. Reprinted by permission of University of Toronto Press and Routledge & Kegan Paul Ltd. Excerpts from *Essays on Economics and Society* by John Stuart Mill, text edited by J. M. Robson (Collected Works of John Stuart Mill, General Editor: F. E. L. Priestley), © University of Toronto Press 1967. Reprinted by permission of University of Toronto Press and Routledge & Kegan Paul Ltd.

Chapter vii   "Table of Diminishing Satisfactions" by Carl Menger, from *Principles of Economics, First, General Part,* trans. and ed. by James Dingwall and Bert F. Hoselitz, with an introduction by Frank H. Knight (Glencoe, Ill.: The Free Press, 1950), p. 127. Reprinted by permission of The Macmillan Company.

Chapter viii   Excerpts from *Principles of Economics,* Vol. I, 9th edition, by Alfred Marshall. Copyright 1948 by The Macmillan Company. Reprinted by permission of The Macmillan Company and Macmillan London and Basingstoke.

Chapter ix   Excerpts from *The General Theory of Employment, Interest, and Money,* by John Maynard Keynes (New York: Harcourt Brace Jovanovich, 1936). Reprinted by permission of Harcourt Brace Jovanovich and Macmillan London and Basingstoke.

Preface

This book is designed to introduce the student of economics and economic theory to the leading economists from the late seventeenth century to the 1930s, men whose theories form part of a rich and complex heritage of economic thought.

Diversities of theory and controversies among economists, as among other social scientists, are inevitable so long as there are different perspectives with regard to the goals and objectives of society. The social and economic facts and values of the real world are many and contradictory. No single interpretation, even one framed within an objectively formulated, quasimathematical logical system, can ever suffice. No one denies that a respectable body of economic theory exists to which many economists subscribe irrespective of their social and political beliefs, but it is also true that social perspectives can and do influence the significance attached to scientific conclusions. The views of those who created and organized basic theoretical systems of economics on the nature and significance of the society they analyzed gave direction to their theories; most of them expressed themselves quite fully on these matters. The objective of this book is to show how the theories of these economists were related to their social and philosophical outlooks and how differences in their theories often stemmed from conflicting evaluations of social priorities.

Although it is impossible to identify here all who have contributed to my own understanding of the history of economics, I would like to express my good fortune in having studied under Professors Joseph J. Spengler and Earl J. Hamilton of Duke University, whose enthusiasm for the history of economic theory was contagious. For suggestions concerning the present manuscript, I wish to thank especially Professors

Kathleen Langley, John J. Hughes, Mark Karp, and Karel Holbik of the Department of Economics of Boston University.

I wish also to thank the Graduate School of Boston University for research assistance and the staffs of the Boston University Mugar Library, the Kress Library of Business and Economics at the Harvard Graduate School of Business Administration, the Library of the University of Toronto, and Cambridge University Library for their help and cooperation. I am particularly indebted to Mr. James Claydon of Cambridge, who clarified a number of points for me.

For help in writing, I thank my wife, Cynthia Webb Burtt, whose literate criticism and historical perspective have been invaluable. Last, but hardly least, thanks are due to Mrs. Jean Whitney, who typed the manuscript.

E. J. B., Jr.

April 1972

Contents

SOCIAL PERSPECTIVES
in the History of
ECONOMIC THEORY

Chapter i

SOURCES OF CONTROVERSY
IN ECONOMIC THEORY

> There is an inescapable *a priori* element in all scientific work.
> Questions must be asked before answers can be given. The ques-
> tions are an expression of our interest in the world, they are
> at bottom valuations.
>
> Gunnar Myrdal, *The Political Element*
> *in the Development of Economic Theory,*
> Preface to the English edition, 1953

I

The history of economic theory is the history of man's attempts to
analyze and understand his economic world—attempts that extend back
to ancient and medieval times. Long before economics became a separate discipline in the latter part of the seventeenth century, social philosophers, ministers of government, and men of affairs struggled to
understand the complexities of the economic behavior of their societies.
Although they advanced various propositions concerning economic behavior, they did not investigate, systematically, the economic aspects
of society as distinct from its political aspects or ethical underpinnings;
nor did they dissociate personal and economic goals. Not surprisingly,
they often disagreed in their analyses and prescriptions of desirable economic policy. Philosophers with different ethical standards, businessmen
with their own personal and organizational goals, would surely arrive at
different conclusions with regard to the nature and significance of economic behavior.

Ever since the seventeenth century, when Sir William Petty first described the field of economics and John Locke claimed that natural laws
governed economic behavior, there have been conflicting theories and

1

schools of economics. Some of the theories and schools have long since faded away; some discredited in one era have been revived in another; while others, for better or for worse, have continued to influence contemporary thinking.

Continued variety in economic analysis should not be surprising. Each age has its own problems of economic organization and of economic relationships among individuals, classes, and governments. In attempting to understand its own economic world, each age uses the tools of analysis in its historical warehouse. If these are inadequate, it invents new ones. Yet not only are there differences among theories from one period to another; at any particular time there is rarely one theory, or set of theories, that is considered definitive. Theories based on different assumptions, with different objectives, and arrived at by different means flourish simultaneously.

The fact that economists differ among themselves, or with their predecessors, does not necessarily mean that their methods are unscientific or that they are not objective in their approach. Three factors contribute to these differences: the difficulty of verifying economic hypotheses; the open-endedness of economic behavior; and, finally, the need for an element of valuation in all economic judgments.

Consider first the problem of verification. A deductive theory is true by definition. But the pertinent question is whether it explains the real world, that is, whether it can predict what will occur or postdict the past by showing that historical events accord with it. Assume two theories, each built upon acceptable but different assumptions, each with its own internally consistent and unassailable logic, but each with opposing conclusions. If economists could experiment under controlled conditions, the question of which theory most successfully explained reality could be tested. Doubters could repeat the experiment themselves. But controlled experiments in economics are generally not possible. The conditions specified for an experiment cannot be made to persist while alternative hypotheses are tried. History cannot be rerun to see if a different monetary policy would have produced greater economic stability. While it is true that modern economics has been developing techniques for examining a group of events to see whether there is sufficient evidence to support a particular hypothesis, the procedure is almost always indirect; the final judgment is almost always conditional.

The open-endedness of economic behavior is a second source of controversy. Economists themselves impose the limits on the area they investigate. Usually an economic action is formally defined as one involving a choice of scarce resources to achieve specified goals, and for most purposes this means activities designed to produce income. In practice, however, the dividing line between economic and noneconomic actions and motives may be drawn differently by different economists. Should goals such as prestige, status, or security, for example, be treated separately from economic motivations (while recognizing that there will be a price for them in terms of resources that must be expended) or should economists push all such considerations aside?

Different decisions on these questions obviously lead to different predictions. Should one expect two prices for the same good to persist in a given retail market? The answer is no, if one assumes that purely economic motivations will override all others. But if habit leads buyers to continue to patronize the firm offering the commodity at a higher price, even though they are aware of the lower-priced alternative, a two-price situation could last indefinitely. If this habitual behavior of the consumer is attributable to noneconomic factors—the friendliness of the clerks at the higher-priced firm, for example—the price differential will measure the magnitude of this noneconomic motive, a differential that could not have been predicted solely on economic grounds.

The third source of controversy in economics is the normative valuations that characterize all analyses of social phenomena. Since ethical norms, value judgments, and philosophical orientations are not amenable to measurement or ranking, a wholly satisfactory bit of analysis considered significant by one economist may be dismissed entirely by another. There is no way by which even an independent and disinterested party can settle the dispute scientifically. Even accredited and honored bodies of academicians, in attempting to evaluate the importance of a scientific discovery, have been known to be surprisingly unreceptive to ideas later deemed important. Leon Walras, one of the world's greatest economists, could not obtain a teaching position in his native France because the authorities did not appreciate his theories. While it is tempting to believe that truth will sooner or later win out, it is important to recognize that each age writes its own history books and stamps upon the contents the value judgments of that age. As these change, so do evaluations of the past. The history of economics is filled with examples of economists whose roles in the development of economics have later been drastically revised.[1] Ricardo demolished Malthus's theory of effec-

[1] References to specific economists are included in the notes after each chapter.

tive demand in the famous glut controversy until John Maynard Keynes, a century later, initiated a small revolution of his own to show that Malthus had been on the right track and Ricardo on the wrong one. The French Physiocrats had been dismissed by generations of economists from Adam Smith on as somewhat interesting but provincial. Yet after a hundred and fifty years it was belatedly recognized that François Quesnay, their founder, had been the first to develop an input-output analysis, a tool that today is of great importance. Sometimes the judgment of history is detrimental even to a generation's own interest. The fact that most economists had rejected blindly such anti-mainstream writers as Sismondi and Karl Marx meant that certain of their insights into the complexities of economic behavior had to be rediscovered in other times and places. Both these writers, for example, used techniques of dynamic analysis, but it was only in the twentieth century that the method won acclaim.

Value judgments affect economists' decisions as to which problems they will analyze, they influence the choice of variables to be included, and they affect the grounds on which the results of investigations are judged. Although the technical problems of verification of hypotheses and the open-endedness of economic behavior are sources of dispute in economic reasoning, conflicts in value judgments are far more fundamental to economic controversy. They affect the method and scope of the science itself.

II

Since the seventeenth century, there have been three stages in the attitude of economists to the place of value judgments in scientific analysis. At first, scientific conclusions were used to support particular governmental policies. The assumption that the value judgments of the economist were desirable for society as a whole to adopt was held not only by the mercantilists, but by the Physiocrats and early classical writers as well. By the end of the nineteenth century, attitudes had reversed. The separation of positive analysis from normative judgments was now held to be the true measure of the growth of a scientific, pure economics. The leading proponents of the new view were Max Weber and Vilfredo Pareto. But by the middle of the twentieth century, the beginnings of a third stage, critical of the methodological orientation of Pareto, had appeared. In the social sciences in general and in economics in particular, it was argued, the valuation process was implicit in all forms of analysis. Among the first of the new critics were Gunnar Myrdal in Sweden and Joan Robinson in Great Britain. In the United States, the new point of view became associated with the criticisms of orthodox economics by John Kenneth Galbraith and more recently with the Union for Radical Political Economics. The position of the Marxists was somewhat ambivalent. Although critical of "scientism" among bourgeois economists, they accepted Marxist economics as "scientific" socialism.

During the first period, which lasted a century and a half, major economists drew no distinction between theory and policy, even though specific analyses were often divorced from considerations of morality, justice, or political or personal advantage. Locke and Petty in England, Francis Hutcheson (who was Adam Smith's teacher in Scotland), and the Physiocrats in France held that economic activities were governed by natural laws and that those laws made possible the scientific study of economic behavior. However, these laws were also viewed as desirable moral laws which, if followed by society, would promote material progress. The natural order was the best possible one; once it was understood, all would see that the divergence of existing political and social institutions from it was the major obstacle to their welfare and would sweep them aside. The view that economic analysis should be divorced from policy was unthinkable to the early writers. They actively promoted doctrines of *laissez-faire,* by which they meant the reform of existing social and political institutions in the interests of greater individual freedom. Locke's analysis of the natural laws that governed interest rates was drawn up to defeat a bill in Parliament. Quesnay's first articles in economics concluded with "Maxims" for government policy. Mercier de la Rivière, a Physiocrat, argued for political liberalism by claiming that in a free economy "the world runs by itself." Although Adam Smith in his *Inquiry into the Nature and Causes of the Wealth of Nations* in 1776 had drifted away somewhat from the philosophy of the benign, natural order, he expressed the vision of economic progress through reform so well that this work has been called one of the major documents of the Enlightenment. To Smith, political economy was the science of the statesman. Although Jeremy Bentham at the turn of the nineteenth century undermined natural law as a basis of economics, he advanced a new philosophy of utility that united economic analysis, morals, and jurisprudence even more firmly than during the heyday of classical economics.

The change in the point of view on policy and economic analysis came during the nineteenth century. Jean Baptiste Say, a critic of the Physiocrats, said in 1803 that a line should be drawn between theory and policy. Although at first British classical economists followed Smith, John Stuart Mill and John E. Cairnes later advanced the idea that the economist as an economist should not, and in fact could not, draw political conclusions. In 1890, John Neville Keynes, a postclassical economist and the father of John Maynard Keynes, distinguished the positive, scientific study of economics from (a) economics applied in order to attain specific objectives within a particular institutional context and (b) the ethical value standards required for policy recommendations.

The "pure science" revolution in economics continued in the twentieth century. Normative content was drained from both ancient and newer economic concepts in the interests of valueless (*Wertfrei*) analysis. Pareto, an Italian, and Weber, a German—both economist-sociologists —were leaders in the new movement. Pareto argued that economics must become a logico-experimental science, with its principles rooted in experience and observation and that it could assume no dogmas, ethical principles, or political exhortations. To Pareto there was no difference between the methodology needed in economics and in natural science.

> Scientific laws are for us . . . nothing more than experimental uniformities. From that point of view there is not the slightest difference between the laws of political economy . . . and the laws of other sciences. . . . [T]he experimental method has had to fight . . . against the methods of introspection, etymology, analysis of verbal expression. . . . In our day the method has been largely banished from the physical sciences. . . . But it is still strutting about in political economy.

Pareto was one of the first economists to argue that hypotheses should be developed for their predictive value and that they should be drawn up in such a way that they could be tested empirically. Thus he stressed the verification problem in economics but claimed its ethical neutrality.

Weber's position was similar but less influential among economists. A *Wertfrei* social science was essential, he said, if social scientists were to avoid confusing the public: "An empirical science cannot tell anyone what he *should* do—but rather what he *can* do." Personal value judgments, unrecognized as such, have in the past affected scientific arguments, bringing "continual confusion."

The new point of view found its clearest expression in a work by Lionel Robbins, *The Nature and Significance of Economic Science,* published in 1932. Economics, said Robbins, deals with the choice of means to achieve given ends. It is "neutral" with regard to the ends themselves, which are value judgments that cannot be scientifically evaluated. In short, the economist cannot say that inflation or deflation is good or bad; he can only point to their consequences without making any editorial comment. He can advise others how to attain their goals, although for personal reasons he may of course refuse to advise someone whose goals he does not support.

This position of ethical neutrality has been challenged, essentially on the grounds that positive economic propositions may in fact have normative implications. Moreover, those implicit value judgments may be more insidious when advanced as scientific conclusions. For example, take the question "Does competition promote maximum welfare?" Yes, say the positivists, presenting arguments to show how equalization of the marginal products of factors of production and equality of costs and prices will yield an optimum equilibrium position, defined in terms of the efficient output of goods at current prices. Critics answer that this argument has normative content similar to the arguments that characterized the older classical economics. The unstated conclusion is still a sermon to the effect that the competitive system is best, and this conclusion is no more valid than any other value judgment. One compelling argument for the critics is the distribution aspect of every allocation problem. A different distribution of resources among individuals will lead to a different pattern of resource allocation; what was efficient is now inefficient. Thus to advance a competitive solution for a particular economy at a particular time on positive grounds is also to support a particular distribution of wealth and hence an implicit value judgment.

The difficulty of recognizing implicit value judgments in positive economics is revealed by the experience of Gunnar Myrdal, whose book *The Political Element in the Development of Economic Theory* was first published in 1929. Myrdal was concerned with the political implications, both implicit and explicit, in the history of economic theory. As he stated in the Preface to the Swedish edition, he found an inconsistency in the theories of Knut Wicksell, that country's famous marginalist. Wicksell argued that the chief cause of dissension in economics was "divergent views and a more or less acute sense of what *ought to be the goal* of the economic evolution of society." He concluded that one should eliminate normative ideas. But at the same time, Myrdal claimed, Wicksell proclaimed the hope that the method of political economy led to "the greatest possible measure of happiness [for] all human beings—of whatever class, race, sex, language or creed." This contradiction between the positive and normative, Myrdal believed in 1929, could only be resolved by a determined effort to eliminate metaphysical elements from positive economics.

Nearly a quarter of a century later, Myrdal changed his mind. In the Preface to the English edition of his book, written in 1953, he admitted a new point of view: "This implicit belief in the existence of a body of scientific knowledge acquired independently of all valuations is, as I now see it, naive empiricism." Without a priori theories, "there are no scientific facts but only chaos." Yet such a theory requires by definition an initial valuation. Social judgments are necessary for observing and analyzing, as well as for drawing political conclusions. Economics, no matter how positivist, cannot escape the valuation process.

The social revelance of the valuation systems of the men who frame theories and draw inferences becomes, then, a fundamental issue in economic theory. It underlies the controversies discussed in the subsequent chapters.

Notes to Chapter i

I

Among the general works on the history of economic theory the most comprehensive and authoritative by far is Joseph A. Schumpeter's *History of Economic Analysis* (New York, Oxford University Press, 1954). A reader does not have to agree with Schumpeter's interpretations to discover and enjoy his scholarly insights. Other good histories for general reference are Eric Roll's *A History of Economic Thought*, 3rd ed. (Englewood Cliffs, N. J., Prentice-Hall, 1956), and Fred M. Bell's *A History of Economic Thought*, 2nd ed. (New York, Ronald Press, 1967).

For a discussion of general problems of methodology and the nature of the science of economics, see Sherman Roy Krupp, ed., *The Structure of Economic Science: Essays on Methodology* (Englewood Cliffs, N. J., Prentice-Hall, 1966).

References to the works of specific economists cited in this section will be found in subsequent chapters.

II

The brief quotation from the French Physiocrat Mercier de la Rivière (p. 5) is from his *L'ordre naturel et essentiel des sociétés politiques* (1767). See E. Daire, ed., *Physiocrates* (Paris, Librairie de Guillaume, 1848), vol. II, p. 617.

Adam Smith's definition of political economy, which appears in the Introduction to Book IV of his *Inquiry into the Nature and Causes of the Wealth of Nations* (1776), was as follows:

Political oeconomy, considered as a branch of the science of a statesman or legislator, proposes two distinct objects: first, to provide a plentiful revenue or subsistence for the people, or more properly to enable them to provide such a revenue or subsistence for themselves; and secondly, to supply the state or commonwealth with a revenue sufficient for the public services. It proposes to enrich both the people and the sovereign. (See the Edwin Cannan edition of *The Wealth of Nations,* New York, Modern Library, 1937, p. 397.)

Said Peter Gay, in *The Enlightenment: An Interpretation,* vol. II: *The Science of Freedom* (New York, Knopf, 1969), p. 368: "Indeed, in its total intellectual style, *The Wealth of Nations* is a cardinal document of the Enlightenment."

Jean Baptiste Say's *Traité d'économie politique (Treatise on Political Economy),* first published in 1803, was a popular work, and the 1821 English translation (based on the fourth edition) was widely used in the United States.

John Neville Keynes's work on methodology, *The Scope and Method of Political Economy* (1890), became the standard book on the subject for the period identified as neoclassical, a period dominated by Alfred Marshall (whose *Principles of Economics* was published in the same year). Both J. N. Keynes and Marshall taught at Cambridge.

Pareto's methodological position is found in various writings. His article "On the Economic Phenomenon, A Reply to Benedetto Croce," originally published in the *Giornale degli Economisti* in 1900, is still of general interest. For an English version, see International Economic Papers, No. 3, translations prepared for the International Economic Association (London, Macmillan, 1953). A sys-

tematic analysis of Pareto's position is made by Vincent J. Tarascio in *Pareto's Approach to Economics: A Study in the History of Some Scientific Aspects of Economic Thought* (Chapel Hill, University of North Carolina Press, 1968). Tarascio also compares Pareto and Weber. The quotation from Pareto on page 6 is from *The Mind and Society,* vol. I, translated and edited by Arthur Livingston (New York, Harcourt Brace Jovanovich, 1935), pp. 52, 59. For the quotation from Weber (p. 6), see his *Methodology of the Social Sciences,* translated and edited by E. A. Shils and H. A. Finch (Glencoe, Ill., Free Press, 1949), p. 54.

In addition to Lionel Robbins' *Essay on the Nature and Significance of Economic Science* (London, Macmillan, 1932), which was written in the spirit of Pareto and Weber, there is a more recent study by T. W. Hutchison, *"Positive" Economics and Policy Objectives* (London, Allen and Unwin, 1964).

Gunnar Myrdal's *The Political Element in the Development of Economic Theory,* translated from the German by Paul Streeten, was published in paperback by Simon and Schuster in 1969. The quotations on pp. 7–8 are from pp. xv and vii, respectively. Myrdal points out that his major research work in the United States, *An American Dilemma—The Negro Problem and Modern Democracy* (1944), played an important role in the change in his position.

Joan Robinson is another economist who has emphasized the role of value judgments in economics: "Perhaps the position is different in the respectable sciences, but, so far as the investigation of psychological and social problems is concerned, metaphysics has played an important, perhaps an indispensable role." (*Economic Philosophy: An Essay on the Progress of Economic Thought*, Garden City, N. Y., Doubleday, 1964, p. 3.) By metaphysics, she means valuations that are unprovable. A metaphysical proposition is "not capable of being tested"; hence it is not a scientific proposition. But it is still a "quarry from which hypotheses can be drawn." (*ibid.*)

Chapter ii

NATURAL-LAW ECONOMICS:

From Petty to Quesnay

. . . it is certain there is such a Law [of Nature] as intelligible and plain to a rational Creature and a Studier of that Law, as the positive Laws of Common-wealths, nay possibly plainer . . . .

> John Locke, *Two Treatises of Government*

We must consider in general, that as wiser Physicians tamper not excessively with their Patients, rather observing and complying with the motions of nature, then contradicting it with vehement Administrations of their own; so in Politicks and Oeconomicks the same must be used.

> Sir William Petty, *Economic Writings*

Positive legislation consists . . . in the declaration of natural laws that constitute the order clearly the most advantageous possible to men joined in society, and one can say quite simply the most advantageous possible to the sovereign, because what is really the most advantageous to the sovereign is [that which is] most advantageous to his subjects. It is only the knowledge of these supreme laws that can assure with constancy the peace and prosperity of an empire.

> François Quesnay, "Le Droit naturel," *François Quesnay et la Physiocratie*

During the seventeenth and eighteenth centuries, a unique combination of forces prepared the way for the new science of political economy. One was the scientific revolution that overturned the ancient categories of physics, astronomy, biology, and mathematics, emphasized observation and experimentation, and promoted a congenial climate for the development of new, imaginative hypotheses. The second was the increasing importance of the market economy, colonial trade expansion, and, in the eighteenth century, the beginnings of the technological revolution, first in agriculture and then in industry. The third force at work was the growth of the philosophy of natural law and natural rights, which made the individual's welfare and property the new measuring rod of governmental policy.

The scientific revolution furnished models of methodology for the new science of economics, the expansion of capitalism and the resultant social conflicts defined the scope, and the natural-law and natural-rights philosophy established a value system for ordering fact and theory.

The idea of economic analysis as a separate field was something new. True, economic concepts had been developed and theoretical relationships between them posited by the medieval writers and even the ancient Greeks. For example, Aristotle's differentiation between two values of a good, its use value and its exchange value, remained part of economic theory until the middle of the nineteenth century. But economics as a science dealing with a class of data that is not wholly within the province of other fields of knowledge and that is subject to stable and logically consistent laws—in short, modern economics—began only in the seventeenth and eighteenth centuries.

The unique development that made this new approach possible was the rise of individualism, or the toleration of, and creation of opportunities for, individual expression and desires for betterment. Negatively, individualism could be viewed not only as a separation but even as an alienation of the individual from society. The market economy was creating an economic division by placing the individual in a position of greater dependence upon objective market forces. The natural-law and natural-rights philosophy expressed the individual's political separation from, and even opposition to, the state.

This transformation in the way individuals could view their relation to the world made it possible to envisage an objective social science of economic behavior. The new discoveries in the natural and biological sciences fostered a new excitement in intellectual circles both in England and France during this period, and it seemed logical to believe that the marketplace too could be shown to exhibit regularities of behavior that could be expressed by laws; that such laws could be examined and compared; that, in short, a science of economics was feasible. Moreover, science was also leading to many practical inventions; the idea that scientific principles could be applied in useful ways was carried over into economics. It is interesting that three of the first writers who viewed economics as a discipline—Petty, Locke, and Quesnay—had been trained in medicine.

A number of writers rose to the challenge of investigating economic behavior. In England during the seventeenth century, Sir William Petty was the first to stake out, somewhat hesitantly, a new science which he called "political arithmetick." John Locke seems to have assumed such a science, although he was more concerned with the independence of the individual from the state. With the eighteenth century, new attempts to describe the field of economics increased, as did the sophistication of the analyses. In France, there were the writings of Boisguillebert (1695, 1707), Richard Cantillon's *Essai sur la nature du commerce en général* (written before 1735 but published in 1755), François Quesnay and his followers, the Physiocrats (Quesnay's first article appeared in 1755), Anne Robert Jacques de Turgot's essay on wealth (published in 1770; in book form in 1776). In Great Britain, the new approach to economics as a field found expression in the economic essays of David Hume (1752), Sir James Steuart's *Principles of Political Economy* (1767), and Adam Smith's *Inquiry into the Nature and Causes of the Wealth of Nations* (1776).

In the development of any new approach, it is not to be expected that individual writers will arrive at similar conclusions. Differences in approach and interests give their work a different orientation, even though all attempted to create a set of principles with which to examine reality as they saw it. Moreover, one would not expect all writers to advocate similar policies solely because they all view economic behavior as a separate discipline. At one time, historians of economic theory did not look beyond Adam Smith for the beginnings of economic theory; it was assumed that only a mercantilist wasteland of erroneous theories and policies had previously existed. That point of view, originally fostered by Smith himself, has fortunately faded. Present historians of science recognize that it is the attempt to build a theoretical system that marks the beginning of a discipline, not its content, or the policies it supports, or even the internal consistency of its doctrines.

Not all the attempts to frame a systematic theory of economics during these two centuries will be discussed here.[1] In this chapter, three

---

[1] Turgot's work is touched on in this chapter in connection with the Physiocrats; Hume's and Steuart's works are considered in Chapter 3 in relationship to Adam Smith's.

Of Boisguillebert and Cantillon—both of whose works are reviewed briefly in the chapter notes—the latter wrote by far the most systematic writers, Petty, Locke, and Quesnay, will be reviewed; in Chapter 3, Smith's system, the most influential of the early ones, will be discussed. What characterizes the first three writers is the relevance and use of natural-law theory in their economic approach. It was this approach in which Smith was raised and which he later modified.

I

Sir William Petty (1623–87) was the first to describe explicitly the field of economics and consciously to apply scientific methods to its study. In terms of content, he was the first to express a form of the labor theory of value and the concept of differential rent, both of which later became major analytical propositions of the British classical school. He had several followers, two of whom, Charles Davenant and Gregory King, achieved widespread recognition.

Petty's education was part practical and part classical; he studied both abroad and in England. His medical studies led to his initial appointment as professor of anatomy at Oxford and in 1652 to a post as Physician-General to the English army during the Irish campaign. Following this conflict, he became the official surveyor of Irish lands forfeited by the rebels for distribution to English soldiers—an operation that led to interminable lawsuits which plagued him for the rest of his life and which also turned his attention to economics. Petty became immersed in Restoration finance. His study of taxes, economic relationships with Ireland, and the trade wars with the French and Dutch led to his first book, *A Treatise of Taxes and Contributions,* published anonymously in 1662. Other books followed, although many did not appear until after the Revolution of 1688. *Political Arithmetick,* written in 1676 and published posthumously, gave his definition of the field of economics and laid down the scientific method he believed so important. *The Political Anatomy of Ireland* (written in 1672 and published in 1691) reflected his medical training, his Irish experience, and his interest in economics. He also wrote *Verbum Sapienti* (1664), in which he attempted to measure the worth of the people of England, and

---

analysis of economic behavior before the Physiocrats. But as his *Essai* circulated only privately, in manuscript form, before 1755, it had little public influence. The Marquis de Mirabeau, Quesnay's loyal supporter, and Turgot (through his teacher, the Viscount de Gournay) had evidently read it. Quesnay may have been influenced by Cantillon's work, but there were many substantial differences in theory between the two, and it was Quesnay's type of analysis that dominated the Physiocratic period.

Quantulumcumque Concerning Money (written in 1682 and published posthumously in 1695).

The three forces described earlier—the new scientific methodology, natural-law theory, and economic analysis—were uniquely joined in Petty's life. As a medical student on the continent, he had learned of the impact that Harvey's discovery of the circulation of blood had in revolutionizing medical theory, met Thomas Hobbes, and perhaps been introduced to the scientific circle of Friar Mersenne, which included, among others, Descartes and Pascal. He became acquainted with the philosophy and scientific methodology of Sir Francis Bacon (1561–1626), the indefatigable exponent of experimentation and induction. Bacon's overall objective was to show the fallacies of existing schools of thought and to prepare the foundation for reconstructed sciences that would restore the sovereignty of man over nature. The desired scientific method was induction. This was first the systematic, objective collection of information by observation and planned experimentation, and then the drawing of axioms, or laws, of higher and higher levels of generalization. The older, misleading axioms of science, he believed, rested on scanty evidence and blind experimentation.

Bacon's influence was strong at Oxford, where Samuel Hartlib and Robert Boyle, both Bacon admirers, were able to translate his hopes into the reality by founding the Royal Society, an organization dedicated to the promotion of science. Petty was friendly with both Hartlib and Boyle and became a charter member of the society in 1662.

As for his political philosophy, Petty had been a friend of Thomas Hobbes, the defender of the all-powerful state, and had worked for and been honored by Charles II during the Restoration. His allegiance to the idea of an absolute monarchy was not inconsistent with the belief in individualism inherent in the new systems of economic analysis. Neither Petty's nor the Physiocrats' embrace of the monarch affected their assumption that the individual, especially the man of property, had certain economic rights; on the contrary, they believed that a powerful monarchy was the most efficient way of protecting those rights. So did Hobbes. Hobbes, who wrote *The Elements of Law, Natural and Politic* in 1640 and published *De cive* in 1642 and *Leviathan* in 1651, argued for absolute political power precisely because he feared that without it the rights of individuals to happiness and even to sheer survival would be destroyed. In the state of nature, each man seeks what he wishes; but as all are equal, each seeking his own goals leads to a war between all men. As the fact of war or threats of war become unbearable, men on rational grounds, said Hobbes, will then by social contract choose a government with the power to maintain order. Hobbes favored an absolute monarchy; he speeded the publication of *De cive* in 1642, he said, because he foresaw the civil wars that were to rack England because governmental power was not absolute.

The individual rights that Hobbes, and also Petty, sought to protect were already being described as the right of individuals to follow their own interests, to make profits, and to use their property as they saw fit. In the sixteenth century, some writers were already defending such rights as legitimate. John Hales, the reputed author of the *Discourse of the Common Weal of this Realm of England,* spoke of the profit motive as a guide to man's actions which governments should heed. The seventeenth-century mercantilists, among them Thomas Mun, Thomas Papillon, and Joseph Lee, believed that the laws of nature governed the actions of traders and that governments should respect such laws. To Petty, and to Hobbes, government was designed not to override those interests but to preserve them.

It was Petty's concern with the problems of Restoration finance that linked his scientific approach and his belief in the importance of individual rights. His *Treatise of Taxes and Contributions* was concerned with the burden of taxes. How could the government raise funds justly and without injuring the individual's future ability to pay? Petty's answer was proportional taxation of individuals' "estates or riches." To know what burden individuals could carry and to eliminate the arbitrary tax assessments productive of injustice, it was necessary to find out how much wealth people possessed. He turned with enthusiasm to the collection of statistics on national wealth and income. Although most of his statistics rested on the slimmest of estimates, he attempted in *Verbum Sapienti* to measure the value of England's wealth and income, and even the value of her people.[2] In *The Political Anatomy of Ireland* (1672), he estimated that country's national wealth, revealed the depths of her poverty, and went on to show how incomes could be raised by an expansion of manufacturing. In *Political Arithmetick,* he attempted to measure the relative wealth and income of England, France, and Hol-

---

[2] Petty put the total value of the country's physical wealth at £250 million. He then assumed that £15 million of the total £40 million of national income was a return on this physical wealth. Using the same interest rate (six percent), he capitalized the remaining £25 million as a return to labor. Thus the value of the country's manpower was £416⅔ million, making manpower more important than physical wealth.

land to show that England's position had not, as some writers had charged, slipped.

In the new scientific spirit of Sir Francis Bacon, Petty now came to his definition of the emerging field of study. In *Political Arithmetick* he committed himself to findings expressed in terms of "number, weight, or measure, to use only arguments of sense; consider only such causes as have visible foundations in nature," leaving "those that depend on the mutable minds, opinions, appetites and passions of particular men to the consideration of others."

Political Arithmetick stimulated statistical studies in England. Although its authorship is in some dispute, *National and Political Observations upon the Bills of Mortality,* one of the first works in demography, is now generally attributed to John Graunt rather than Petty. Graunt was, however, Petty's friend, and Petty undoubtedly influenced him and may have collaborated actively with him. Gregory King's estimates of the English population in 1688 are still considered authoritative. King also produced a pioneering quantitative study of the demand schedule for corn that was not appreciated until the twentieth century. Political arithmetic, however, later fell out of favor; and Adam Smith's deprecatory comment concerning it in 1776 served to further dampen interest in quantitative economic analysis.

None of Petty's hypotheses had more effect on the subsequent development of economics than his labor theory of value, a theory whose implications were not fully understood for another two centuries. Petty's theory evolved from his examination of the politically explosive problems of taxation in Restoration England. He first considered the basic causes of wealth. Not unexpectedly, given the society of his day, he found two, labor and land: "Labour is the Father and active principle of Wealth, as Lands are the Mother." (*Treatise,* I, p. 68) This proposition could be interpreted in two ways: as meaning that both factors were equally important or that labor is the determining factor, and "lands" only a passive one. Petty himself interpreted it both ways but generally ran into trouble with the first approach. The problem was that it seemed essential, in Petty's view, to establish a par of exchange between labor and land like that between gold and silver. This was difficult to do, for although land had a market value, that value was a capitalization of land rents at a going rate of interest. What determined rents, and what determined the rate of interest? As Petty was searching for explanations more fundamental than monetary forces, he switched to the second interpretation, that it was the quantity of labor required to produce goods which determined their value. Given normal conditions, labor established the "natural" price of a good:

> If a man can bring to London an ounce of silver out of the earth in Peru, in the same time that he can produce a bushel of corn, then one is the natural price of the other; now if by reason of new and more easie mines a man can get two ounces of silver as easily as formerly he did one, then corn will be as cheap as ten shillings the bushel, as it was before at five shillings *caeteris paribus*. (*ibid*. I, pp. 50–51)

Petty used the same hypothesis in another connection: The "Wealth, Stock, or Provision of the Nation," he said, was the "effect of the former or past labour." (*Verbum Sapienti,* I, p. 110)

It is perhaps idle to speculate whether Petty was aware of the political implications of his analysis. What he was saying was that in the highly structured society of his day, dominated by the landed nobility, the labor of workers, merchants, and artisans gave them a prior claim, as both a cause and a measure of wealth, on the national income. This was a natural law that should not be ignored by kings or nobles. Petty was not really challenging regal authority. Kings, he believed, would govern better if they recognized the true nature of wealth.

This interpretation of Petty's position is supported by his own emphasis on the stability of the value of goods as determined by labor. He compared their natural price with the market, or "political," price, as he called it. The latter fluctuated temporarily due to changes in demand and supply; the former tended to prevail in the long run.

Petty's argument that land rents were a surplus and not a true cost of production was related to his theory of value. He argued that the cultivation of land for the production of corn (i.e., grain) required outlays for seed, other expenses, and the farmers' own subsistence. When these costs (in corn) are deducted from the yield there remains a surplus which is the "natural and true rent." This surplus of real goods that arose in agriculture was price-determined, not price-determining. As the value of land was simply the capitalization of rents at the going rate of interest, land values, the economic basis of the nobility and gentry, were dependent upon natural economic forces over which they had little or no control.

Despite his allegiance to Bacon's inductive method, Petty's theories were neither logically worked out nor tested empirically and systematically. He later modified his own theory of value by stating that it was not the quantity of labor that determined value but rather the daily food requirement of the adult male. In this way he attempted to establish a relationship between land and labor as joint determinants of value. He was unsuccessful because lands of differing fertilities produced different quantities of food, and his device of averaging production over a period of time was unsatisfactory.

Even though he might have been hard-pressed to support his case with a specific, logical argument, Petty strongly believed that he could generalize the conclusions of his natural-law approach to economic behavior. He did not believe that governments should regulate interest rates; he argued that regulation would not work because of "the vanity and fruitlessness of making Civil Positive Laws against the Laws of Nature. . . ." (*Treatise*, I, p. 48) In a discussion of Dutch competition, he claimed that the low interest rates there were an "effect" of that country's wealth and "not the Fruit of their contrivance." (*Political Arithmetick*, I, p. 261) As for laws prohibiting the exportation of money and bullion, he claimed that such laws were "against the Laws of Nature, and also impracticable." (*Quantulumcunque*, II, p. 445)

One can speculate that Petty was interpreting the experience of civil laws that failed to achieve their objectives as evidence of underlying forces that he called natural. "We must consider in general," he said, "that as wiser Physicians tamper not excessively with their Patients, rather observing and complying with the motions of nature, then contradicting it with vehement Administrations of their own; so in Politics and Oconomicks the same must be used." (*Treatise*, I, p. 60) Petty was by no means an ardent advocate of *laissez-faire*, ready to let the market settle all questions. Like a good physician, he would tamper with the economy when necessary, but he would act only in accordance with the natural laws that independently controlled it.

Petty did not advance a theory of economic progress. Such a theory came later. The point is important because Petty, through his inductive generalizations, had correctly perceived the building blocks of the theory of progress. Like the Physiocrats in the following century, he felt that increasing agricultural output through technological change would expand the wealth and income of the nation. (*Verbum Sapiente*, I, p. 118) Like Adam Smith nearly a century later, Petty extolled the virtues of increased productivity through the division of labor in manufacturing (*Another Essay in Political Arithmetick*, 1682, II, p. 473) as well as the advantages of large urban industrial concentrations. Petty urged inventiveness (he made several practical inventions of his own) and believed government should subsidize the cost of education and research for the advancement of knowledge. (*Treatise,* I, p. 20) His embryonic benefit-cost analyses for government outlays indicated yet another way government could promote progress. (His analysis of the costs of the plague that struck London in 1665 and the benefits that could have been obtained had it been avoided are described in *Verbum Sapienti,* I, pp. 109ff.)

But Petty did not put the blocks together; the idea of progress had not yet been born. Although a case was being made for government support of the individual's pursuit of material goals, the idea that individualism, if given free rein, would create an upsurge in material benefits for society as a whole did not come until the eighteenth century.

II

John Locke (1632–1704) is well-known for his philosophy of empiricism and his political theories of natural law and natural rights; he is less well-recognized for his theories of economics. Although incomplete, they also reflected his belief in natural laws based on human behavior that had predictive value and could be generalized. Locke's approach to economics was scientific. Raised in the academic tradition, he studied at Christ Church, Oxford, and became a lecturer in moral philosophy. However, he also studied medicine, knew Boyle and other Oxonian scientists, and was a member of the Royal Society. Appointed family physician to Lord Ashley, later the Earl of Shaftesbury, Locke became an advisor on economics and other matters of state policy. It was in a 1668 memorandum prepared for Lord Ashley on proposed interest-rate legislation that he first applied natural-law assumptions to economic analysis. But this concern with economics was soon overshadowed by his interest in politics. Political unrest and the Reaction of 1683 drove him into voluntary exile in Holland. It was upon his return to England after the Revolution that he established his preeminence in philosophy with his *Essay Concerning Human Understanding* (1690). At the same time he published *Two Treatises of Government,* his major work in political theory, but the book appeared anonymously and Locke's authorship did not become generally known until after his death.

In the early 1690s Locke returned to a consideration of economic problems as an advisor to Lord Somers, Lord Chancellor under William III, and as a member of the powerful Board of Trade. In the interest-rate controversy which reemerged as a Parliamentary issue, Locke expanded his earlier memorandum opposing the reduction in the legal interest rate into *Some Considerations of the Consequences of the Lowering of Interest and Raising the Value of Money* (1691). In a paper on money in 1695, he contributed to the debate over recoinage and influenced the legislation passed the following year.

Locke's scientific approach to economics stemmed from his interest in the revolution in the natural sciences, especially medicine, and from his early studies in natural law. The legitimacy of the application of scientific reasoning to social problems seemed to him indisputable. In his 1668 memorandum on interest rates, he spoke of the "natural" rate of interest, and of laws of the market which could be known and analyzed. The exchange values of goods were "intrinsic," determined by supply and demand (which he called scarcity and vent). He held that money was subject to the "same laws of value." The *prices* of goods (in contrast to their *values*) were set by the amount of money in circulation relative to the amount of goods. Although this quantity theory of money had been expressed a century earlier by Jean Bodin, Locke gave it a new dimension when he said that the "quickness" of circulation of money also affected its value. This velocity was, he added, in turn related to the expenditure patterns of the public, including their liquidity preferences. All these relationships Locke considered "natural," and not to be violated by positive laws.

Locke's attack on proposed legislation to reduce the interest rate also used natural-law terminology. In both the late 1660s and early 1690s, the proposal to reduce the maximum legal rate of interest from six to four percent had been advanced as the best means of improving England's position in world trade, especially with respect to the Dutch. Sir Josiah Child, the head of the East India Company, had supported the reduction on the grounds that the lower rate would encourage traders, enable them to meet foreign competition, and stimulate employment. In short, low interest rates could lead to an increase in England's national wealth.

Locke's reply, both in his 1668 memorandum and later in 1691, showed his confidence in the power of natural laws. Low interest rates were the result of wealth, not its cause. The legal rate should be set in accordance with the natural (i.e., market) rate, because it cannot be regulated in any other way. ". . . it will be impossible, by any contrivance of law, to hinder men, skilled in the power they have, over their own goods . . . to purchase money to be lent them, at what rate soever their occasions shall make it necessary for them to have it." Man borrows not from pleasure but from need and will pay proportionately. The skillful "will always so manage . . . to avoid the prohibition of your law."

A legal reduction in interest below the natural rate would also create injustice. While bankers and others would pocket gains by avoiding the law, the "uninstructed," such as widows and orphans, would receive only what the law allowed. As a law contrary to people's interests would be evaded, perjury would be rewarded; and "faith and truth," that "great bond of society," would be undermined. Finally, he said, an arbitrary reduction would be injurious. If the interest rate is below the natural rate, some lenders will "chuse rather to hoard up their money than venture it abroad." This will lead to a decline in trade, especially in foreign exports, and a loss of gold and silver to the nation. With a reduction in the domestic monetary supply, ultimately the rate of interest must rise.

Locke's analysis of the market mechanism was innovative, but how did it relate to the natural law? His belief in such laws may have given him confidence and inspired others; at least the bill in Parliament did not pass. How did one know what the natural laws were? Or was the use of the word "natural" simply conventional and idiomatic, as the use of "naturally" is today?

Presumably Locke himself would have been able to answer this question. His *Essay Concerning Human Understanding* is concerned precisely with epistemology, or the theory of knowledge. Yet it was in this regard that Locke the philosopher denied what Locke the natural-law theorist asserted. As a philosopher of understanding in the British empirical tradition begun by Bacon and continued by Hume and Mill, Locke reasoned that man learned only through his senses. Man was a *tabula rasa,* with no innate ideas. As it was to his own interest to do whatever would permit him to avoid pain and increase his gains, he would learn about the world by experience. Although Locke stated that natural laws might exist, his psychological theories essentially excluded them on the grounds that they were innate ideas, not perceivable by the senses.

But Locke as a political theorist contradicted this view. He did not use experience to justify the existence of natural laws. In *Two Treatises of Government,* he claimed that natural laws and natural rights existed prior to the formation of governments, prior to recorded human knowledge itself. They could be known only through reason. "The Law of Nature . . . is the Law of Reason." In one stroke, he made reason, not experience, the source of knowledge about the laws of nature, on which he rested his case for representative democracy, the institution of private property, men's right to act in their own self-interest, and all the rest of the value judgments associated with the philosophy of economic individualism. According to Locke the political theorist, all men were the handiwork of God and therefore free and equal. Unlike Hobbes, he believed there was a fundamental order to social life, the effect of natural laws that manifested themselves in the state of nature, before governments were formed. Yet governments built upon the consent of rational men were necessary to interpret and enforce the law of reason and to preserve lives, liberty, and property. Locke's celebrated theory of property rested upon his belief that as man had property in his own person, in his labor and the work of his own hands, whatever he mixed his labor with became his property. Although this concept is juridical and not an economic theory of value, Locke seems to have had something like a labor explanation of value in mind. "Labour indeed" he says, "puts the difference of value on every thing."

In his economics, Locke did not resolve the contradiction in the interpretation of what is "natural" as what is an observable regularity of behavior and what is natural because it is reasonable. The empirical approach assumed that economic laws were tentative, hypothetical, and subject to test. The rational approach meant that laws were final, absolute, and incontrovertible. Later writers who used natural-law concepts were no more successful than Locke in escaping this ambiguity.

III

The natural-law approach to economics found its most complete expression in France in the eighteenth-century writings of François Quesnay and his followers. This group became the first school of economists; they advanced a theoretical system of economic analysis and economic policy to which they gave the name Physiocracy, the rule of nature.

Quesnay (1694–1774), a surgeon and writer of essays on medicine, first came to Versailles in 1749 as a physician (to Madame de Pompadour and later to Louis XV). He was over sixty years of age when he became interested in agricultural and economic matters. He wrote his first analyses of economic problems, "Fermiers" and "Grains," for Diderot's *Encyclopédie* in 1756 and 1757 respectively. Not wishing to indulge his position as royal physician, he signed his son's name to the articles. His analytical *Tableau économique,* which contained a flow diagram of the French economy, was published in 1758 and 1759 in three different editions. His other writings consisted of explanations and defenses of the *Tableau,* statements of government policy, and shorter articles; he wrote no single treatise.

Quesnay had many able disciples, of whom the Marquis de Mirabeau (1715–1789) was one of the most important. Mirabeau had written a popular commentary on French economic conditions, entitled *L'Ami des hommes ou traité de la population,* in 1756 but became convinced that Quesnay's position was more scientific. An energetic and voluble spokesman, he praised Quesnay's *Tableau* as the third most important invention in the world (after writing and money) and recruited others to the Physiocratic cause. He wrote *Théorie de l'impot* in 1760 and *Philosophie rurale,* a textbook of Physiocracy, in 1763.

Other members of the school included Mercier de la Rivière, who wrote on Physiocratic political and philosophical doctrines; DuPont de Nemours, the able editor of the Physiocratic journal *Les Ephémérides* (who later came to the United States); Le Trosne, a lawyer; and the Abbé Baudeau.

Anne Robert Jacques de Turgot (1727–81), who as Comptroller-General held the highest government post in France from 1774 to 1776, was only partially associated with the Physiocratic school. He attended some of their meetings and helped support their publications, but he maintained a distance from them intellectually and differed with them on a number of theoretical points. His principal work, *Réflexions sur la formation et la distribution des richesses,* was written in 1766. It was published in *Ephémérides* in 1770 and in book form in 1776.

When Quesnay turned to economics, his approach was that of a physician examining a sick patient. The economy of France was ailing, the masses were impoverished, there was little hope of improvement either in rural or urban areas, and the financial position of the crown was going from bad to worse. Like Petty and Locke, Quesnay the physician sought to make a diagnosis and offer prescriptions consistent with the laws that governed healthy bodies. But unlike the seventeenth-century natural-law economists, he did not want simply to restore the patient to good economic health; he wanted to make France better and better.

The eighteenth century vision was revolutionary: Unlimited progress in terms of physical, economic, and even intellectual well-being was considered desirable, possible, even inevitable. Welfare in this world was a worthy goal, with which worries about spiritual welfare in the next world need not interfere. The basis of this new attitude was the scientific revolution, which opened up the vista of a continuously growing body of knowledge that could be used to benefit society, and a belief in the perfectibility of man and his institutions. The prognostication of future progress was based on the further assumption that man's reason would enable him to advance such compelling arguments for institutional reform that the weight of public opinion would bring about the required transformations.

The idea of progress permeated the writings of the Physiocrats. Turgot had expressed the idea of man's perfectibility in his *Discourses* (1750). He was one of the earliest French writers on this theme (the first being the Abbé de Saint Pierre). But it was Quesnay's version that most Physiocrats followed. In his article "Natural Right," Quesnay began, as others of his day did, with a supreme being who fashioned the natural order and its laws, which are "immutable and indisputable and the best laws possible" and the "foundation of the most perfect government." (II, p. 740) Human legislation must conform with these laws, or the penalty for transgressions will be social and economic ills.

Although Quesnay's followers assumed that their master had somehow "revealed" those natural economic laws, Quesnay himself was hardpressed to justify his version of the laws of nature, especially when critics read the book of nature differently. His argument was the modified Cartesian one that "evidence" came through reason and ultimately through divine revelation. ("Evidence," II, p. 423) Although he believed that empirical information obtained through the senses also supported his theories, the natural-law argument was uppermost. Whether it promoted or hindered acceptance of Physiocracy at the time is debatable. Later the argument was recognized as irrelevant. But the system of natural law nevertheless helped give direction to Quesnay's theoretical curiosity and guide his analysis.

Quesnay translated the new and spreading idea of progress into a theory of economic growth. This theory consisted of a capital-investment mechanism in agriculture that increased productivity, a macro analysis of intersectoral commodity and money flows, and a program of governmental reform. The overall theory was related to the French economy both structurally and quantitatively. The population was divided into three key economic categories: farmers (tenants), proprietors (landowners), and the merchants and manufacturers ("the sterile classes"). Quesnay then attempted to estimate actual output and rents (the net product of France) and to indicate how much they would increase if conditions were the "best possible."

Quesnay's theory that economic growth results from capital investment in agriculture was based on the assumption that agriculture alone was productive, since it alone produced an economic surplus. As wages, interest, and profits under competitive conditions to entrepreneurs (whether farmers, artisans, or merchants) were costs, and as rents in agriculture were the only true surplus, agriculture was, by definition, the only truly productive economic activity. The Physiocrats called land rents "the net product"—the gift of God. Although trade and manufacturing paid their own way by recovering their costs, they did not yield rents and hence were unproductive. (The Physiocrats called such industries "sterile," a term hardly designed to win support from the business community.) Quesnay found empirical data that he believed justified his assumption of the productivity of agriculture. Writing at a time when the new agricultural techniques were proving successful, but before the industrial revolution had begun to demonstrate the possibility of increased productivity in manufacturing, Quesnay carefully documented the effects of better farming methods. In "Fermiers," he weighed the relative economic advantages of horses over the traditional oxen. He compared their initial costs, their average working life, the number required to cultivate a given plot, their speed and efficiency, their requirements for pasturage and feed in winter, the amount of manure they produced, and their susceptibility to accidents and disease. Horses, he concluded, were far more advantageous. And he went on to point out other types of investments that could be made by farmers, all of which required capital as well as freedom from outside interference.

The Physiocrats defined three types of "advances," or capital: *avances foncières* (the original investments required to clear the land), *avances primitives* (fixed capital, including buildings, horses, and farm equipment), and *avances annuelles* (essentially the circulating capital expended annually for wages, seed, fertilizer, and so on). Although the first type was no longer important, nothing, said Quesnay, should hinder large investments in the other two.

Quesnay believed that the farmers, who were the capitalist-entre-preneurial class, should be encouraged in every way possible to make investments and to introduce new methods. They should be free of unjust taxation—in fact, free of almost any tax. Since markets for agricultural products should be expanded at home and abroad in order to yield a *bon prix* (i.e. the best possible price that covered all costs), *laissez-faire* was believed to be good for agriculture. More revenue made available more capital for investment, more investment led to a higher net product, and a larger net product meant national prosperity. Quesnay had constructed a model of economic progress.

Quesnay's diagram illustrating his theory was a major theoretical innovation. He devised an analysis of the intersectoral flows of money and goods through the economy as a whole in the form of a chart, which he called the *Tableau économique* (the *Economic Table*). The table, modified somewhat in later editions, showed the flow of goods and expenditures among the three sectors of the economy. These sectors were, first, the proprietors (including the king) who received the rent, or net product; second, the productive class of farmers; and third, the sterile class of manufacturers and businessmen. The model assumed a given annual investment of capital in agriculture, a rate of productivity based upon the best techniques of agricultural production, and specific ratios for the amount of output going to the proprietors and sterile class. Quesnay demonstrated the circular flow of goods in exchange for money among the three classes of society and how funds returned to the productive class so that the next annual round of outlays could begin. He showed how, at full capacity, an equilibrium between national output and expenditures could be maintained.

Quesnay illustrated these exchanges in two ways. The original table, called "the zigzag," began with an annual advance of 2000 million livres (to simplify calculation) by the productive class. This provided a payment of 2000 million to the proprietors as net revenue. Proprietors spent their money on two types of goods: Half their income was spent on agricultural goods from the productive class and half for manufactured goods from the sterile class. Each of these two classes, in turn, would spend half their income on products of their own sector and half on the goods of the other class. Each expenditure induces production of an equivalent amount of output and income, except in the case of agricultural production, where a new net product would result, equal in size to the additional outlays. The process of exchange continued to the limit of the geometric progression, by which time the productive class had regained its 2000 million livres. These advances also produce a net revenue of 2000 livres. The total of 2000 million livres received by the sterile class is equal to the value of its output.

The second method of presentation, used by Mirabeau and by Quesnay in his "Analysis," was a table in which the aggregate purchases were summed for each class. With slight adjustments, this becomes an input-output table, with which today's students are more familiar. (See Table 1.) In this instance, the table includes transactions (not income), and the figures are in milliards of livres. Of the output of five milliards in agriculture, two are used by farmers for subsistence, seed, fertilizer, and

Table 1

Transactions Table for *The Tableau Économique*
(VALUE OF REAL GOODS IN MILLIARDS)

| | Purchasing Industry | | | |
Producing Industry	*Farmers*	*Proprietors*	*Artisans*	*Total Production*
Farmers	2	1	2	5
Proprietors	2	0	0	2
Artisans	1	1	0	2
Total Purchases	5	2	2	9

Source: Adapted from Almarin Phillips, "*The Tableau Économique* as a Leontief Model," *Quarterly Journal of Economics,* vol. LXIX (1955), p. 141.

other annual costs, and three by the other two classes: The proprietors consume one milliard of food and the sterile class purchases two milliards for raw materials and subsistence. The proprietors in the modern input-output table are viewed as producers of rental services worth two milliards, all of which are purchased by farmers. The sterile class (artisans) produces two milliards of goods. These manufactured goods, half of which are consumed by proprietors and half by farmers, "pay" for the two milliards of agricultural goods. The proprietors' rent "pays" for their subsistence and manufactured goods they consume. The farmers thus receive a total of three milliards, two of subsistence and seed (i.e. agricultural goods) and one of manufactured goods. The three together constitute their capital investment: two milliards in the form of an annual advance (*avances annuelles*) for labor and noncapital items and one milliard for depreciation of fixed capital (*avances primitives*). (Since the estimated annual rate of depreciation was ten percent, the amount of such capital would be ten milliards.) The third type of capital investment, *avances foncières,* was not included in the table.

Quesnay used the table to illustrate what would happen to aggregate output if proprietors did not spend their income in the proportions he had assumed. He showed that reductions in outlays for agricultural goods would reduce the aggregate level of output, while an increase in expenditures for agricultural goods would raise total output.

Quesnay's diagnosis of the ills of France was made for the purpose of recommending a cure. He saw nothing unscientific about policy suggestions. On the contrary, he believed that the natural-order philosophy was by definition a guide and analysis to action. In his article on "Natural Right," he stated his acceptance of the idea that natural laws were both physical and moral and had been designed by the creator to be the best possible laws for mankind. Society's laws—which he called positive —should conform to these natural laws. As Quesnay and the other Physiocrats liked to put it, sovereigns really should not pass laws; they should only "declare" the natural laws to be the laws of the land. Only "ignorance can . . . favor the introduction of positive laws contrary to the regular and annual production and distribution of wealth in a kingdom." (II, p. 740)

Obviously the Physiocrats felt that ignorance was only too prevalent, for they sought thorough reforms of the existing institutional structure and new government objectives. The need for reform, however, brought them to a more fundamental question. They were not followers of Hobbes, who had held that in the state of nature there had been continual warfare, but of Locke, who had found in that state peace and happiness. What institutions and policies caused the divergence of the actual world from the true natural order and led to impoverishment rather than wealth? The Physiocrats' answer was the ironic one that the growth of property in land not only led to the emergence of man from the state of nature but also disrupted its peace and unity. Such property increased wealth, but as wealth increased so did the temptation to take goods from others; moreover some individuals were unjustly prohibited from access to goods. These inadequacies and injustices in the state of nature made government necessary to provide stable institutions that would safeguard property and contractual rights. Police protection was necessary to make property secure, and courts and judicial procedures were required to resolve disputes. Although property in land was the basis of prosperity, Quesnay did not dispute the possibility that the natural course of historical development might be injurious. Not only ignorance but monopoly groups bent on achieving selfish goals through the avoidance of competition and private and public actions that caused a misdirection of economic resources were sources of harm to society.

Quesnay presented his arguments for specific policies which, if followed by governments, would make the greatest advantages of the natural order available to society in the form of maxims. "Grains" contained 14 maxims; the first edition of the *Tableau économique* contained 22, and his *General Maxims of the Economic Government of an Agricultural Kingdom,* published in 1767, contained 30. Other Physiocrats expounded the proper policies of governments in different ways; yet on most points they agreed with Quesnay.

As the natural order pertained to all of society, Quesnay did not limit himself to a study of economic relationships but undertook to examine the directives of nature with respect to the proper form of government, its rightful functions, and the proper form of institutions. With respect to the nature of government, he was no revolutionary. He believed in a single, sovereign authority over all individuals, and unlike Montesquieu he found the idea of countervailing power baneful, a source of "discord among the great and of oppression among the weak." (*"Maximes générales,"* II, p. 949) The only natural form of government was a single sovereign, or as other Physiocrats put it, a "despot," but a legitimate not an arbitrary one who intervened only to perform the necessary functions of government and to prevent violations of the natural laws. The proper form of government was to be, in short, very much like the hereditary monarchy which then ruled France.

The direct functions of government were minimal: to preserve the natural rights of citizens, including their property rights; to provide a system of courts for the resolution of disputes; to engage in public works to encourage commerce, such as dredging harbors; and to establish a system of education. Quesnay did not view unfavorably the expenditures of the monarch and his court for consumption goods. Lack of spending, he pointed out, could in fact be harmful, as it would reduce the level of national income by restricting the circular flow. But a misdirection of spending could also be harmful, if too much of the king's resources were spent on manufacturing at the expense of agriculture. In particular, Quesnay decried spending for luxuries because it meant a misallocation of outlays that benefited the sterile classes rather than the truly productive class of agricultural entrepreneurs. Government spending should, of course, not exceed its revenues. Quesnay denounced borrowing on the grounds that governmental debt set up a flow of income to financiers, a financial class that "knew neither king nor country" and would use its pecuniary wealth in ways likely to be inimical to the best interests of society. (i.e., it would not make agricultural investments).[3] (*"Maximes*

How the crown spent its income was one problem; how it raised *générales,* II, p. 956)

---

[3] Turgot differed with Quesnay in his analysis of capital investment, money markets, and the rate of interest. In general, Turgot was willing to allow freedom in such markets on the grounds that capital would flow into those fields where the returns were greatest, so that eventually the rate of return would be equalized, to the advantage of society. Quesnay was not willing to trust the market in this regard, believing that the interests of agriculture would be mistakenly neglected by the bankers.

funds was another, in many ways more difficult. Like his predecessors Vauban and Boisguillebert, Quesnay believed that the tax structure of France was oppressive and destructive to the modernization of agriculture. Taxes were imposed arbitrarily, the revenues to the crown were far less than the taxes taken from individuals because private tax collectors obtained excessive fees, gains in income through private initiative were deliberately taxed, and the multiplicity of taxes frustrated those who sought to expand their businesses. Quesnay attempted to devise an equitable system of taxation that would encourage capital investment in agriculture and at the same time produce adequate revenues for the crown. He decided upon the single tax.

Quesnay's theory of taxation fitted neatly into his theory of the unique productivity of agriculture, which said that the net product in the form of land rents was a true surplus and not a cost of production. A tax on rents would not interfere with the proper circulation of goods or discourage individual initiative; on the contrary, it would give farmers hope if they knew that what gains they made for themselves would not immediately be appropriated by the tax collectors. A tax on wages, on the other hand, would lead to a rise in wages because workers had to live, and a tax on profits would hinder capital investment. A tax on manufacturing would have to be shifted to others, and eventually to the agricultural net product, because there was no surplus to be absorbed. But a tax on rents would harm no one—except the landlords. That was the rub. The crown and the nobility were the largest proprietors and had no wish to tax themselves. At the beginning of the century Boisguillebert had advocated a reduction in taxes to help the producers of "real wealth," namely the farmers. His argument was that if the farmers paid fewer taxes they would grow more produce, so that rents and taxes would eventually be larger; in the long run everyone would benefit. Quesnay's argument was similar, except that he advocated a tax solely on rents. The gains to the economy as a whole would eventually lead to general prosperity and a larger net product after taxes for the monarch.

Quesnay and other Physiocrats discussed but did not agree upon the exact rate of taxation needed. Baudeau suggested a tax on rent of about thirty percent; Quesnay's figure was somewhat higher, between a third and a half of the net product.

Quesnay's attitude toward individual freedom was somewhat ambiguous. Both he and his followers argued for state protection of individual rights, rights of property, and free exchange, yet they were not always ready to give the individual his head completely. Quesnay argued for competition, the reduction of tariff barriers, and the abolition of restraints on monopolies; on the other hand, he could not quite accept actions that might lead to "over-investment" in the sterile industries to the detriment of agriculture. He could not accept "over-expenditure" on luxuries, which also meant a misdirection of funds to the sterile industries. (Luxury, said Mirabeau, is "the disguise of the misery of a nation in decadence.") Still, the overwhelming force of their arguments was for *laissez-faire, lassez-passer*. Although Quesnay did not define precisely what he meant by "the greatest possible competition," he believed that lack of it caused a misallocation of investments and restricted consumption outlays below the desirable level. Turgot ardently supported free competition as fundamental to the economic health of a nation—he attributed the phrase *laissez-faire, laissez-passer,* to his teacher, Vincent de Gourney, a businessman well informed on the economic writings of his day. As Minister of Finance and Commerce of France from 1774 to 1776 Turgot introduced free trade in grains and attempted to abolish the monopoly power of the guilds. After he was driven from power, the reforms were repealed, not to be reinstituted until after the French Revolution.

Quesnay, like other reformers of his day, had an unlimited faith in reason. "If the light of reason illuminates government, all positive laws injurious to society and the sovereign will disappear." It is by the application of reason that

> man can acquire the knowledge which is necessary to him, by which he can . . . obtain the physical and moral goods essential to the nature of his being. Reason is to the soul as eyes are to the body; without eyes man cannot enjoy the light, and without light he can see nothing. ("Natural Right," II, pp. 741–742)

But reason had to be taught, and Quesnay advocated a system of education in which Physiocratic principles would be the curriculum. "The first positive law, the law fundamental to all other positive laws, is the institution of public and private education in the laws of the natural order." (II, pp. 740–741) Once properly instructed, men would put the necessary reforms into effect, not because they were told to do so, but because they would recognize that it was in their own best interest to do so. Thus Quesnay, like reformers generally, sought to enlighten others as to their own self-interest.

But Quesnay and his school were not particularly successful in enlightening others. A few heads of state were interested in their reform programs, and various Physiocrats became advisors in foreign countries. Mirabeau was invited by Karl Friedrich, the Musgrave of Baden, and by Gustavus III of Sweden to formulate a reform program. Mercier de la Rivière visited Russia at the request of the Empress Catherine and also went to Sweden. However, few changes were introduced and most of them were short-lived. In France, the high point of Physiocratic influence was reached during Turgot's government; with his fall from power the prestige of the Physiocrats generally declined.

The economic and political ideas of the Physiocrats also came under attack from critics who themselves commanded impressive followings, such as the Abbé Galiani, François Forbonnais, the Abbé de Mably, and Voltaire. Especially vulnerable to criticism were the Physiocratic doctrines of the unique productivity of agriculture, the "sterility" of manufacturing and commerce, the single tax on rents, and the justification for a hereditary monarch. In Great Britain, Adam Smith's criticisms (in *The Wealth of Nations*) of the Physiocratic doctrines effectively blunted their influence there.

It was undoubtedly true that the Physiocrats lost their audience with the implied deprecation of the role of manufacturing in economic development, especially at a time when that sector of the economy was beginning to undergo the fundamental, progressive changes later characterized as the Industrial Revolution. But the dismissal of the Physiocratic theory also meant that Quesnay's insights into the circulatory nature of the flow of goods within the economy as a whole were passed over and neglected. Adam Smith did not appreciate the value of Quesnay's analysis; in fact, he did not understand it; he dismissed Quesnay's "arithmetical formularies, which by way of eminence he peculiarly distinguishes by the name of the OEconomical Table." (*Wealth of Nations,* p. 637) The *Tableau,* with its assumption of productivity solely in agriculture, was basic to Quesnay's analysis because it emphasized those relationships which, in his interpretation of the natural order, had the highest social value. Smith's value system was different; since the *Tableau* did not fit into his vision of the economic world, it was not important.

IV

Natural-law philosophies, the new discoveries in science (particularly in medicine), and the growing complexities of the expanding world of commerce and trade formed the environment in which the new science of economics was born. Each in his own way, Petty, Locke, and

Quesnay sought explanations of economic problems and scientific statements of economic relationships. Their work helped to establish the idea that stable economic laws which could be analyzed objectively governed market behavior. They agreed that such laws were related to human welfare and should be respected by government policymakers. But despite their belief that economic laws were part of the natural order, they did not agree upon what those laws were. They differed in their approaches, they used different analytical tools, and they recommended different policies. The laws of nature did not lead unequivocally to the principles of the new science either by deduction or by empirical revelation.

Notes to Chapter ii

At one time, the pre-Smithian writings of the seventeenth and eighteenth centuries identified as mercantilist were simply condemned by economic historians as fallacious in theory and erroneous in their policy prescriptions. Exceptions to the indictment were reserved for those few who anticipated doctrines of free trade. Fortunately this attitude has now changed, and the period of two or more centuries is no longer regarded as monolithic or as one in which a given set of doctrines uniformly dominated all the countries of western Europe. There were national differences, conflicts in economic opinion within nations, and considerable modifications of ideas over time.

One of the questions that has now been raised is to what extent and in what ways mercantilist writers contributed to the development of economics as a discipline. J. J. Spengler has said that "the mercantilists brought into the arena of discourse many issues that had tended to escape critical examination as long as economic theorizing was concerned

largely with questions of commutative and related justice." Moreover the mercantilists "played an important part in determining the scope and concerns of classical economic analysis and in drawing attention to problems which the classical writers later ignored." ("Mercantilist and Physiocratic Growth Theory," in Bert F. Hoselitz, ed., *Theories of Economic Growth*, New York, Free Press, 1960, p. 17).

Some historians have emphasized the mercantilists' development of analytical tools which later economists refashioned. (For example, see Schumpeter's *History of Economic Analysis* for careful and detailed assessments of both major and minor figures of the period from this standpoint.) More to the point with respect to the development of scientific thinking in economics is William Letwin's *The Origins of Scientific Economics* (Garden City, N. Y., Doubleday, 1965), in which attention is given to English writers, especially Petty, Locke, and Sir Dudley North.

Those who seek the more traditional approach to mercantilism, however—and it is still widely held —should begin with the book that began it all, Adam Smith's *The Wealth of Nations,* book IV, chs. 1–8. Gustav Schmoller's *The Mercantile System and Its Historical Significance,* should be read next to ensure a counterbalancing point of view. The most comprehensive modern version of the doctrine is Eli F. Heckscher's *Mercantilism,* trans. by Mendel Shapiro, rev. ed. edited by E. F. Söderlund (New York, Macmillan, 1955), 2 vols. The revised edition is especially interesting because of Heckscher's analysis (vol. II, pp. 340–358) of the sympathetic interpretation of mercantilist monetary policy presented by John Maynard Keynes in *The General Theory of Employment, Interest, and Money* (New York, Harcourt Brace Jovanovich, 1936), pp. 333–351.

I

The works of Petty have been recently reprinted. All references in the text to his writings are from Charles Henry Hull, ed., *The Economic Writings of Sir William Petty,* Reprints of Economic Classics (New York, Kelley, 1963, 1964), 2 vols. Extensive summaries of Petty's background and his economics are given in Letwin, *op. cit.,* ch. 5; Eric Roll, *A History of Economic Thought,* 3rd ed. (Englewood Cliffs, N. J., Prentice-Hall, 1956), pp. 98–112; E. A. J. Johnson, *Predecessors of Adam Smith: The Growth of British Economic Thought* (New York, Prentice-Hall, 1937), ch. xiii. Hull's Introduction is also useful. For a full biography, see Emil Strauss, *Sir William Petty* (London, Bodley Head,

1954). Some of Petty's ideas are also expanded in his correspondence.

The development of natural-law philosophy in seventeenth-century Europe is associated primarily with Hugh Grotius (1583–1645), Thomas Hobbes (1588–1679), Samuel von Pufendorf (1632–94), and John Locke. The natural-law tradition, of course, begins with Greek writers such as the Epicurians and Stoics and the Roman jurists; it was elaborated in the comprehensive philosophical systems of Thomas Acquinas and the medieval schoolmen. The issue that separated seventeenth century thinking from these earlier ideas was the designation of the individual as the final authority and decision-maker. With Locke, the church was excluded from playing a role: The individual was of divine origin and that was enough. Government became the instrument of individuals, which should not attempt to remake them. For a summary of the historical roots of liberalism and its development during the mercantilist period, see William D. Grampp, *Economic Liberalism* (New York, Random House, 1965), especially vol. I, *The Beginnings.* For a shorter account, see Alfred F. Chalk, "Natural Law and the Rise of Economic Individualism in England," *Journal of Political Economy* (1951), vol. 59, pp. 332–347.

Petty's analyses were largely directed toward very practical problems, and England had many of these in the 1660s. There was the costly three-year war with the Dutch that broke out in 1664, the plague that struck in 1665 with a loss of life estimated by Petty at 100,000 in London, and the devastating 1666 London fire that wiped out a fourth of the city's homes. Petty's attempts to measure these disasters in terms of the population affected and property destroyed, however fanciful his estimating procedures may appear to modern economists, were pioneering not only in the development of statistics but also in the recognition that quantitative estimates could form a basis for evaluating priorities. For example, he contrasted war costs and domestic social losses, using a unique cost-benefit analysis. Continuing his analysis of the value of the nation's manpower (see footnote 2), he pointed out that if the population totaled six million persons, then each person was worth 69 pounds: "From whence it follows, that 100,000 persons dying of the Plague, above the ordinary number [i.e., the normal death rate], is near 7 Millions loss to the Kingdom; and consequently how well might 70,000 £ have been bestowed in preventing this Centuple loss?" (*Verbum Sapienti* I, 109) A levy of £70,000 per month had been imposed earlier by Charles II as a special assessment for prosecution of the war with Holland.

II

The best treatment of Locke's economics is in Letwin, *op. cit.,* ch. 6. For a discussion of the interest-rate controversy with Sir Josiah Child, see also Letwin's ch. 1 as well as his monograph *Sir Josiah Child, Merchant Economist* (Publication #14, The Kress Library of Business and Economics, Boston, Baker Library, 1959).

Locke's 1668 manuscript on interest is reprinted in Letwin's *Origins;* the quotation on the natural rate of interest is from p. 299. The other quotations on interest rates are from Locke's *Consequences of the Lowering of Interest, and Raising the Value of Money,* in *The Works of John Locke* (London, Ward, Lock, n. d.), pp. 560, 564.

For his work on government, see Peter Laslett, ed., *John Locke, Two Treatises of Government,* rev. ed. (New York and Toronto, Mentor Books, New American Library, reprint authorized by Cambridge University Press, 1963). Laslett's introduction is especially valuable in pointing out the implications of the inconsistencies in Locke from the point of view of political theory. The quotation on reason is from Book I, 101, p. 253.

Those who have commented on Locke's methodological inconsistencies in the *Treatise* and the *Essay Concerning Human Understanding* (Harold Laski, Bertrand Russell, and Carl Becker, to mention a few) have been noneconomists. Economists have not seemed to be aware of the methodological problems. This is unfortunate because Locke's inconsistency helps to unravel the problem of his labor theory of value.

As the text points out, Locke expressed what was essentially a cost-of-production theory of value, with prices determined by supply and demand. But this was the analysis that appeared in his writings on interest rates; it was not the analysis that appeared in the *Treatise of Government.* The first approach may be considered, methodologically, in the spirit of the *Essay,* namely, as an inductive generalization of price behavior. In contrast, Locke in the *Treatise of Government* was concerned with the laws that governed the state of nature, which was hardly available for observation. Using "reason," he postulated his famous theory of property in Chapter V of the *Second Treatise:*

> . . . every Man has a property in his own Person. . . . The Labour of his Body, and the Work of his Hands, we may say, are properly his. Whatsoever then he removes out of the State that Nature have provided, and left in it, he hath mixed his Labour with, and joyned to it something that is his own, and thereby makes it his Property. (See the Laslett edition, pp. 328–329.)

Locke's approach to a labor value theory may have influenced Adam Smith's famous deer-and-beaver example of the labor theory of value in the state of nature. Locke wrote: "Thus this Law of reason makes the Deer, that Indian's who hath killed it; 'tis allowed to be his goods who hath bestowed his labour upon it, though before, it was the common right of every one." (*ibid.*, p. 331)

Locke made estimates of the relative contributions of land and labor to the value of goods:

> for 'tis Labour indeed that puts the difference of value on every thing; and let any one consider, what the difference is between an Acre of Land planted with Tobacco, or Sugar, sown with Wheat or Barley; and an Acre of the same land lying in common . . . he will find, that the improvement of labour makes the far greater part of the value. I think . . . that of the Products of the Earth useful to the Life of Man 9/10 are the effects of labour: nay, if we will rightly estimate things as they come to our use . . . we shall find, that in most of them 99/100 are wholly to be put on the account of labour. (*ibid.*, p. 338)

Since Locke probably wrote this particular chapter in 1679, why did he not use the labor theory in his later economic writings? One can only speculate that the revolutionary implications of the *Treatise* and its labor theory no longer suited his purposes as an official of the government of William III in the 1690s. The more conservative, objective demand-and-supply analysis of prices was more appropriate to the new situation. It should also be noted that Locke's interest in "labor" did not extend to the propertyless laborer. As Commissioner of the Board of Trade in 1697, he proposed forced labor for vagabonds, impressment into the navy, and child labor at an early age. (See Grampp, *op. cit.*, I, 71.) It was only labor related to property that mattered. In the *Treatise*, he wrote that riches would differ as men applied their own labor in differing amounts and skill:

> God gave the World to Men in Common . . . but it cannot be supposed he meant it should always remain common and uncultivated. He gave it to the use of the Industrious and Rational, (and Labour was to be his title to it;) not to the Fancy or Covetousness of the Quarrelsome and Contentious. (*Second Treatise,* Laslett, *op. cit.*, p. 333.)

He had no objection to large holdings. The accumulation of wealth by an individual, said Locke, is perfectly reasonable so long as it does not result in the oppression of others or waste.

III

The works of Quesnay have been collected by August Oncken, *Oeuvres économiques et philosophiques de F. Quesnay* (Paris, Peelman, 1888). This volume was reprinted by Scientia Verlag Aalen in 1965. Another and more complete collection, *François Quesnay et la Physiocratie*, has been published by the Institut National d'Études Demographiques (Paris, 1958, 2 vols., with commentaries by Louis Salleron). References in the text to Quesnay are from this edition. An older selection of the writings of Quesnay and other Physiocrats is contained in Eugéne Daire, ed., *Physiocrates, Quesnay, Dupont de Nemours, Mercier de la Rivière, l'abbé Baudeau, Le Trosne* (Paris, Guillaumin, 1846). The lack of English translations of the Physiocratic works, which has undoubtedly hindered familiarity with their ideas in English-speaking countries, has been partially overcome with translations of some of Quesnay's articles prepared by Ronald L. Meek for his valuable *Economics of Physiocracy: Essays and Translations* (Cambridge, Mass., Harvard University Press, 1963). In addition to Meek, other books in English on the Physiocrats include Henry Higgs, *The Physiocrats* (London, Macmillan, 1897), and Max Beer, *An Inquiry into Physiocracy* (London, Allen and Unwin, 1939). For a comprehensive annotated bibliography, see *François Quesnay et la Physiocratie*, I, pp. 317–392.

French science of the seventeenth and early eighteenth century was dominated by Réné Descartes, the French philosopher and scientist, rather than Bacon. Descartes' method was deductive, not inductive. He sought to wipe the mind clean of old ideas and create a logical system of laws deduced from a few first prin-ciples. As Herbert Butterfield said of him, "His vision of a single universal science so unified, so ordered, so interlocked, was perhaps one of his most remarkable contributions to the scientific revolution." (*The Origins of Modern Science 1300–1800*, rev. ed., New York, Free Press, 1957, p. 125) Descartes' principal work, the *Discourse on Method*, had a powerful impact on the development of many fields, including economics. Quesnay's analytical work in the *Tableau* represents the type of tight logical analysis that fits the Cartesian scientific model. This is not surprising since in his medical works Quesnay considered himself a follower of the Dutchman Boerhaave, the great medical authority of the period, who gave up theology for medicine because he was so taken with Cartesian theories. Philosophically he considered himself a follower of Malebranche, who also considered himself an interpreter of Descartes. (See Jean Sutter, "Quesnay et la médecine," and Akiteru Kubota, "Quesnay, disciple de Malebranche," in *François Quesnay et la Physiocratie*, esp. pp. 172f. and 202. (The relationship of Boerhaave to Descartes is noted in Butterfield, *op. cit.*, p. 175.)

The step from appreciation of the beauty and power of a unified science to the belief that it could be used for the benefit of humanity was a short one, and it was quickly followed by a second, crucial to the eighteenth century—namely, that increased scientific knowledge would automatically improve the human condition. This idea of unlimited and inevitable progress became a hallmark of the Enlightenment that underlay the economics of the Physiocrats and Adam Smith as well. This point was made by Thorstein Veblen in "Preconceptions of Economic Science I," *The Place of Science in Modern Civilization* (New York, Viking Press, 1930), pp. 86ff. For a more general, though even older treatment, see J. B. Bury, *The Idea of Progress* (London, Macmillan, 1928).

The French predecessors of Physiocratic economics included Vauban, Boisguillebert, and Cantillon. Seigneur de Vauban (1633–1707), a military engineer, was concerned with the widespread rural poverty in France. In *Projet d'une dixme royale* (1707), he advocated a single tax similar to that propounded later by the Physiocrats. Sieur de Boisguillebert (1646–1714), a lawyer, produced estimates of the French national income that indicated a substantial decline since 1660. In a collection of his writings entitled *Le Detail de la France* (1707), he proposed tax reforms, support of agriculture, and freer trade. (The phrase he used was *"laisser faire la nature"* —to give nature free rein.) Boisguillebert dealt with macroeconomics; his primary concern was the expansion of aggregate demand by tax reductions. His analysis of prices and costs was similar to that later used by Quesnay. For a discussion of his works, see Hazel Van Dyke Roberts, *Boisguillebert, Economist of the Reign of Louis XV* (New York, Columbia University Press, 1935).

The most important predecessor of the Physiocrats was Richard Cantillon (1680–1734), whose *Essai sur la nature du commerce en général* circulated privately in France before being published in 1755. A Parisian banker of Irish background, Cantillon had written the *Essai* in London in English, translating it into French for a friend just before his untimely death. It was a brilliant exposition of the market system of prices, money, and foreign trade. His anticipation of the species-flow mechanism in nearly all the details attributed to David Hume was not recognized until William Stanley Jevons, over a century later, established Cantillon as the undisputed author of the *Essai* and revealed that it had been written nearly two decades before Hume. Jevons' article, "Richard Cantillon and the Nationality of Political Economy," first appeared in *Contemporary Review* (January 1881); it is reprinted in Henry Higgs' edition of the *Essai, Richard Cantillon, Essai sur la nature du commerce en général,* with an English translation (London, Macmillan, 1931). J. J. Spengler calls Cantillon the "principal forerunner of both the classical and neoclassical schools." (See his "Richard Cantillon: First of the Moderns," *Journal of Political Economy* (August, October, 1954), reprinted in Joseph J. Spengler and William R. Allen, *Essays in Economic Thought: Aristotle to Marshall,* Chicago, Rand McNally, 1960, p. 105.)

Cantillon followed Petty on value and in his emphasis on the importance of population (labor) in production. He stressed the flow of funds within the economy, the importance of social structure, and the dominant role of the outlays of landed proprietors in the national economy. Quesnay developed the idea of circular flows but emphasized the productivity of agriculture alone. For a description of Quesnay's shift from acceptance to rejection of Cantillon's assumption that profits in industry were a part of surplus, see Meek, *op. cit.,* pp. 16ff.

Why the Physiocrats did not accept the idea of the productivity and net profit of industry outside agriculture has been the subject of lingering controversy. (See, for example, Meek, "The Interpretation of Physiocracy," *op. cit.*, ch. V, Beer, *op. cit.*, and Leo Rogin, *The Meaning and Validity of Economic Theory* (New York, Harper & Row, 1956), esp. pp. 49–50.) Much of the criticism of this school stems from the fact that later economists saw things differently. Were this criterion of consistency with subsequent findings applied universally, then only the very latest ideas could be considered "scientific," and not even for very long.

Chapter iii

THE ECONOMICS
OF INDIVIDUALISM:

Adam Smith

Without any intervention of law . . . the private interests and passions of men naturally lead them to divide and distribute the stock of every society, among all the different employments carried on in it, as nearly as possible in the proportion which is most agreeable to the interest of the whole society.

Adam Smith, *The Wealth of Nations*

Every increase or diminution of capital . . . naturally tends to increase or diminish the real quantity of industry, the number of productive hands, and consequently the exchangeable value of the annual produce of the land and labour of the country, the real wealth and revenue of all its inhabitants.

Capitals are increased by parsimony, and diminished by prodigality and misconduct.

ibid.

In *An Inquiry into the Nature and Causes of the Wealth of Nations* in 1776, Adam Smith presented the most impressive system of economic analysis to appear during the eighteenth century and one of the most influential of any century. He expressed the spirit of the Enlightenment with all its optimism, belief in progress, and appeal to the common man. *The Wealth of Nations* contained history, social philosophy, and above all a system of economic propositions concerning welfare. Private interest, Smith held, did not undermine the common good, and using all his scholarly abilities as well as an incisive, sometimes biting, phraseology, he launched an attack on government restrictions on individual self-interest as inimical to economic well-being and revealed the potential for economic development through investment.

With markets free of government controls, Smith argued that savings promoted capital investment, and capital investment led to an increased division of labor, greater productivity, and rising real incomes. In laying down principles that governed the value of goods and the distribution of income among landlords, capitalist-entrepreneurs, and workers, Smith introduced theoretical issues that were to dominate subsequent economic controversy.

In keeping with the spirit of his age Smith made no attempt to separate his judgments about the nature of society from his analytical propositions: To him, freedom of trade was both a scientific necessity and a moral virtue; the idea that capitalists should be thrifty and increase their investments was both morally and economically justifiable.

Although later economists have criticized his moral imperatives and found inconsistencies in his theories, *The Wealth of Nations* remains a great seminal work. Its value judgments and even its inconsistencies may well have contributed to its vitality and amazing success.

I

Adam Smith (1723–90) absorbed and interpreted the intellectual and commercial revolution that swept Scotland during his lifetime. Born in Kirkcaldy, he attended Glasgow University where he learned about ethics, natural law, and economics from Francis Hutcheson, who held the chair of moral philosophy he himself later occupied. The natural-law theories then current in Glasgow were those of Grotius and Pufendorf, rather than Locke; but their message of a peaceful and harmonious natural order was similar. Hutcheson was one of the first Scottish writers to expound the ideas that the individual himself could determine what was ethically good, without first acquiring a knowledge of God, and that individual happiness was the measure of goodness. As an early exponent of such principles, Hutcheson was accused during Smith's student days of teaching ideas subversive of church doctrines. He was tried by the local Presbytery but was acquitted and allowed to continue teaching.

After Glasgow, Smith went to Oxford where he stayed for six years. He found the atmosphere there frivolous and backward (he was reprimanded for reading Hume) and happily returned to Scotland without his degree, which would have required taking religious orders. He came to know David Hume through Edinburgh's circle of intellectuals. A philosopher and economist who extended Locke's empiricism to the point of doubting even such concepts as cause and effect, Hume modified Smith's attachment to natural-law concepts and encouraged him to draw his generalizations about human behavior from the study of history.

Smith was appointed to the chair of logic at Glasgow University in 1751 and the following year professor of moral philosophy, the position formerly held by Hutcheson. Smith's lectures included material that eventually became the basis for his two books. His lectures on ethics were developed into *The Theory of Moral Sentiments,* published in 1759, a book that attracted widespread attention at home and abroad, going through six editions. In his lectures on jurisprudence, Smith discussed "police, revenue, and arms," expanding the problems of "police," which included "cheapness of commodities" along with security and cleanliness, to those policies that promoted wealth and abundance. These lectures eventually grew into *The Wealth of Nations.*

At Glasgow, Smith did not confine himself only to teaching and writing; he participated in community life. He was a founding member of the Glasgow Literary Society which included David Hume and the inventor James Watt, as well as various professors and local business people, and a Political Economy Club. The flourishing town of Glasgow was his laboratory, where he learned firsthand many of the facts of trade, commercial practices, and effects of governmental regulations.

In 1764, Smith terminated his professorship at Glasgow and accepted an invitation from Charles Townshend (the colonial minister of Great Britain who later imposed the tea duty that brought a strong reaction from American colonists) to tutor his stepson, the Duke of Buccleugh. Impressed with Smith's *Theory of Moral Sentiments,* Townshend asked him to take the young Duke abroad for several years to complete his education in the style then fashionable for young members of the nobility. The salary of £300 a year with traveling expenses while abroad and a pension of £300 a year for life afterwards was so attractive that Smith could not refuse. Abroad for two and a half years, mainly in Paris, Toulouse, and Geneva, Smith and his pupil met many leading French thinkers, including Voltaire and the Physiocrats, particularly Quesnay and Turgot. Although much of *The Wealth of Nations* had been formulated by the time he met the Physiocrats, Smith nonetheless thought highly of them and was influenced by them in a number of ways. He would have dedicated *The Wealth of Nations* to Quesnay had the latter not died two years before. Although he rejected the Physiocratic theory that land was the sole source of wealth, Smith later accepted the ideas that agriculture was more productive than manufacturing, that agriculture came first in the natural order of economic development, and that the production of material goods was more important than the provision of services. He used the Physiocratic view of output as an annual flow but failed to understand the importance of Quesnay's *Economic Table*.

Smith began writing *The Wealth of Nations* at Toulouse; after his return to London and then Kirkcaldy, he continued his work at home with his mother, who outlived her husband by sixty years. The publication of Sir James Steuart's *Principles of Political Oeconomy* in 1767 prevented Smith from using a similar title for his own work. Although the words were well known, Steuart was the first to publish a book with such a title in English. Smith and Steuart knew each other but held different views on economics. Steuart is sometimes referred to as the "last of the mercantilists" because of his espousal of a favorable balance of trade—or more specifically, a favorable balance of labor. (He was the first to use the adjective favorable in this connection.) Steuart was a government interventionist, but he was not a mercantilist in the sense that he confused precious metals with wealth or money with capital. Stripped to its essentials, his theory was that a beneficial equilibrium of prices and trade relationships would not develop automatically. He posited a theory of stages of economic development and believed that different types of governmental policy were required during each stage. In *The Wealth of Nations,* Smith made a point of not referring to Steuart's work.

Smith spent a total of twelve years writing *The Wealth of Nations.* When it was published in 1776, it was well received. Two years later he was appointed Commissioner of Customs in Scotland by Lord North, then Prime Minister. North, it is said, generously made the appointment, even though Smith was a member of the opposition party, because Smith's tax recommendations made it possible for him, when he was at his wits' end for more revenue to carry on the American war, to successfully impose two new taxes. As Commissioner of Customs, Smith, the free-trade authority, ironically spent most of his remaining years supervising the enforcement and collection of tariffs.

II

Adam Smith's economics of individualism rested on the proposition that if individuals were free to follow their own self-interest and to engage in exchanges advantageous to themselves, not only the individuals but society as a whole would gain. If governments impeded such exchanges, individual welfare would diminish. To this fundamental proposition, he added one proviso. Exchanges must take place in open markets exposed to competition from others, because monopoly was injurious and led to less desirable allocations of society's resources and hence lower levels of welfare.

Smith's attempts to support this proposition were remarkably comprehensive, especially if one considers his arguments in *The Theory of Moral Sentiments* as well as those in *The Wealth of Nations*. There are good reasons to treat both books as part of Smith's total system, although they differ in minor details. Essentially, Smith gave three major arguments. The first, expressed in *The Theory of Moral Sentiments,* was that the drive for economic self-interest did not, or at least not necessarily, undermine the important moral values of society. The second was that either monopoly or government intervention in markets would diminish the welfare of individuals. The third was that the individual who invested his savings in new capital investment would raise the level of welfare of others. Proofs of the last two arguments comprise the bulk of *The Wealth of Nations*.

The question of the relationship of self-interest to other virtues, an ancient one in philosophy, had been raised again by the new theorists of natural law. Except for Hobbes, the major natural-law philosophers of the seventeenth century held to the metaphysical belief that there was a "natural" tendency for the individual, despite his pressing wants and drives, to live harmoniously with his fellow men. Hutcheson accepted this principle, and Adam Smith in his *Theory of Moral Sentiments* followed Hutcheson, although with certain modifications. Smith believed in a beneficent natural order. "The idea of that divine Being, whose benevolence and wisdom have, from all eternity, contrived and conducted the immense machine of the universe, so as at all times to produce the greatest quantity of happiness, is certainly of all the objects of human contemplation by far the most sublime." (*Theory of Moral Sentiments,* p. 210)

There is a benevolent quality to social relationships, said Smith, but this is not due to an inborn moral sense, as Hutcheson would have us believe, nor to enlightened self-interest, as Hume argues. Rather it is the result of sympathy, a feeling that can be found even in an impartial and uninvolved observer.[1] Sympathy is the basis of benevolence, and benevolence can moderate self-interest.

[1] The role of the impartial observer curiously befitted Adam Smith himself. A man who never married, whose father died before he was born, and who lived alone with his mother at Kirkcaldy for so many years (she died in 1784), Smith was in many ways the detached spectator.

Benevolence alone is not enough, however. Smith was fully aware that the unrestrained pursuit of individual self-interests could under certain conditions be destructive of society. Neither he nor Hutcheson, for example, supported the propositions of Bernard de Mandeville, who in *The Fable of the Bees* had shocked his contemporaries by praising self-indulgence. In that poem (subtitled "Private Vices, Public Virtues") Mandeville had written:

> . . . luxury
> Employ'd a million of the poor
> And odious pride a million more:
> Envy itself and vanity
> Were ministers of industry.

Hutcheson disapproved of this argument on moral grounds; Smith disputed the invitation to spending. Prudence was a more fitting virtue. Individuals should take care of themselves and their families. In one place, Smith said that as the "Author of Nature" makes it his business to be concerned with universal happiness, the individual should be more "humble" and worry only about his own affairs. The great issues of universal happiness would take care of themselves, thanks to the "great Director of Nature." (*ibid.,* note to Pt. II, Sec. I, ch. V, p. 110)

Finally, he said, there must also be justice if society is to exist in a harmonious way.

> Beneficence . . . is less essential to the existence of society than justice. Society may subsist, though not in the most comfortable state, without beneficence; but the prevalence of injustice must utterly destroy it. (*ibid.,* p. 125)

By justice, Smith meant the observance of those laws that make a man's property and person secure. Injustice was injury, and violations of the law, no matter how small, may lead to even worse violations. "The thief who imagines when he steals from the rich that they will never miss what he takes . . . is no longer to be trusted, and no man can say what degree of guilt he may not arrive at." (*ibid.,* p. 250)

Smith did not question the "justice" of the unequal distribution of wealth and income. The poor through sympathy share vicariously the pleasures of the rich, and the rich should not disparage the poor. "Do they [the rich] imagine that their stomach is better, or their sleep sounder, in a palace than in a cottage?" (*ibid.,* p. 70) Inequality was part of the natural order.

When Providence divided the earth among a few lordly masters, it neither forgot nor abandoned those who seemed to have been left out in the partition. . . . In what constitutes the real happiness of human life, they are in no respect inferior to those who would seem so much above them. In ease of body and peace of mind . . . the beggar who suns himself by the side of the highway, possesses that security which kings are fighting for. (*ibid.,* p. 265)

With a phrase made famous in *The Wealth of Nations,* Smith in *The Theory* argues that the rich "are led by *an invisible hand* [*italics added*] to make nearly the same distribution of the necessaries of life" that would have occurred were all property equally divided, and thus "without intending it, without knowing it, advance the interest of the society."

In short, although Smith recognized that self-interest could be a danger to society's happiness, it was not a great danger. Desirable social values had their source in sympathy, and society could exist without it. The protection of life and property was more important to survival. The greedy should be admonished and urged to be prudent, but the actions of the wealthy were probably in the best interests of society.

III

Although most of the value judgments in Smith's *Theory* appear again in *The Wealth of Nations,* his task in the second book was far more difficult. His objective was to show that economic freedom did in fact promote the interests of society, whose structure he did not question. That structure consisted not of the Physiocrats' three classes but rather of those classes that characterized the Scottish economy: landlords who received rent; merchants, master-manufacturers, and farmers —the capitalist-entrepreneurs—who were paid profits on their capital; and the workers employed on farms or by firms, who received wages for their efforts.

To Smith, there was no doubt that the capitalists were the dynamic force in the economy. The Glasgow merchants and businessmen were the "projectors," the "enterprisers," the savers and investors. This class, he said, was distinguished by its "acuteness of understanding," whereas the landlords, "whose revenue costs them neither labour nor care" were "too often, not only ignorant, but incapable of that application of mind" needed to foresee and understand the consequences of public regulations. As for the workers, their economic condition and lack of education impaired their judgments. (pp. 249–250)

But the dynamic class of capitalists was not to be allowed a completely free hand. However valuable they were to society in promoting economic growth, their self-interest, said Smith, also tended to produce undesirable social ends. By narrowing competition and raising their profit rate above the natural level, they could impose an "absurd tax upon the rest of their fellow-citizens." Because they have an interest that is "never exactly the same with that of the public . . . they have generally an interest to deceive and even to oppress the public, and . . . have, upon many occasions, both deceived and oppressed it." (p. 250)

Smith, the impartial observer, provided an answer to the problem of a class that had the power to bring both gain and harm to society. That answer was competition. Competition would prevent the capitalist from pursuing his natural tendency to restrict markets and raise prices to the disadvantage of others. This solution, however, raised further questions. If competition was necessary to ensure the adaptation of self-interest to the social good, then was it not a "flaw" in natural order if competition did not develop "naturally" as a controlling force? In many passages, Smith simply assumes that enough competition exists to promote the social interest. In his analysis of opulence arising from an increased division of labor, he states that this development is not the result of intent but of a "certain propensity in human nature which has in view no such extensive utility; the propensity to truck, barter, and exchange one thing for another." (p. 13) He neglects to add that competition must somehow be created. Similarly, the famous statement that it "is not from the benevolence of the butcher, the brewer, or the baker, that we expect our dinner, but from their regard to their own interest" (p. 14) makes sense only if competition prevents consumer exploitation.

In his analysis of the allocative function of the market, Smith is more explicit. Only when there is competition—Smith calls it "perfect liberty"—will consumer demands lead firms to produce goods which can be sold at a price that will just cover the costs of bringing together the land, labor, and capital necessary for their production. Such a price is a *natural* price; the mechanism through which the "quantity of every commodity brought to market naturally suits itself to the effectual demand." (p. 57)

By "perfect liberty," Smith meant the freedom of individuals to make capital investments and to enter or leave any trade or occupation as they pleased. (See pp. 56, 62, 99.) But such freedom did not develop "naturally." On the contrary, the lack of such freedoms was the main target of *The Wealth of Nations*. Its principal objective (in terms of economic reform) was to wipe out the restraints that hindered competition. The "obvious and simple system of natural liberty establishes itself of its own accord," but only if all forms of preferential treatment and restraints are abolished. (p. 651) Apparently, the system was neither "obvious" nor "natural."

The underlying, perverting influence, of course, was government policies that went beyond the limits consistent with natural liberty. Although the natural course of economic development led from agriculture to manufacturing and foreign commerce, Smith claimed that "this natural order of things . . . has, in all the modern states of Europe, been, in many respects, entirely inverted." (p. 360)

Governments had attempted to stimulate foreign commerce through a mercantile system, as Smith called it, a system of controls and subsidies that distorted the allocation of resources. Urged on by foreign merchants who would benefit from such policies, states sought to accumulate gold and silver through devices to promote a favorable balance of trade. Governments did not recognize that free trade would enable people to buy those amounts of goods (including gold and silver) that they actually needed, and that aggregate output levels would be higher. Restraints on the importation of goods through quotas or tariffs interfered, according to Smith, with the freedom of individuals to use their capital as they saw fit and channeled it into ventures less profitable for society as a whole. Encouraging exports through a system of bounties, although it seemingly encouraged business activity, actually forced trade in directions that otherwise could not be supported. Smith criticized the colonial system on the grounds that it promoted monopolies. He attacked apprenticeship rules and other restrictions that hindered the free flow of labor on the grounds that what obstructed the flow of labor constrained the flow of capital into the most useful channels.

Smith's argument for free trade was that interference with the capitalists' investment decisions was detrimental to the public interest. This was the rationale for Smith's economic individualism. He did not use Hume's theory—of which he was well aware—that given a freely fluctuating system of foreign exchange bullion would be distributed automatically among nations, whether they had gold or silver mines or not, through price-level adjustments. Except in one place (pp. 415–416), Smith did not use his earlier impressive argument for free trade, that widening the extent of the market would increase the division of labor and raise productivity and income. The general tenor of his argument was, in fact, the exact opposite, namely that subsidization of a widening trade in foreign markets led to an overextension of capital that was detrimental to domestic investment. The aggregate return on capital was therefore less than it would otherwise have been, and less revenue meant less savings; smaller savings in turn meant less investment, so that ultimately wages at home would have to drop. (See p. 577.)

The parodox in Smith's position was that if governments had been wrong to listen to the merchants and master-manufacturers who sought restrictive trade policies, whose recommendations could they accept? Certainly not those of the landlords or workers. In the end, Smith could appeal only to the government. Political economy, he said, was "a branch of the science of a statesman or legislator." (p. 397) It was the statesman, above the pressures of interest groups, who could see the long-run consequences of economic actions and remove the barriers to progress. When Smith in another place refers to "that insidious and crafty animal called a statesman or politician," he is talking about a person concerned with "the momentary fluctuations of affairs." (p. 435)

Yet a philosopher-statesman who could be an impartial observer and yet manage affairs of state was too much to hope for, and Smith was willing to forego "perfect" liberty while pressing for improvements. "If a nation could not prosper without the enjoyment of perfect liberty and perfect justice," he said (talking of the theories of the Physiocrats), "there is not in the world a nation which could have ever prospered." (p. 638) In the end, he appealed to the statesman's own self-interest. Abolish restraints, he said, and you will be "discharged from a duty" (p. 651) and freed of attempting to regulate industry with results that will never be successful. The minimum duties of the sovereign—the protection of the security of society, the prevention of injustice, and the establishment of essential public works that cannot profitably be provided by private individuals—are consistent with the system of natural liberty. These duties are complex enough without adding to them. (Book V, which contains Smith's recommendations on expenditures, taxes, and public debts, is primarily concerned with minimizing the importance of the government sector.)

IV

Smith's most important argument for economic individualism was that self-interest, if its tendency to seek government protection through monopolistic restrictions is restrained, will automatically promote the well-being of the entire society and lead to unending economic progress.

The underlying desire for economic betterment and the psychological propensity to be thrifty, according to Smith, were the keys to growth. These Scottish virtues did not have to be supplemented by a reform of the class structure of his society (in many ways Smith was quite conservative) in order for the mechanism of progress to take hold; at most, what was needed was a strengthening of the moral will to be prudent, cautious in investments, and thrifty.

The theory Smith presented to demonstrate the mechanics of growth leaves much to be desired. He is often inconsistent: there are gaps in his analysis; assumptions are made and then abandoned. These contradictions have been the source of unending discussion from the days of Say (1803) and Ricardo (1817) to the present. (Paul Douglas, an economist who examined Smith's theories of value and distribution on the 150th anniversary of *The Wealth of Nations,* wrote that "it might seem to be the path of wisdom to pass these topics by in discreet silence.") Yet all his commentators concur that Smith's theories were a goldmine of ideas for later economists. That Smith's theories cannot stand alone is perhaps the reason he is more often quoted than analyzed, a popular folk hero of believers in the moral philosophy of economic individualism rather than an economist's economist.

Nonetheless, there were several basic concepts Smith insisted upon, and it would be a mistake to concentrate on the accompanying inconsistencies and miss what he was attempting to do. His argument consisted of three essential steps, all developed within the first two books of *The Wealth of Nations.*

The first step was the assumption, taken from Petty and Locke, that labor was the source and measure of value. Smith tells us in the very first sentence of the Introduction and Plan of Work that "the annual labour of every nation is the fund which originally supplies it with all the necessaries and conveniences of life which it annually consumes." (p. lvii) In primitive societies where labor is the only factor of production, the "whole produce of labour belongs to the labourer." (p. 47) In an economy where there is capital as well as labor, the owner (or capitalist) demands profits; the worker "must in most cases share" the output with him. When the landlord appears on the scene, the worker must also "give up" a further portion of what he produces. (p. 49) Later, writing about wages Smith says:

> No society can surely be flourishing and happy, of which the far greater part of the members are poor and miserable. It is but equity, besides, that they who feed, cloath and lodge the whole body of the

people, should have such a share of the produce of their own labour as to be themselves tolerably well fed, cloathed and lodged. (p. 79)

If Smith believed that the worker produced the country's wealth, as he indicated in these passages, he did not claim that workers should receive all of it. Nor did he argue that the value of goods was determined by labor.

He did believe that the value of goods was best measured by labor; his interest here was essentially in how to measure aggregate income. He recognized that real income consisted of the "necessaries, conveniences, and amusements of human life." (p. 30) Money, which most people used as a measure of income, was unsatisfactory as a means of comparing income in different times and places because its value could change substantially. In the sixteenth century, for example, the "discovery of the abundant mines of America reduced . . . the value of gold and silver in Europe to about a third of what it had been before." (p. 32) If some other commodity (e.g., a bushel of wheat) is chosen as a measure, the same problem of variation in the value of the measuring rod could still occur. It showed how corn would still be a variable yardstick.[2]

If gold, silver, and wheat were not invariable measures of wealth, what could be used? Smith's solution was to use units of labor. "Labour . . . is the real measure of the exchangeable value of all commodities." (p. 30) The "real" price of a commodity is its command over labor; its "nominal" price is its command over money.

Command over labor was not a simple concept however. At first, Smith interpreted it as a command over "toil and trouble"—labor's disutility, as it later came to be called. Recognizing that a measure had to be invariable to be useful and that different kinds of labor involved differences in hardship and skill, Smith believed that he could convert all types of labor into units of a given quality by using actual wage differentials. (A $4 man hour could be assumed to be the equivalent of two man hours of common labor worth $2 each.) With this procedure, Smith argued, the adjusted unit of labor was constant "at all times and places."

[2] Today's method of getting an index of real income by dividing money income by some index of the price level is an attempt to resolve Smith's problem with statistical tools that were not available when Smith wrote. But even this method is not wholly satisfactory. There are no absolute answers to the problems raised in the choice of an index, the method of weighting, the handling of qualitative changes in goods, the introduction of new commodities, and so on.

"In his ordinary state of health, strength and spirits; in the ordinary degree of his skill and dexterity, [a man] must always lay down the same portion of his ease, his liberty, and happiness." (p. 33) Of course, the real wage level may change, but not the measuring rod of "pain" per man hour.

Smith soon abandoned this standard for units of labor, however, in favor of dealing with labor as a commodity, the value of which he had already admitted could change like any other commodity. This altered the nature of his analysis in ways that he had not intended. The amount of labor commanded by goods now varied inversely with wages; they commanded less labor at a higher wage, and more at a lower wage. The question of wage levels upset Smith's absolute measuring system and led him into the thicket of income distribution.[3]

Determining the "cause" of value was a different problem from measuring it. As economic writers from Aristotle on had recognized, the principal theoretical issue that arose from the division of labor was the explanation of the ratio at which one good was exchanged for another. Smith sided with those who found an explanation of exchange values in the cost, not the demand, side of the market. Although all goods have utility, he said, it is a "paradox of value" that some goods with great use value, like water, have low exchange values, while some goods with a low use value, like diamonds, have a high exchange value. Therefore, he concluded, use values do not determine exchange values. This bit of logic became dogma for most members of the British classical school.

In his analysis of the value at which any one commodity can be exchanged for another, Smith began with an economy in which labor was the only scarce factor of production. In his deer and beaver example, he said that if it required, on the average, two days to kill a beaver and one day to kill a deer, the ratio of exchange of beaver for deer would

---

[3] The question of income distribution was at the bottom of the long discussion by later economists of why the amount of labor commanded by goods exceeded the amount embodied in their production, at least in economies where there were income claimants other than labor. If where 100 units of labor, at the wage of a dollar a unit, are required to produce goods with a value of $200, then the amount of labor commanded is 200 units, even though the input is 100. The "excess" represents the amount of labor commanded by profits and rents, which together account for the additional $100 of costs. Had Smith (and later economists) considered the ratio of labor expended (100 units) to labor commanded (200), it would have been clear that he was discussing not a measure of income, but labor's share of the national output—i.e., the distribution of income.

be one to two. Goods would be exchanged in proportion to the amount of labor required to produce them. But this straightforward labor theory of value lasts for little more than one page in *The Wealth of Nations*. In a two-factor economy, where capital and labor are both scarce, it appears that capital now requires a payment; otherwise it will not be used. This payment, made not for the labor of the capitalist in managing the enterprise but as a return on the stock of capital, we call profit. In a three-factor economy, where land is privately owned, the landlords, who "love to reap where they never sowed," also demand a payment in the form of rent. The value of commodities in most societies, therefore, has three components—wages, profit, and rent. The value of any particular good depends on the amount of each factor used in its production times the factor price. This answer to the question of exchange value led Smith to the theory of income distribution. He did not systematically discuss factor proportions.

The second step in his argument was that capital raised labor's productivity. He defined capital as circulating capital (money, provisions, raw materials, semifinished goods, and finished work in the form of inventories) and fixed capital (machines, buildings used in business, improvements of land, and the abilities of members of society). Capital puts labor to work both by direct advances of circulating capital (provisions) and by making available fixed capital (tools and other equipment) to work with. In general, Smith assumed that as more capital was advanced to workers, more labor would be employed and the output (income) of society would increase. He recognized, however, that the productivity relationship was more complex than appeared on the surface.

In the first place, Smith made a distinction between productive and unproductive labor. Productive labor adds to the capital stock of a country; unproductive labor does not. He measured income in terms of goods and excluded services. An unproductive laborer produces services, which "generally perish in the very instant of their performance, and seldom leave any trace or value behind them for which an equal quantity of service could afterwards be procured." (p. 315) On the other hand, a productive worker's wages cost his employer nothing. He adds value to the goods on which he works; when the employer sells the finished goods, he receives a price that not only covers the cost of the worker and the material but returns a profit. The "unproductive" workers, including, as well as menial servants, the king himself, his court, and the military forces, even though they are not productive perform useful services. Yet the implication of the analysis is clear: A shift of labor from unproductive occupations to productive ones will enhance per capita income.

However, an increase in capital outlays for hiring productive labor could go on only so long before wages would rise. Only the existence of unemployment (which Smith did not discuss) and the transfers from unproductive to productive occupations could offset a wage increase in the short run. When wages began to rise, would this mean that capital investment would no longer lead to increases in output? Not at all, said Smith. Higher wages encourage workers' industry.

> A plentiful subsistence increases the bodily strength of the labourer, and the comfortable hope of bettering his condition, and of ending his days perhaps in ease and plenty, animates him to exert his strength to the utmost. Where wages are high . . . we shall always find the workmen more active, diligent, and expeditious. . . . (p. 81)

Moreover in the long run the "liberal reward" for labor will encourage an expansion of the population, "as nearly as possible in the proportion which the demand for labour requires." (p. 80) To complain of increasing population "is to lament over the necessary effect and cause of the greatest public prosperity." (p. 81)

The third way capital investment increased output was by the division of labor. "The greatest improvement in the productive powers of labour and the greater part of the skill, dexterity, and judgment with which it is any where directed, or applied, seem to have been the effects of the division of labour." (p. 3) With this sentence Smith began his famous Chapter I of Book I, on the division of labor. Division of labor meant specialization and greater productivity. In a pin factory, for example, the unspecialized worker could make one pin per day, but certainly not twenty. On the other hand, in a small "manufactory" with ten men each specializing in a part of the pin-making operation, the output would be upward of 48,000 pins a day, or 4800 per worker instead of one or even twenty.

The possibility for increasing the division of labor and raising per capita income, however, is limited in two ways. It is limited, first, by the extent of the market. (Smith had in mind the geographical extent of markets especially; no isolated village was going to devote its labor resources to producing 48,000 pins.) It is also limited by the amount of capital; no producer will devote himself to preparing and selling a particular commodity unless he has accumulated a store of goods (i.e., capital) to subsist on in the interim or someone else has made such an accumulation and will advance it to him. Capital accumulation is therefore a necessary condition for the division of labor. "As the accumulation of stock must, in the nature of things, be previous to the division of labour, so labour can be more and more subdivided in proportion only as stock is previously more and more accumulated." (p. 260)

In this argument, Smith refers not to higher capital/labor ratios but to changes in the "production function," that is, improvements in the organization of work, changes in workers' skills, and technological change. He did not make a separate analysis of the effects of capital accumulation on output with and without technical changes. In the language of the nineteenth-century economists, he was discussing the law of increasing returns.

V

Savings is the source of the capital that puts labor in motion and increases the wealth of a nation.

> Parsimony, by increasing the fund which is destined for the maintenance of productive hands, tends to increase the number of those hands. . . . It tends therefore to increase the exchangeable value of the annual produce of the land and labour. . . . (p. 321)

To Smith, the best way to view the economy was through the eyes of the capitalists. The aggregate amount of goods in society consisted of a vast accumulation of capital, both circulating and fixed, plus goods "reserved for immediate consumption." When capitalists as a whole engaged in production they advanced capital to productive labor, with the expectation that the circulating capital (except money) and the maintenance costs of the fixed capital would be returned to them with a profit. That profit (plus rents to landlords) was "revenue," or the social surplus. Economic growth could occur only if this surplus was saved and not "dissipated." Revenue maintains the consumption of capitalists and landlords, but the more modest the consumption and the less unproductive labor these classes employ, the more savings, or new additions to capital, there will be and the higher the rate of economic growth will be.

Smith's theories of the distribution of income had been important to the determination of natural prices of individual goods; they were now revealed as vital to the mechanism of economic growth. What laws governed wages (circulating capital), and the profits and rents that made up the revenue of society? Smith's answers were suggestive, but neither precise nor rigorous.

Smith's concept of capital led him to what became known as the *wage-fund theory*. As the capitalists advanced wage-goods (i.e., a part of the circulating capital) to workers, the resulting average wage was simply the aggregate of those goods divided by the number of hired workers: An increase in the amount of capital thus raised wages; a larger number of workers decreased wages. Smith laid down no principle that would govern the size of the wage fund except to state that more savings led to more investments and hence to higher wages. The principle governing the supply of labor was a rough statement of the long-run subsistence theory of wages. Wages, he said, could not be less than the amount on which the worker could subsist and raise a family large enough so that a son would survive to replace him in the labor force. Referring to Cantillon's estimates (without comment), he concluded that the worker and his wife would have to earn somewhat in excess of their own subsistence in order to support their children. (Cantillon had estimated that a family would have to consist of four children, half of whom were male and half of whom would die before reaching maturity.) Smith did not commit himself as to how low the wage rate could go except to say that the minimum rate was "the lowest . . . consistent with common humanity." (p. 68) However, he believed that in Great Britain, "the wages of labour [were] more than what is precisely necessary to enable the labourer to bring up a family." (p. 74) With wages higher than the subsistence level, mortality rates would be reduced and the population would grow. Smith did not believe that such an increase in population was necessarily undesirable. In one place, he wrote, "The most decisive mark of the prosperity of any country is the increase of the number of its inhabitants." (p. 70) He was aware, of course, that an increasing supply of labor would reduce wages, ceteris paribus; but he generally held to the view that if new capital could be invested more rapidly, both the rate of wages and the population would increase, a situation which seemed to him an optimum one. Yet there is also in Smith the implication that eventually the growth rate must taper off. A country with great wealth could not increase its investments at the old rate, and since the supply of labor would eventually rise more rapidly than new investment, both wages and the rate of profit would fall. This situation, which anticipated the stationary state of Ricardo and Mill, seemed far off to Smith. "No country ha[d] ever yet arrived at this degree of opulence." (p. 95)

Profits, in Smith's analysis, included both interest (a return on capital) and compensation for risk. Both were "costs" that had to be covered in the long run if capital were to remain employed in any industry. To the key question of what determined the economy's rate of profit as a return on capital, he gave no definite answer. His basic theory seemed to make the return on capital dependent on the amount of competition among owners of stock.

> When the stocks of many rich merchants are turned into the same trade, their mutual competition naturally tends to lower its profits; and when there is a like increase of stock in all the different trades carried on in the same society, the same competition must produce the same effect in them all. (p. 87)

The increase in stock causes profits to fall and wages to rise; one is the inverse of the other. Smith abandoned his hope for an independent theory of profit on which to build a cost-of-production theory of value. Although his discussion of changes in profit rates, rather than levels, reveals his fascination with the impact of economic growth, he also believed that a very wealthy country would probably have low rates of profit; in fact, interest rates might be so low that only the wealthiest people could afford to live on interest. This was not necessarily undesirable; it would force men of "small or middling fortunes," who otherwise might do nothing, to enter the business world. (p. 96)

Why profits should go down as wages rise Smith does not make clear. He seems to assume that the aggregate output from the employment of a fixed supply of labor is also fixed, and that the more labor receives the less there will be for the capitalists (after payment of rents). But this explanation fails when one considers the opening argument of *The Wealth of Nations,* in which an increase in the division of labor raises the productivity of labor. Under such circumstances, rising wages would not be inconsistent with constant profit rates; hence Smith's analysis is indeterminate.

On rents, Smith presented several theories, all incomplete. One argument followed up Petty's hints that rent is not a cause of price, but a result. Rent, said Smith at one point, "enters into the composition of the price of commodities in a different way from wages and profits." (pp.

147–148) This theory, of course, is inconsistent with his original argument that the natural price of a good is the result of adding together its three independently determined components—wages, profit, and rent. Smith also suggested that rent "is naturally a monopoly price." (p. 145) Such a price, he had previously (and erroneously) explained, was the "highest which can be got." (p. 61) The landlord charges an amount that leaves the farmer only enough to cover his costs and ordinary profits.

Smith finally described rent as an opportunity cost, the price that had to be paid for a particular piece of land to be used in the production of one crop rather than another. The more profitable crops would be successful in competing for the land. Smith used this approach to rent in his comparison of alternative uses of land (for growing grain for bread and for raising cattle for "butcher's-meat"). (pp. 148–149) As sophisticated as this theory was, it lacked completeness, according to modern standards, because of Smith's inadequate theory of the demand for goods.

It was the first, differential, rent theory that eventually became a part of classical economic doctrines. On the basis of hindsight it is evident that Smith himself favored this theory in his long examination of the history of rents and food prices and in his digression on silver. He not only appreciated the fact, later developed by Ricardo, that agricultural rents were dependent on the prices of agricultural goods rather than an independent cause of those prices; he also saw that with increases in population and wealth the "real" prices of "rude produce" would tend to rise in comparison with the prices of manufactured goods. This would happen not only because of the scarcity of certain types of agricultural resources but because the division of labor, which reduced real prices, could be carried out to a greater degree in manufacturing than in agriculture. With such economic progress, not only rents would rise; the exchange value of the landowner's output compared with that of manufactured goods would rise also. The landlord, in short, would gain twice.

Smith's theories of distribution did not provide the independent explanations of wages, profit, and rent necessary for the determination of costs of production and the exchange values of goods, nor were they an adequate explanation of the size of society's net revenue. Yet the conclusion that greater revenue would bring a greater rate of saving and investment was clear enough. Since his objective in the last analysis was to lay down maxims by which the wealth of nations could be increased, Smith was concerned that wrong policies and practices would reduce and misuse society's revenue.

Several of his strictures concerning policies that reduced the size of the surplus for investment have already been noted. He opposed public spending, except a bare minimum for necessities, because this meant supporting the idle and unproductive. Public prodigality could, he believed, destroy a nation by diverting too much revenue from profitable capitalist investments. Misdirecting capital into foreign commercial ventures instead of allowing it to move freely into more profitable domestic fields also reduced the available revenue.

Another mercantilist policy that reduced the revenue available for investment was based on a misunderstanding of the nature of money. Although hard money was a commodity, which could be bought and sold like any other, it also had a peculiar feature. Although it was part of the nation's circulating capital, it did not, like other types of capital, earn a profit that could be used to put labor in motion. Money had to be deducted from the computation of "either the gross or the neat revenue of any society." (p. 274) It was the "great wheel of circulation" but was itself a dead weight on society's resources because its increase, other things being equal, reduced the amount of capital that could be used to employ labor. For this reason, Smith urged the substitution of banknotes for hard money. Paper money would be a satisfactory medium of exchange, and the gold and silver not required for circulation could be exchanged abroad for other goods that could increase the employment of productive labor.

Even if the proper policies were followed economic growth would not occur unless those who received the revenues invested them productively. Smith seems to have been of two minds about the propensity to save. In one respect, he believed there was a natural drive to save that overcame all obstacles:

> The uniform, constant, and uninterrupted effort of every man to better his condition, the principle from which public and national, as well as private opulence is originally derived, is frequently powerful enough to maintain the natural progress of things toward improvement, in spite both of the extravagance of government, and of the greatest errors of administration. (p. 326)

Although, he said, the "profusion of government" had "undoubtedly . . . retarded the natural progress of England . . . it had not been able to stop it." And the reason? Capital had been "silently and gradually accumulated by the private frugality and good conduct of individuals." (pp. 328–329). In this passage, Smith came closest to accepting the idea of inevitable progress.

On the other hand, Smith believed that the natural tendency to save and invest in productive labor should not be left alone but positively encouraged—not only by exhortation but even by government intervention. Evidently one could trust the natural propensity for good conduct only up to a point. Reverting to his role of moral philosopher, Smith made a passionate plea for "parsimony," denouncing "prodigality and misconduct." (p. 321) The prodigal, he said, "perverts" the process of saving and investment (p. 322); yet in another place, he labels the saver a "public benefactor" and the spendthrift a "public enemy." (p. 324) Smith went beyond even moral suasion. The promotion of capital investment, he believed, was even more important than the freedom of the individual. The government, he said, should set a maximum rate of interest only somewhat above the lowest market rate. If the legal rate was too high, then savings would be more likely to be diverted to the wrong uses. The wrong group of people would be able to outbid the "sober people." A "great part of the capital of the country would thus be kept out of the hands which were most likely to make profitable and advantageous use of it, and thrown into those which were most likely to waste and destroy it." (pp. 339–340)

Notes to Chapter iii

References to Smith's works are from *The Theory of Moral Sentiments,* with a Biographical and Critical Memoir by Dugald Stewart (London, Bell & Sons, 1887), and *An Inquiry into the Nature and Causes of the Wealth of Nations,* ed. by Edwin Cannan (New York, Modern Library, 1937). Notes of Smith's earlier lectures have been published as *Lectures on Justice, Police, Revenue and Arms* (1763), ed. by Edwin Cannan (Oxford, Clarendon Press, 1896).

I

The principal sources of biograph-ical data on Adam Smith include John Rae, *The Life of Adam Smith* (London, Macmillan, 1895), reissued in 1965; *Reprints of Economic Classics* by Augustus M. Kelley, New York, with an introduction by Jacob Viner which contains new material; William Robert Scott, *Adam Smith as Student and Professor* (Glasgow, Jackson, 1937); and Dugald Stewart, *Biographical Memoirs of Adam Smith, Ll.D.* (1793) in Stewart's *Collected Works* (Edinburgh, 1858). The latter two references have been reissued by Kelley. A more recent biography is by E. G. West's *Adam Smith* (New Rochelle, N. Y., Arlington House, 1969). For a general review of his background, see C. R. Fay, *Adam Smith and the Scotland of His Day* (London, Cambridge University Press, 1956).

The 150th anniversary of *The Wealth of Nations* was the occasion for an informative series of lectures by John Maurice Clark, Paul H. Douglas, and others, published as *Adam Smith, 1776–1826* (Chicago, University of Chicago, 1928). The essays by Douglas on Smith's theory of value and by Jacob Viner on Smith and *laissez-faire* are of special interest. The quotation on p. 43 of the text is from page 77 of Douglas's essay.

Preparations are currently underway at the University of Glasgow for celebrating the bicentenary of *The Wealth of Nations;* all known works and correspondence of Smith will be reedited and published in conjunction with this event. (See West, *op. cit.*, p. 213).

Smith's intellectual debt to Francis Hutcheson and David Hume is well known. In addition to the biographies listed above, see Cannan's "Editor's Introduction" to *The Wealth of Nations*, pp. xliv–li, for a discussion of Hutcheson's influence and W. L. Taylor, *Francis Hutcheson and David Hume as Predecessors of Adam Smith* (Durham, N.C., Duke University Press, 1965).

Hutcheson's major work, *System of Moral Philosophy,* although published posthumously in 1755, was in manuscript as early as 1737 and was probably the basis of the lectures attended by Smith. Hutcheson published a *Short Introduction to Moral Philosophy in Three Books, Containing the Elements of Ethicks and the Law of Nations,* first in Latin in 1745, and then in English in 1747. In the shorter work, the three parts of moral philosophy were the "Elements of Ethics," the "Elements of the Law of Nations," and the "Principles of Oeconomicks and Politicks." In *System,* there was a similar breakdown of subject matter, but "Civil Polity" replaced "Oeconomicks and Politicks." Hutcheson dealt with economic matters in the two sections on the laws of nations (or jurisprudence) and civil polity. The order and content of Smith's materials in his *Lectures* of 1762–63 resembled Hutcheson's arrangement of subject matter. His *Theory of Moral Sentiments* closely paralleled Hutcheson's "Elements of Ethics."

Smith's lectures on political economy followed Hutcheson's organization in considerable detail, especially on the division of labor and taxation. He differed from Hutcheson on interest rates. (Hutcheson accepted the older view, called "mercantilist" by later critics, that interest was determined by the supply of and demand for money.) He originally agreed with Hutcheson's reasoning on the determination of exchange value in his lectures in 1762 and 1763; he also accepted Pufendorf's view that the price of a commodity reflected the use or pleasure it afforded and its scarcity.

Smith seems to have acquired the labor theory from David Hume (1711–76). In his essay "On Money," Hume had written that it is "the stock of labour in which consists all real power and riches," that "everything in the world is purchased by labour; and passions are the only causes of labour." (See David Hume, *Essays Moral, Political, and Literary,* vol. I, p. 293.)

Hume also influenced Smith's interest-rate theory. He said interest was not a monetary phenomenon but was determined by changes in real savings, the rate of economic progress, and the "manners and customs" of the people. Short-run changes in the amount of money may affect interest rates in the short run; but in the longer run these basic factors eventually reassert themselves.

Smith differed from Hume on several issues. He did not use Hume's argument against mercantilist balance-of-trade policies, nor did he agree with Hume on the luxury issue. A controversy had arisen during the early years of the century over the desirability of spending to promote high levels of economic activity. Like Boisguillebert in France, Bernard de Mandeville (1670–1733) in England emphasized the public virtues of private spending. His 1705 poem *The Grumbling Hive: or Knaves Turn'd Honest,* enlarged and republished in 1714 as *The Fable of the Bees,* became famous for its thesis that private vice led to economic activity and more employment. Hume took a middle position. He said that luxury, if carried too far, could be "pernicious" to society, but it was still preferable to sloth, and on balance the luxurious ages in history wère those marked by economic progress and individual liberty. The antiluxury position was supported by Hutcheson and the Physiocrats. The former argued against Mandeville on the grounds that a high level of consumption did not require vice or pride. Aggregate demand would be maintained because income "not wasted in luxury [would] be devoted to useful prudent purposes." (Quoted in Taylor, *op. cit.,* p. 104.) The Physiocrats, although they wanted outlays to be high, criticized luxury spending on sterile industries. In *The Wealth of Nations,* Smith held that luxury consumption would reduce savings, the source of capital.

Hume probably contributed to Smith's intellectual development by his generally critical approach to the problem of epistemology. As did Locke, Hume rejected innate ideas, but he went even further and denied that one could determine even cause-and-effect relationships. He was willing, however, to assume such relationships on the basis of observed juxtapositions of one set of experiences with another. The emphasis on empirical observations and customary behavior was repeated in his historical works and in his study of the social and economic aspects of society.

II

The relationship between Smith's *Theory of Moral Sentiments* and *The Wealth of Nations* has received little attention from economists (the late Jacob Viner being the outstanding exception). Those who have attempted to relate one work to the other have frequently concluded that Smith gave more emphasis to the benevolence of the natural order and its divine origin in the *Theory* than *The Wealth of Nations.* In the later work, it is argued, despite references to the "invisible hand" and similar manifestations of a belief in natural harmony, Smith's analysis lacked his earlier uncritical trust in beneficent natural laws, that in fact he saw many "flaws" in the natural order and was well aware of "serious conflicts between private interests and [the] interests of the general public."

(Viner, *Adam Smith, 1776–1926,* p. 138) Viner notes that references to a deity are almost entirely absent in *The Wealth of Nations* (*ibid.,* pp. 126–127), and that references to harmony are qualified by such words as "frequently" or "in most cases." (p. 128) Yet given all the exceptions, Viner notes that Smith had a strong prejudice against government activity. "His philosophical speculations about a harmonious order in nature undoubtedly made it easier for him to reach a laissez faire policy" (p. 140); and whatever "evils of unrestrained selfishness" might exist, they were "better than the evils of incompetent and corrupt government." (p. 142)

The Wealth of Nations might contain occasional exceptions to natural harmony not found in *The Theory of Moral Sentiments,* but Smith's basic opinions concerning economic individualism remained constant throughout all his writings.

III

Smith's criticisms of mercantilism were considerably different than those of Hume and Sir James Steuart, also Scottish economists. Hume stated his concept of the self-regulating mechanism that governed the international flow of gold and silver first in a letter to Montesquieu in 1749 and then in an essay on the balance of trade in his *Political Discourses,* published in 1752. He pointed to the effects of a change in the monetary supply within a country on prices. It makes no difference, he said, how much money is in circulation: The price level will rise or fall in proportion to an increase or decrease in the quantity of money, and no one will be either better or worse

off. If in an open economy there is an initial inflow of specie into a country, prices will rise, hindering exports and stimulating imports. The resulting outflow of specie lowers the internal price level until it is in equilibrium with the price levels of other countries. As a result of this interplay of economic forces, free trade will promote an optimum international distribution of monetary supplies, so that no country need concern itself with gold reserves. Moreover, no nation need concern itself with taking trade away from other countries. The more prosperous all nations are the better off any one nation will be, because it is the progressive and expanding international division of labor that brings marked benefits.

This equilibrating mechanism of specie flows was Hume's answer to the mercantilists, but it was an argument Smith never used in his *Wealth of Nations.* It did not fit his hypothesis that capital was more profitably employed at home than abroad. (See Frank Petrella, "Adam Smith's Rejection of Hume's Price-Specie-Flow Mechanism; A Minor Mystery Resolved," *Southern Economic Review* (January 1968), vol. xxxiv.)

Sir James Steuart (1712–80) was born in Edinburgh, attending the university there and entering the profession of law. He embarked on a political career in the service of Prince Charles and the Jacobite cause. The disaster at Culloden Moor in 1746 forced him into exile, where he remained until 1763, working on his book, *Principles of Political Oeconomy.*

Steuart defined political economy as both an art and a science. It was an art when it provided "food, other necessaries, and employment to every one of the society"; it was a science when it examined the principles that govern society. The subjects he treated included population, agriculture, trade, industry, money, coin, interest, circulation, banks, exchange, public credit, and taxes. His theory, which saw differences in periods of economic development, was historical and dynamic and led the German historical school of the nineteenth century to see him as a predecessor of their methodology and point of view. According to Steuart, society evolved from a slave to an exchange economy, from a system of infant industries to one of foreign trade, and from a trade-based economy to autarchy. Each stage called for different policies. In the foreign-trade period there were three substages—infancy, manhood, and old age—each a logical and necessary outgrowth of previous conditions. Furthermore, at any given time various countries may be in different stages of economic development; such a situation requires policies different from those that would be required if all nations had reached the same level of development. Steuart accepted also the analytical approach to economics. He was, in fact, one of the first writers to explicitly use the procedure of stating simplifying assumptions and then gradually introducing complexities to see what the effect of each would be. As for his trade policy, he argued that the best way for a nation at certain stages of its economic development to promote its own welfare was by restrictive trade policies. Trade tends to improve the relative position of those nations that are frugal and industrious if they can export more than they import. Nor does a truly favorable balance neces-

sarily entail payment with precious metals: A country can use its favorable trade position to support a larger population, expand its shipping, acquire more durable commodities, or make other nations its debtors. However, Steuart explicitly rejected Hume's theory that a nation need not concern itself with the flow of precious metals. He claimed that different nations have different interests and different rates of saving which lead to different rates of economic development. Trade policies must be designed to prevent the actions of other countries from having adverse effects on the nation. He also urged adoption of domestic policies that would preserve a "proper balance" between town and country, population and resources, rich and poor, and between stagnation and a too rapid rate of change.

The differences between the two Scottish economists never led to a debate or confrontation. In a letter dated September 5, 1772, Smith said of Sir James' book: "Without once mentioning it, I flatter myself that any fallacious principle in it will meet a clear and distinct confutation in mine." (See Rae, *op. cit.*, pp. 253–254.)

It should be noted, however, that Smith himself did recognize four reasons for governmental intervention in foreign trade. One was to protect an industry necessary for the national defense. (For example, the British gave shipping an absolute monopoly in foreign trade.) A second was to set a tariff on a commodity equal to a domestic tax imposed on the same commodity. A third was the possible use of tariffs in retaliation for the imposition of tariffs by other countries. The fourth was the desirability of reducing tariffs slowly in order to prevent the hardship that might accompany dislocations of trade resulting from a sudden abolition of protective duties. In the last two cases, however, intervention should be carefully scrutinized to make certain that the tariffs would be only temporary. (See *Wealth of Nations*, pp. 429ff.)

IV

Smith's theory of the division of labor (even his pin-manufactory example) was drawn from other sources, as were many, if not most, of the concepts in *The Wealth of Nations*. The division-of-labor concept can be traced back to Plato, Aristotle, and especially Xenophon, although their theories lacked the dynamism and the vision of unending progress that marked Smith's approach. It was a standard topic in the eighteenth century, when many writers, following Petty, were impressed by mechanical inventions such as watches, pumps, and sawmills which used this principle. Smith's pin-factory example was drawn from the French *Encyclopédie* (1775), vol. V. He gave three reasons for the gains in efficiency created by the division of labor: the greater dexterity made possible by specialization, the time saved by concentrating on one operation, and the use of machinery invented by workmen. All three reasons had been described in an *Encyclopédie* article in 1751. (See note by Cannan, *The Wealth of Nations*, p. 7.) The relationship of reduced costs of production to market expansion had been expressed by the anonymous author of a perceptive tract entitled *Considerations on the East-India Trade* (London, J. Roberts, 1721).

Even Smith's later exposure of the evils of the division of labor seems to have been anticipated. What Smith wrote was: "The man whose life is spent in performing a few simple operations . . . has no occasion to exert his understanding. . . . He naturally loses . . . the habit of such exertion, and generally becomes as stupid and ignorant as it is possible for a human creature to become." (*Wealth of Nations*, p. 734) Smith also criticizes the division of labor as producing a lack of martial spirit. Similar views in this regard had been expressed by Adam Ferguson (1723–1816), a professor of moral philosophy at the University of Edinburgh who had written one of the first critiques of Smith's *Theory of Moral Sentiments*. Although the relationship between Smith and Ferguson had been friendly, when the latter's analysis of the division of labor appeared Smith "became enraged" because he felt his ideas had been plagiarized. (See David Kittler, *The Social and Political Thought of Adam Ferguson*, Columbus, Ohio State University Press, 1965, p. 75, n. 35.) Ferguson, like Sir James, is not referred to in *The Wealth of Nations*. Although Ferguson denied that he had borrowed anything from Smith, the issue of plagiarism is less important than the fact that both professors of moral philosophy had found deficiencies in the natural order of industrialism, but they disagreed as to their importance. Smith felt that the government should do something to correct these deficiencies. (p. 735) That "something" was presumably to educate the public, which could, he believed, be done for a "very small expense." Ferguson, on the other hand, generally viewed a "profit economy," motivated by self-interest, as destructive of social virtues.

V

As a number of statements quoted in the text show, Smith was sympathetic toward the worker. Empathetic would perhaps be a better word, for Smith, while expressing concern, was nonetheless reluctant to offer the worker anything but a "free market." He was unwilling to allow an expansion of government assistance and a firm advocate of self-reliance and prudence in all matters. A close inspection of his analysis of the worker's lack of bargaining power, often cited as evidence of his sympathetic understanding of the worker, reveals that he was actually making a case for support of the investment process, not the worker. He argued that the worker, being poorer than his master, could not hold out as long, and that masters "are always and every where in a sort of tacit, but constant and uniform combination, not to raise the wages of laborer above their actual rate." (pp. 66–67) This statement by itself seems to imply that Smith believed labor was being exploited. But he immediately goes on to point out that whenever there is a high demand for labor, the "scarcity of hands occasions a competition among masters, who bid against one another, in order to get workmen, and thus voluntarily break through the natural combination not to raise wages." Moreover, workers in such a situation would "have no occasion to combine in order to raise their wages." (p. 68) In short, the answer to their lack of bargaining power was a high rate of capital investment, which comes about through policies that promote private savings, and a free labor market. Smith may have been suspicious of entrepreneurs and men of wealth, but the policies he advocated assumed that they were the unquestioned prime movers in the process of raising the level of economic welfare.

Chapter iv

THE POLITICAL ECONOMICS OF THE NEW CAPITALISM:

Ricardo vs. Malthus

On rent:

> It follows . . . that the interest of the landlord is always opposed to the interest of every other class in the community.
>
> Ricardo, *Essay on the Influence of a Low Price of Corn on the Profits of Stock*

> Is it [rent] not a part . . . of that surplus produce from the land, which has been justly stated to be the source of all power and enjoyment; and without which . . . there would be no cities, no military or naval force, no arts, no learning, none of the finer manufactures . . . and none of that cultivated and polished society, which . . . elevates and dignifies individuals . . . ?
>
> Malthus, *Inquiry into the Nature and Progress of Rent*

On savings and investment:

> M. Say has . . . most satisfactorily shewn that there is no amount of capital which may not be employed in a country, because a demand is only limited by production.
>
> Ricardo, *Principles of Political Economy and Taxation*

> . . . The principle of savings, pushed to excess, would destroy the motive to production.
>
> Malthus, *Principles of Political Economy*

On unproductive expenditures:

> A body of unproductive labourers are just as necessary and as useful with a view to future production, as a fire . . . .
>
> Ricardo, *Notes on Malthus*

> . . . it is absolutely necessary that a country with great powers
> of production should possess a body of unproductive con-
> sumers.
>
>   Malthus, *Principles of Political Economy*

Although Adam Smith had urged capital investment and innovation, he could not have foreseen the magnitude and speed of the Industrial Revolution that transformed British society in the fifty years after the publication of *The Wealth of Nations.* The rise of the factory system, based on new textile machinery and the steam engine; the burgeoning cities, fed by a booming birth rate and an influx of population driven from the countryside by enclosures of agricultural land—these were manifestations of the revolutionary changes created by the rush of private capital to take advantage of new methods of production. The rapid restructuring of the economic base of British society, which upturned tradition and challenged established centers of power, set in motion a turbulent half-century as various groups struggled to adjust and reshape British economic and political institutions to fit the emerging economic realities.

British classical economics grew out of those political struggles. Following in broad outlines the theory and policy of Adam Smith, classical economists argued for complete freedom for private capital. Their objective was political; it could be achieved only if control of the machinery of government (then in the hands of the landlords) shifted to the manufacturers and merchants. Paradoxically, it seemed, a policy of *laissez-faire,* or government noninterference, could be achieved only through political action.

The classical economists participated both in political conflicts and in the controversies over pivotal economic issues such as free labor markets, monetary neutrality, and the abolition of the Corn Laws (which gave tariff protection to the landlords). The classical writer Jeremy Bentham made the reform of Britain's legal and political institutions a lifelong goal; David Ricardo, and later John Stuart Mill, were members of Parliament; and most of the economists of the period supported the great Reform Act of 1832, which finally reduced the landlords' representation in Parliament. Although the first steps in freeing the labor market from the Combination Acts came earlier, in 1825 and 1826, most of the economists' major political victories came after the Reform

Act was passed. The denial of public assistance to the able-bodied unemployed, a goal long-sought by Malthus, was finally achieved with the
Poor Law Amendment of 1834. Ricardo's proposals for banking and
monetary reform were incorporated in the Bank Charter Act of 1844,
over a decade after his death. And the bastion of the landlords' economic power, the Corn Laws, was finally toppled in 1846.

The political struggle over control of the development of industrial
capitalism precipitated a brilliant burst of theoretical analysis, probably
unmatched in any other short period of time. David Ricardo was acknowledged as the chief exponent of the economics of the new industrialism. In the fourteen years from his first letters on economics to the
Morning Chronicle to his untimely death at the age of 51 in 1823, he
rose to preeminence as an economist and gave a new direction to the
science of political economy. Ricardo was a deductive thinker who
moved without hesitation from premise to conclusion. One of the first
of many model-builders, he argued with the single-mindedness of one
who knows his logic is rigorous and therefore true. He refused to recognize any difficulties in applying analytical propositions to government
policy and assumed that failure to follow policy prescriptions resulted
only from ignorance, a condition which, with patience, could eventually
be overcome.

Thomas Robert Malthus was unsympathetic to the rapid transformation of the British economy because it endangered the landlord-
dominated social structure. He challenged Ricardo on many aspects of
theory and policy; yet his position was an anomalous one, for he himself had contributed to Ricardo's classical economics with his theory of
population and wages and (to some extent) his theory of rent. Nevertheless, Malthus began to find himself at odds with his good friend
Ricardo over such doctrines as free trade, theories of value and profits,
and the ability of the competitive system to absorb without a depression
as much savings and investment as the capitalists decreed.

Malthus's criticisms won few friends. As John McCulloch, a follower of Ricardo, remarked:

> I do not know how Mr. Malthus Book [*The Principles of Political
> Economy,* in which he attacked Ricardo's theories] has sold in Lon-
> don, but I know it has not sold well here—It is the text book—the
> very gospel indeed—of a few landlords who have read it in order to
> find arguments to defend our factitious system. . . . (Sraffa, VIII,
> p. 312)

Malthus's theory that the competitive system could not automatically maintain full employment remained a footnote in the history of economic analysis for a century, when his theory of effective demand was rediscovered and praised by John Maynard Keynes and reformulated into a modern theory of macroeconomics.

The Ricardo-Malthus controversy reveals something of the relevance of political viewpoints to scientific success. The value judgments of Ricardo, who was sympathetic to greater freedom from governmental restrictions for capitalist enterprises, and Malthus, who supported the traditional landed estates, undoubtedly influenced their choice of issues for analysis, which elements they took into consideration, and what kinds of evidence they accepted for analytical or empirical propositions. Yet neither Malthus nor Ricardo could be accused of deliberately reasoning from personal advantage. Malthus was a professor of history and political economy at Haileybury, a college supported by the East India Company, a commercial enterprise, while Ricardo, after winning a fortune on the London stock exchange, had invested in land. Said Malthus:

> It is somewhat singular that Mr. Ricardo, a considerable receiver of rents, should have so much underrated their national importance; while I, who never received, nor expect to receive any, shall probably be accused of overrating their importance. Our different situations and opinions may serve at least to show our mutual sincerity. . . . (*Principles,* pp. 222–223)

Ricardo had two points in his favor: His theory withstood considerable criticism, and his policy recommendations were eventually supported by political victories. What alterations were made came in another era when different value judgments were the order of the day.

I

Thomas Robert Malthus (1766–1834) opened the post-Smithian era of economics in 1798 with his pessimistic *Essay on Population,* a devastating attack on the Enlightenment and its faith in progress through reason and the reform of institutions. Malthus fastened on the idea that attitudes of reform, rather than benefiting society, were so far removed from an appreciation of social realities that they would accelerate the inherent tendency of the world toward widespread misery. He believed that the most critical and overlooked factor was the threat of overpopulation. "[The] power of population is indefinitely greater than the power in the earth to produce subsistence for man"; thus there is a tendency for population to increase faster than food supplies. The positive checks to overpopulation are famine and misery; any set of policies designed to improve the economic condition of the masses without at the same time requiring them to work to produce essential foodstuffs would be doomed because they would simply raise more children and intensify the population pressure on the always limited means of subsistence.

With this analysis, Malthus abandoned the atmosphere of the Enlightenment in which he had been raised—his father Daniel had been a prominent liberal and had entertained various well-known figures such as Hume and Rousseau—for a small but growing public who believed that institutional reform based on the rights of man was dangerous. One of the primary factors behind the change was the French Revolution of 1789, which had seemed initially to herald the triumph of reason over corruption but had instead brought anarchy and terror. Fears of revolution and bloodshed spread to other countries, strengthening those who believed that any democratic reform led inevitably to the destruction of society. Strongly affected by those fears, Malthus directed his *Essay* specifically against two exponents of the doctrine of human perfectability, the English political writer William Godwin and the French philosopher the Marquis de Condorcet.

In his *Inquiry Concerning Political Justice,* published in 1793 and revised in 1796, Godwin had claimed that the institutions corrupting society were property, government, and marriage, and that with their abolition evil could be rooted out of the world. Condorcet said much the same thing. Godwin had also attempted to refute the objection to the possibility of improving economic conditions made by Robert Wallace, who had raised the specter of population pressure in 1761. Godwin saw no reason why the mind could not eventually control the passions and regulate the number of births. In fact, he claimed that the human lifespan might be so prolonged through improvements in medical science that men would cease to propagate and the human race would consist only of adults.

Malthus would have none of this argument. He believed the "perpetual tendency in the race of man to increase beyond the means of subsistence" to be "one of the general laws of animated nature," and he used two numerical progressions that captured the imaginations of his readers with their simplicity to illustrate his point. Without limitations on the means of subsistence, he said, the population of a country could easily double every 25 years (as it had in America) and therefore would increase in a geometrical ratio. But the increase in the production of foodstuffs from the same land under the best conditions could not be that high; its ratio was "evidently arithmetical."

> [the] human species would increase in the ratio of—1, 2, 4, 8, 16, 32, 64, 128, 256, 512, &c. and subsistence as—1, 2, 3, 4, 5, 6, 7, 8, 9, 10, &c. In two centuries and a quarter, the population would be to the means of subsistence as 512 to 10: in three centuries as 4096 to 13, and in two thousand years the difference would be almost incalculable. . . . (p. 13)

The tendency of population to outrun food supplies, which is restrained by the positive checks of misery and vice, makes poverty inevitable, a natural law beyond hope of institutional control. The abolition or reform of current institutions, as suggested by Godwin, would remove from regulation the growth of population and provisions and make matters worse. Without marriage, there would be no moral obligation on the part of parents to support their children. Without property, man would feel no need to exert himself productively. Without governments, or with utopian governments dedicated to equality, industry would be demoralized. Malthus admitted that there might be evils in the present distribution of private property, but he saw no way to improve society by institutional reform. "The principal argument of this essay [on population]" he said, "only goes to prove the necessity of a class of proprietors, and a class of labourers," a system which he believed characterized all civilized society.

The response to the *Essay* was immediate. Many were swayed by Malthus's arguments and welcomed his refutation of reformism. Others denounced him. In any event, his fame was established, and in 1805 he accepted an appointment as professor of history and political economy at Haileybury College, operated by the East India Company to train its future functionaries. Malthus was now Great Britain's foremost political economist.

Malthus modified his population theory beginning with the second edition of the *Essay* in 1803. In certain ways this modification undermined his original theory (a fact he failed to recognize); in other respects the theory remained intact. What he introduced in 1803 was a new type of check on population, a "preventive" check. Through moral restraint, individuals could postpone marriage and voluntarily reduce the size of their families. (However, Malthus did not approve of birth control.) Such action would raise their standard of living; if enough individuals exercised such prudence, the population pressure would be eased and the wage level could rise. Malthus in effect apologized to his readers for not having recognized this possibility in his first edition, admitting that he had written "on the impulse of the moment" at a time when he was in the country and few materials were within his reach. (*Essay on Population,* p. xxxv) His subsequent travels and study, however, had convinced him that subsistence levels in different countries varied considerably, and that in some cases the population pressure was reduced.

The preventive check conceded much to Godwin: A change in individuals' attitudes could enable living standards to rise above the poverty level. But Malthus conceded nothing with respect to institutional reforms. Poverty or the lack of it was the responsibility of the individual alone, not society. And he continued his campaign to repeal the Poor Laws, a system of relief that he insisted caused the indigent to remain lazy and produce more children for the relief roles.

Ricardo and other classical economists incorporated Malthus's analysis of population and wages into their theoretical systems. Labor was not a political factor at the time, and there seemed no reason to give the problem more thought. Ricardo assumed that in the long run wages equaled the subsistence level and that this level was dependent on cultural factors. In the short run, wages might be above the subsistence level, even "for an indefinite period"; (*Principles, Works,* I, p. 95) but this was the result of a high rate of investment, as Smith had recognized. In the long run the level of subsistence could be shifted upward only if workers' tastes were changed so that they preferred "comforts and enjoyments" and were willing to keep their families small. He accepted as "a truth without which admits not a doubt" Malthus's dicta that the poor had only themselves to blame for their impoverishment and the Poor Laws should be repealed. (I, pp. 106–107)

Although Ricardo might agree with Malthus on wages, it seems obvious in retrospect that the two would be likely to disagree on other matters. Ricardo the businessman and financial genius would be unlikely to accept Malthus's belief that a class system consisting only of landlords and laborers was the mark of a stable and civilized society.

Ricardo (1772–1823) had been raised in a family with banking and financial connections. He had received a practical education in financial matters from his father, a successful member of the London stock exchange, and had spent two years in Amsterdam (he went there at the age of 12) acquiring from relatives further training in commercial affairs. Upon returning to London, he worked with his father on the exchange and soon revealed an ability to calculate rapidly and make sound decisions under pressure. When at 21 he married a young woman who was a Quaker and gave up the Jewish faith, he was disowned by his father. Undaunted, he relied on his own abilities and reputation and soon became a financial success. By the age of 43 he had made one of the largest fortunes on the London exchange and was able to retire, investing some of his funds in landholdings. Malthus was correct in stating that Ricardo often espoused policies not in accord with his own personal interest. The Parliamentary reforms he advocated would have prohibited men from entering Parliament by a route he himself had followed. (In 1819 he purchased a seat representing Portarlington, an Irish borough which he never visited.)

Ricardo first emerged as a national figure in economic analysis during the bullion controversy on the causes of the rise of prices during the Napoleonic war period. The government had suspended payment of Bank of England banknotes in gold with the Restriction Act of 1797; it would not resume specie payments at a fixed ratio until 1821. After the suspension, prices in Great Britain began to rise, slowly at first, then faster; and in foreign exchange markets the price of gold in terms of the irredeemable British notes also increased. At a time when there was no index of prices to indicate price level changes, questions arose concerning the extent of price rises and their causes. In 1809, in a series of letters to the *Morning Chronicle,* elaborated in a pamphlet entitled *The High Price of Bullion, A Proof of the Depreciation of Bank Notes* published the following year, Ricardo argued that there had been an overissue of notes by the Bank of England and that their value in relation to gold bullion had fallen. The remedy, he said, was to repeal the Restriction Act and resume convertibility in gold. As the public sought to redeem its notes in gold, the reduction of specie reserves at the bank would force a reduction in the amount of notes issued, and the level of commodity prices would fall.

In Parliament, where the controversy was being investigated, the Bullion Committee of the House of Commons, chaired by Francis Horner, finally submitted a report sympathetic to the views of the bullionists, including Ricardo. Although the report was not acted upon favorably at the time by Parliament, Ricardo had established his position on monetary theory and policy, he had demonstrated his method of analysis, and he had acquired a reputation as a leading analyst of economic matters.

His position on the bullion controversy was that the premium on gold did not indicate that gold had risen in value, but rather that the paper money which was exchanged for it had fallen in value. He believed that this drop in value was due to an overissue of the banknotes and that a given amount of gold purchased the same quantity of goods as it had previously. The inflation was injurious and could be remedied by a return to the gold standard. Ricardo's argument, as elaborated both during this controversy and later, was based on a strict quantity theory of money. Changes in the amount of money in circulation affected the general level of prices; they did not affect the relative prices of goods. This argument was not precisely the same as Horner's, and certainly different from that of the leading monetary analyst of the time, Henry Thornton, who helped write the Bullion Report. Unlike Thornton, Ricardo did not admit that changes in the quantity of money could affect interest rates, except temporarily. In Ricardo's mind, it was important to establish conceptually the idea that changes in the amount of money did not affect the "real" economy. This point was basic to his general advocacy of *laissez-faire:* Because the real forces governing distribution and relative prices cannot be altered by monetary intervention in the long run, governments should avoid attempts to manipulate money for any fancied gains; such attempts will only create uncertainty and hamper capitalist investment.

Ricardo's deductive method of reasoning led to certain adverse comments. When Charles Bosanquet charged that Ricardo was only a theorist, as he had not presented any empirical evidence to support his conclusions, Ricardo replied:

> But, when the principles of a currency, long established, are well understood; when the laws which regulate the variations of the rate of exchange between countries have been known and observed for centuries, can that system be called wholly theoretical which appeals to those principles, and is willing to submit to the test of those laws? (*Reply to Mr. Bosanquet's Practical Observations on the Report of the Bullion Committee,* in *Works,* III, p. 160)

Ricardo had an abundance of factual financial information to illustrate his principles; but he did not consider it necessary to test his conclusions specifically as working hypotheses. To his opponents, his method seemed very much like pulling principles out of thin air and then refusing to consider alternatives. To his friends, the beauty of his logic made the truth of his conclusions indisputable. In subsequent controversies, the same aspects of Ricardo's method continued to arouse the same emotions.

The bullion controversy launched Ricardo's economic career. He met James Mill, who introduced him to Jeremy Bentham and drew him into the circle of philosophical radicals who played such an important role in sparking economic reforms. Malthus introduced himself to Ricardo in 1811, and their subsequent friendship proved close and enduring despite disagreements on theory and policy. Ricardo met the French economist Jean Baptiste Say in 1814 when the latter made a brief trip to Great Britain.

II

Few political events have had a more immediate and direct effect on the development of economic theory than the Corn Law debate in Parliament in 1814 and 1815. The issue was whether the landlords' proposal to increase the tariffs on imported grains to protect their profits from the expanded cultivation of lands made necessary by the Napoleonic wars would injure or benefit the British economy. The prospect of an early end to the hostilities, bringing with it the possibility of a sudden flood of imports of cereal grains from Europe, had convinced the landlords that they were threatened with financial disaster. Through their political control of Parliament, they were able in 1815 to boost the scale of duties. Business interests, on the other hand, were convinced that the Corn Laws gave special treatment to a favored few at their expense.

In the controversy that developed between Malthus, who supported the landlords, and Ricardo, who led the attack against them, it quickly became apparent that the legislative issue had been translated into a contest in economic analysis. The central issues were the nature of rent, the theory of income distribution in a developing economy, and the meaning of national economic welfare. Malthus developed the differential rent theory in his *Inquiry into the Nature and Progress of Rent* (1815), wrote two pamphlets on protectionism, and continued his analysis of distribution as related to economic progress in *Principles of Political Economy* in 1820. Ricardo, on the other hand, found Malthus's differential rent theory the missing link in his own analysis of distribution and used it to support his criticisms of the landlords in *An Essay on the Influence of a Low Price of Corn on the Profits of Stock* (1815). At the urging of James Mill, Ricardo elaborated upon this pamphlet, producing a theory of value and analyses of taxation that appeared in 1817 in *Principles of Political Economy and Taxation,* his great exposition of classical economics.

The differential rent theory must be considered the creation of Malthus, even though the concept had been anticipated by others and became known to future generations as the Ricardian theory of rent. In his 1815 pamphlet, Malthus began by observing that agricultural land, like machinery, was of different grades.

> The most fertile lands of a country, those which, like the best machinery in manufactures, yield the greatest products with the least labour and capital, are never found sufficient to supply the effective demand of an increasing population. The price of raw produce, therefore, naturally rises till it becomes sufficiently high to pay the cost of raising it with inferior machines, and by a more expensive process; and, as there cannot be two prices for corn of the same quality, all the other machines, the working of which requires less capital compared with the produce, must yield rents in proportion to their goodness. (*Inquiry*, pp. 33–34.)

He went on to point out that as a society prospers and its population grows the increasing demand for corn means that land of poorer quality must be brought under cultivation. Not only must the price of corn rise to cover the higher costs of production; rents must also rise on the lands already under cultivation.

Malthus interpreted this analysis of rent to mean that increasing rents and rising corn prices were measures of economic progress. His argument, similar to that of the Physiocrats, was that the fertile lands yielded a surplus which represented their productivity; they were the foundation of the economy because they provided the necessaries of life not only for those who worked them but for others. As for agriculture in general, it produced necessaries which had the "peculiar" quality of "being able to create their own demand." There could be no overproduction of subsistence.

Malthus's support of the Corn Laws was based, first, on the fear that without tariff protection Great Britain would be more dependent on foreign foods and therefore more subject to the whims of foreigners (who might decide to limit their food exports to suit their own purposes). In addition, he believed that higher rents enabled landlords to make permanent improvements in the productivity of their acres, equivalent to creating new land, and that such additions to wealth encouraged domestic food production. Finally, he felt that if the Corn Laws were repealed manufacturing would grow at the expense of agriculture. Not only would this lead to a transfer of workers out of agriculture, reflecting the increasing dependency on foreign foods and discouraging agricultural improvements; the rapid expansion of manufacturing would itself be detrimental. His argument was twofold: First, manufacturing led to a concentration of employment in the cities where conditions for the populace were unhealthful; and second, manufacturing employment was essentially unstable, reflecting the capriciousness of tastes for luxury items, and hence led to the possibility of worker unrest. (The latter argument Malthus later expanded into his theory of gluts.) Finally, he contended, the evils of industrialization undermined the great nonpecuniary advantages that accompanied a society built on a landed class. With economic progress, he said in his *Principles,* rents can never be diminished; and they "will always afford a fund for the enjoyments and leisure of the society, sufficient to leaven and animate the whole mass." Malthus could not understand why Ricardo, with his purchase of lands maintained by rents, could not appreciate the virtues of the landed gentry.

Ricardo's reply to Malthus in his 1815 *Essay on Profits* consisted of a new theoretical model of the long-run distribution of national income among the three classes (landlords, capitalists, and workers) in a competitive economy. To Ricardo, his model demonstrated unequivocally that a rise in rents adversely affected the level of profit in the system and that the welfare of society as a whole hinged directly on profits. He presented first a highly simplified economy in which there were three classes: the landlords, who owned the land but did not work it; the capitalists, who were tenant farmers; and the workers, hired by the capitalists. This one-industry economy produced corn (i.e., food), which was all the workers needed for subsistence. The produce resulted from the application of a "dose" (to use James Mill's later appropriate terminology) of labor and capital in a fixed proportion. In the "first settling of a country rich in fertile land," said Ricardo, the produce from a dose of capital and labor pays the costs of circulating capital (mostly wages) and replaces the depreciation of fixed capital; what is left is profit. As society grows newer lands must be cultivated, and as these lands will eventually be less fertile than those previously farmed, the output per additional input-dose will be less. Workers on the marginal land with the lower output must still receive a subsistence wage, however; consequently the amount of the marginal output remaining as profit will be smaller. Moreover, the rate of profit on the marginal dose of capital and labor will be less. As Malthus correctly showed, said Ricardo, rent will now rise on the original, fertile land for two reasons: The price of the output will be the same no matter where produced, and the rate of profit throughout the economy will fall until it equals the rate of profit on the marginal land.

> Rent then is in all cases a portion of the profits previously obtained on the land. It is never a new creation of revenue, but always a part of a revenue already created. (IV, p. 18)

In an economy where nonfood commodities are also produced, their costs will not increase and will probably decrease with technological improvements. In the agricultural industries, the need to cultivate less fertile land will raise costs and hence the exchange value of food. The landlord thus winds up, as a result of economic expansion, not only with greater "corn rents" but with more purchasing power since each bushel brings him more of other commodities. Since rents are a transfer of profits to landlords, and since rising food prices affect everyone, the interest of the landlord, said Ricardo, "is always opposed to the interest of every other class in the community." (IV, p. 21)

Furthermore, to increase profits, there must be a fall in the value of food; and this can occur only through (1) a fall in real wages, (2) improvements in agriculture, or (3) the importation of corn at a cheaper price. If real wages remain at the subsistence level, only the other two events can offset a long-run tendency for general profits to fall. Implicitly assuming that the demand for agricultural products was inelastic, Ricardo argued that technological changes would enable farmers to produce the same output from less land; thus the value of food would fall and lead to a rise in profits as the result of the reduction of rents. Since the free importation of grains would accomplish the same objective, he then asked why, if landlords wished to prohibit the importation of grain, should they not also (to be consistent) ban all technological improvements, rather than urging technological change as Malthus had done.

As for dependency on food from other countries, Ricardo saw little harm in it. If land is like machines, he said, why should machines of poor quality be maintained when the produce from better ones abroad is available? Moreover, he pointed out, if foreign countries have expanded their cultivation to sell produce to Great Britain, they will be unlikely to endanger their own economies by refusing to export.

On the other hand, the importation of cheap food would lower rents and raise profits and hence benefit "farmers, manufacturers, merchants, or capitalists." But would not the gain to these groups be exactly offset by the losses to landlords? Not at all, said Ricardo. Capital would be withdrawn from the poorest land and would be employed in the manufacture of such commodities as would be exported in return for the corn. Such a distribution of part of the capital of the country, would be more advantageous, or it would not be adopted. This principle is one of the best established in the science of political economy. . . . (IV, p. 32)

There was no doubt that the material output of society would be increased by employing more capital in manufacturing where the law of diminishing returns did not apply, instead of in agriculture, where it did. The noneconomic advantages claimed by Malthus for a landlord-dominated society were hardly worth considering if they meant a lower overall output. (By output, Ricardo meant net output, or that portion of total production returned to capitalists over and above the cost of labor and replacement capital.)

Ricardo's analysis of distribution dominated his *Principles of Political Economy and Taxation,* published two years later in 1817. The book was written, in fact, to elaborate the very theory Mill had found so profound. Said Ricardo in the preface,

> The produce of the earth . . . is divided among three classes of the community, namely, the proprietor of the land, the owner of the stock or capital necessary for its cultivation, and the labourers by whose industry it is cultivated. . . . To determine the laws which regulate this distribution is the principal problem in Political Economy. . . . (I, p. 5)

Although the laws were essentially the same as those he had already laid down, he introduced two new concepts. One was a definition of rent that made clear distinction between the capitalist and the landlord in terms of economic functions. "Rent," he said, "is that portion of the produce of the earth which is paid to the landlord for the use of the original and indestructible powers of the soil." (I, p. 67) The actual rent which the landlord collects from the tenant farmer, however, often included not only the land rent but a return on capital investments in the form of permanent improvements of the land and buildings. Since these returns were true profits, Ricardo rebutted Malthus's contention that it was the landlords who increased the fertility and productivity of land. To Ricardo, this was impossible by definition; only the capitalists created new wealth.

Ricardo also introduced the concept of the stationary state. Like Smith, he was concerned with the effects of economic progress, through capital investment, on each group's share of the national income. His model of distribution provided a definitive description of these effects.

With investment, money wages would rise, population would grow, and more land would be cultivated to provide subsistence. As land of decreasing fertility was farmed, rents to landlords would inexorably rise. As population caught up with the increasing capital investment, real wages would tend to settle at the subsistence level so that workers would have neither gained nor lost. But deduction of the same subsistence wage from the no-rent, marginal, and increasingly inferior land that had to be cultivated to meet the needs of the larger population would leave less and less for the capitalist. (The fall in profits was actually a drop in the rate of profit; since Ricardo assumed a constant capital/labor ratio, after some point even aggregate profit would fall.) When the rate of profit fell low enough (not necessarily to zero), the capitalists would have no motive for further accumulation because it would not "afford them an adequate compensation for their trouble, and the risk which they must necessarily encounter in employing their capital productively." (I, p. 122)

At that point, the system would expand no further. Ricardo thought that such a state of affairs was a long way off, unless, of course, unwise policies such as the prohibition of cheap food from abroad were adopted and aborted the natural course of economic development.

III

Ricardo and Malthus disagreed on the theory of value. Ricardo's overriding concern with distribution led him to an embodied-labor theory of value; Malthus's increasing interest in problems of aggregate output caused him to develop a demand-and-supply theory, in which a good's value was measured by the amount of labor it could command. Although both theories had their roots in the work of Adam Smith, each writer added theoretical innovations to support his own purposes.

In Chapter I of his *Principles,* Ricardo introduced a labor theory of value that integrated his entire argument on distribution. Essentially what he was attempting to do was to explain the exchange ratios of reproducible commodities in a competitive economy in the long run. By an exchange ratio he meant the ratio at which the quantities of two goods exchanged in a market. If the price of wheat was $3 a bushel and a pair of shoes $12, the ratio for shoes would be 4 to 1. If the price of wheat rose to $4 a bushel the ratio would fall to 3 to 1; in terms of shoes, the exchange ratio of wheat would rise from 0.25 to 0.33. The same change in ratios would have occurred if, instead of the price of wheat rising, the price of a pair of shoes fell from $12 to $9.

Ricardo believed that exchange ratios were best explained by the relative amounts of labor required to produce goods. Value, he said, depends on "the difficulty or facility of production." (I, p. 273) The more labor a good required, the harder it was to obtain and hence the higher its value.

Smith had said the same in his deer-and-beaver example, but Ricardo went beyond Smith in claiming that the labor theory did not have to be abandoned when capital was introduced as a second factor of production. Capital in fact consisted of past labor; hence its contribution to the value of output could be measured in terms of labor. Savings in labor time, whether in active labor or in the labor embodied in capital, would reduce the exchange value of any commodity.

Ricardo recognized that capitalists did not concern themselves with the relative quantities of labor a good required but with costs of production. Yet this made no difference to his theory of value. Given the going rate of wages and profit, the comparative costs of production reflect the relative amounts of labor time involved. (Rent, to Ricardo, was not a cost; it was price determined.)

Ricardo pointed out that there were exceptions to this theory, but he considered them minor. In the first place, labor was not a wholly adequate measure of the difficulty of production. Skilled labor could produce more than unskilled. Ricardo agreed with Smith on this point and felt that labor units should be standardized for measurement purposes by converting skilled labor into homogeneous units of unskilled labor, in accordance with a system of weights derived from existing wage differentials.

Second, Ricardo realized that the value of certain types of goods could not be determined by the labor theory. These were (a) nonreproducible goods such as "rare statues and pictures, scarce books and coins, wine of a peculiar quality"; (I, p. 12) (b) goods produced under monopolistic conditions (since supply was not controlled by the costs of production); and (c) the prices of goods in the short run. In all three instances, demand and supply factors determined prices. In the third case, Ricardo said, deviations of market prices from natural prices (i.e., costs of production) lead to reallocations of resources in accordance with shifts in demand and supply; but the solution to this type of problem seemed obvious and did not interest him. "Having fully acknowledged the temporary effects which . . . may be produced on the prices of commodities . . . by accidental causes . . . we will leave them entirely out of our consideration." (I, pp. 91–92) The reason he gave for so limiting the discussion was "we are treating of the laws which regulate natural prices, natural wages, and natural profits . . ."; in other words, distribution problems were best explained not by short-run but by long-run forces.

Third, Ricardo acknowledged that changes in the rate of profit (i.e., the rate of interest) as well as changes in labor requirements might affect the relative value of goods. This would occur, however, only when the capital/labor ratios among different industries were not identical. If they were identical, then changes in profit rates would have no effect on exchange values: Changes in costs of production would still reflect the relative amounts of labor employed. However, if some industries employed more capital goods than others, and profits fell, their costs would be reduced relative to costs in industries that employed less capital and more labor. Ricardo noted three situations in which this could occur: where there were differences in the proportion of circulating and fixed capital; where there were differences in the durability of fixed capital; and where there were differences in the turnover of capital. He correctly perceived that the problem arose because the elapsed time from the beginning of a new capital investment to the final payoff would be variable, and because time was valuable. Commodities "will be valuable, not exactly in proportion to the quantity of labour bestowed on them . . . but something more, to compensate for the greater length of time which must elapse before the most valuable can be brought to market." (I, p. 34) However, he considered the divergence from labor values a small one. The natural rate of profit changed slowly (and inversely) as a result of permanent changes in the natural price of wages. Such changes corresponded with population expansion that required the cultivation of less fertile lands. Even then, a large change in profits would modify exchange ratios only slightly; the effect would be nothing like the immense changes in value that resulted from differences in the amount of labor required to produce a good. (See Ricardo's letter to Malthus, October 9, 1820, VIII, p. 279.)

The labor theory of value strengthened Ricardo's theory of distribution. If as the population expanded less-fertile lands were cultivated, the value of food would have to rise relative to manufactured goods. If 200 man-days initially produced 100 bushels of wheat on this marginal land and now produces only 80, the amount of labor per bushel has risen from 2.0 to 2.5. If the cost of production of manufactured goods has remained the same, the exchange value of wheat will rise and the position of the landlords will be substantially improved. Moreover, the landlords will now obtain more rent (for the reasons explained in section II); in this case, the land previously marginal yields a rent of 20 bushels of wheat. On the other hand, the rate of profit will fall. If a subsistence wage for the same workers in each case is equal to 50 bushels, the amount of the marginal product available as profit will fall from 50 to 30. In Ricardo's terminology, the "natural price" of labor's subsistence, which rises by a fourth (from 2 man-days per bushel to 2.5), will force the profit rate to decline.

Finally Ricardo argued, the adverse effect of a rise in wages cannot be offset by a rise in prices. Although Adam Smith at one point had indicated that since wages were a cost of production an upward movement of wages would cause an upward movement of prices (see *Wealth of Nations,* p. 86), Ricardo disagreed. No rise in prices could save the profit rate from falling; it was relative values that were important, not the absolute level of prices. Assume, he said, that a country is on a gold standard and that there is a domestic gold-mining industry. A general rise in wages cannot disturb the long-run exchange ratios of commodities, including gold. If there is a rise in prices, the balance of trade will become unfavorable; gold will flow out of the country and wage-and-price relationships will return to their previous position. If the country has no mines, a similar outflow will occur if the internal price level is out of line with world prices. If a country were not on the gold standard, wages might push the price level up, depending on the government's monetary policy. Even if prices were allowed to rise, however, the *gold* prices of goods would remain unchanged, because any fall in the value of paper money would be offset by a premium on gold in foreign markets.

On September 25, 1820 Malthus wrote to Ricardo: "You assert that with few exceptions the quantity of labour employed on commodities determines the rate at which they will exchange for each other. This is a *proposition;* and one that is not well founded. . . ." (VIII, p. 261) In *The Principles of Political Economy,* and in later writings, Malthus presented a demand-and-supply approach to value, rather than the labor theory with its cost-of-production analysis. A demand-and-supply approach was more useful, he said, because it could be applied to all commodities, whether reproducible or not; because it was relevant in both the short and long run; and because it explained costs of production. Costs of production, he said, are only a "necessary condition" to the supply of a commodity. As the "component parts of this cost are themselves determined by the same causes which determine the whole, it is obvious that we cannot get rid of the principle of demand and supply by referring to the cost of production." (p. 84)

Malthus was on the trail of a theory not fully expressed until the end of the century, the neoclassical theory of value. It followed a line of development begun by Smith and extended by the Earl of Lauderdale and J. B. Say in 1803. For example, Say said: "The value of every commodity, rises always in a direct ratio to the demand, and in an inverse ratio to supply." Malthus was only continuing a tradition. Ricardo himself pointed out in his *Principles* that the demand-and-supply theory had already "become almost an axiom in political economy"; and as a result, he went on to say, it was a "source of much error in that science." (I, p. 382)

Malthus contended that the labor theory was an oversimplification. He wrote to Ricardo on October 26, 1820:

> . . . when you reject the consideration of demand and supply in the price of commodities and refer only to the means of supply, you appear to me to look only at the half of your subject. No wealth can exist unless the demand, or the estimation in which the commodity is held exceeds the cost of production: and with regard to a vast mass of commodities does not the demand actually determine the cost? How is the price of corn, and the quality of the last land taken into cultivation determined but by the state of the population and the demand. How is the price of metals determined?
>
> Do fifty oak trees valued at 20£ each contain as much labour as a stone wall in Gloucestershire which has cost 1000£. (VIII, p. 286)

Ricardo was somewhat nettled by Malthus's letter and replied, in a letter the following month, that no, the oak trees do not contain as much labor as a stone wall, and continued, "let me ask you. . . . Did you ever believe that I thought fifty oak trees would cost as much labor as the stone wall?" (VIII, p. 302) Ricardo felt that he had already clearly provided for the case of nonreproducible goods, just as he had provided for cases where demand influenced prices. His reply to Malthus on demand was:

> I do not dispute either the influence of demand on the price of corn and on the price of all other things, but supply follows close at its

heels, and soon takes the power of regulating price in his own hands, and in regulating it he is determined by the cost of production. (*ibid.*)[1]

The differences in opinion on value between Malthus and Ricardo stemmed from divergent views of the objective of political economy. In Chapter XXI of his *Principles*—a chapter that could well have been incorporated into his first chapter on value—Ricardo distinguished between value and riches. The latter dealt with the abundance of goods (i.e. aggregate output), or as Smith called it, the "necessaries, conveniences, and amusements" that persons enjoy. Ricardo was more interested in value, which, he said, depends not on abundance, but on the obstacles to production. Malthus on the other hand was concerned with abundance; thus he emphasized absolute prices, not relative values.

Ricardo stated their differences in a letter written on October 9, 1820:

> Political economy you think is an enquiry into the nature and causes of wealth—I think it should rather be called an enquiry into the laws which determine the division of the produce of industry among the classes who concur in its formation. No law can be laid down respecting quantity, but a tolerably correct one can be laid down respecting proportions. (VIII, p. 278)

Malthus replied in his letter of October 26, 1820 that such a definition seemed to be "very confined; and if it be just, I should say that political economy would be at once converted from a science which I have always considered as the most practically useful . . . into one which would merely serve to gratify curiosity." (VIII, p. 286)

---

[1] If the cost function of a reproducible good in manufacturing is constant (i.e., a horizontal straight line), then Ricardo was right: the demand curve determines only the quantity produced, not its price. For agricultural commodities with rising cost curves, the highest marginal cost determined price. Ricardo could claim, correctly, that supply alone determined prices in this case too, but only if the demand for subsistence was absolutely inelastic given the size of the population. Although Ricardo often made such an assumption, at other times he admitted that high food prices might cause a worker to reduce his consumption of foods and purchase more of other types of goods. In such cases, demand elasticities would affect output as well as the natural price of agricultural products. Ricardo's fascination with strong cases relevant to the problem of distribution undoubtedly led him to oversimplify the theory and to neglect the implications of loopholes he believed unimportant.

IV

The fundamental difference in the judgments of Malthus and Ricardo concerning the desirability of the expansion of industrialism culminated in their controversy over gluts. Malthus believed that unrestrained capital investment would lead to overproduction and economic stagnation. Ricardo, on the contrary, argued that there was no inherent limitation on the ability of capital investment to promote economic growth until a stationary state was reached. The controversy was waged primarily with the tools of economic analysis in an atmosphere marked by patience, sincerity, and respect, not by ideological confrontations. Yet the fact that neither man could fully appreciate the nature of the other's analysis revealed how profoundly their value judgments concerning the goals of society as a whole had affected their theoretical vision.

The dispute technically centered on Say's Law of Markets, which denied the possibility of a "general glut." That law, which Ricardo believed to be an indisputable principle of economics, had been developed by Say in his *Traité d'économie politique* (1803) and by James Mill in *Commerce Defended* (1808) to answer arguments supporting high levels of spending. Those arguments reflected the lingering influence, in both France and England, of Physiocratic theory, justifying as they did landlord and governmental outlays not only for investment but also for consumer goods and services. Say and Mill advanced a counterproposition—which became known as Say's Law—that there was no need for any special policy to bolster the aggregate demand for goods because production would always generate an equivalent demand for the goods produced. Although there could be no *general* overproduction of goods, a *partial* glut might occur if a particular commodity were overproduced. But such a situation would automatically correct itself given competition and factor mobility: When one commodity had been overproduced and was selling at a loss, another would be underproduced and selling at a price high enough to attract the unemployed resources. Aggregate demand would always be sufficient.

Say's Law had two implications. One was that the economy behaved in a way that would be apparent in a barter economy, where money did not veil the true exchange value of goods. Like Smith, the adherents of this law believed that money was only a medium of exchange, not an asset valuable for its liquidity. Since money could neither be consumed nor earn interest, hoarding was irrational. The second implication, and the one stressed by Ricardo, was that there could be no limit due to lack of demand on the amount of savings that capitalists might wish to invest (except in the distant stationary state). As savings meant investment outlays, and as investment outlays meant the purchase of factors of production and receipt of income by resource suppliers, aggregate demand would always equal total supply.

Malthus presented his case against Say's Law first in his letters to Ricardo and then to the public with his *Principles of Political Economy* in 1820. First, he believed that the evidence refuted the proposition that there could be no general glut. In a letter to Ricardo on January 20, 1817, he wrote:

> . . . I really think that the progress of society consists of irregular movements, and that to omit the consideration of causes which for eight or ten years will give a great *stimulus* to production and population, or a great *check* to them, is to omit the causes of the wealth and poverty of nations,—the grand object of all enquiries in Political Economy. (VII, p. 122)

In his *Principles,* Malthus saw the depression that had descended upon England after the Napoleonic wars as further evidence that a general glut was not only possible but had occurred right under Ricardo's eyes. There had been a great fall in prices and profits; unsold goods filled the warehouses, and attempts to export them only succeeded in glutting the foreign markets. As the population continued to grow, augmented by "disbanded soldiers and sailors," wages also fell, while unemployment rose. According to Malthus, this situation was not due to the difficulties of the transition from war to peace, which he could not believe would "require [as] much time as has now elapsed since the war"; moreover, where were "the understocked employments, which, according to . . . theory, ought to be numerous, and fully capable of absorbing all the redundant capital . . . ?" (II, p. 442)

Second, Malthus claimed that from a theoretical point of view there must be a deficiency of purchasing power if capitalists invested their revenues in productive labor. The demands of productive labor alone would not be enough to purchase the goods produced. Say's Law, he said, was "utterly unfounded" (II, p. 306) because it did not take into consideration "effectual demand":

> If we compare them [commodities], as we certainly ought to do, with the numbers and wants of the consumers, then a great increase of produce with comparatively stationary numbers and with wants

diminished by parsimony, must necessarily occasion a great fall of
value estimated in labour; . . . both the power of accumulation
and the motive to accumulate would be strongly checked. (II, p.
309)

To support his case, Malthus seized upon an admission by Ricardo
that there was one situation, albeit hypothetical, in which a glut could
occur. In his *Principles,* Ricardo wrote, "If every man were to forego
the use of luxuries, and be intent only on accumulation, a quantity of
necessaries might be produced for which there could not be any immediate consumption. Of commodities so limited in number there might
be a universal glut. . . ." Both demand and profits would be low.
Ricardo attempted to make clear that "this admission does not impugn
the general principle" of Say's Law because man's wants are not restricted to the consumption of subsistence: "Adam Smith has justly
observed 'that the desire of food is limited in every man by the narrow
capacity of the human stomach, but the desire of the conveniences and
ornaments of building, dress, equipage, and household furniture seems
to have no limit or certain boundary.' " (I, p. 293) As there are no
limits to these demands, Ricardo concluded that the exception only
went to prove the rule that capitalists could save and invest without fear
of any unintended general overproduction.

To Malthus, Ricardo's exception exposed the fallacy in Say's Law.
If a glut could be avoided only by increasing the demand for luxuries,
then how could Ricardo persist in his erroneous belief that higher rates
of savings would be desirable? Would not more frugality be inconsistent
with the need for more luxury spending? Malthus himself, of course,
had fallen into the trap of the oversaving fallacy, a trap which Ricardo
had inadvertently prepared with his example of overproduction in a
single-industry economy. Oversaving can occur only when there are no
new investments to match.

But Malthus had a third argument against Say's Law. This was not
that there were too many goods produced but that the attempts to invest at too high a rate would increase the level of wages and so lower
the rate of profit that there would be no further inducement to invest
and the economy would stagnate. In many respects, this was Malthus's
most important argument, and he stated it in his preface:

Adam Smith has stated, that capitals are increased by parsimony,
that every frugal man is a public benefactor, and that the increase of
wealth depends upon the balance of produce above consumption.
That these propositions are true to a great extent is perfectly un-

questionable. . . . [B]ut it is quite obvious that they are not true
to an indefinite extent, and that the principles of saving, pushed to
excess, would destroy the motive to production. . . . The two extremes are obvious; and it follows that there must be some intermediate point, though the resources of political economy may not
be able to ascertain it, where, taking into consideration both the
power to produce and the will to consume, the encouragement to
the increase of wealth is the greatest. (II, pp. 7–8, 10)

Ricardo, who liked a strong statement with a minimum of exceptions, had taken the position in his *Principles* that a high rate of saving
and investment could not reduce profits and hence could not discourage
further investment. He admitted two exceptions, but one he buried. The
first was that "no accumulation of capital will permanently lower profits
unless there be some permanent cause for the rise of wages." (I, p. 289)
The "permanent cause" for a wage increase was, of course, the rise in
the natural price of labor as society was forced to cultivate less-and-less-
fertile land. But only when the stationary state was reached would the
era of capitalist expansion come to an end.

The second exception was that capital investment might "for a
limited period" cause wages to rise (and hence profits to fall). Ricardo
elaborated this point only briefly: "I say excepting for a limited period,
because no point is better established, than that the supply of labourers
will always ultimately be in proportion to the means of supporting
them." (I, p. 292) With this statement, he dismissed the importance of
the short-run effects of capital investment on profits, relying on the
long-run tendency of the population to increase if wages were bid upward.

Malthus, the population expert, needed no urging to pick up the
implication of Ricardo's exception. "A country is always liable to an
increase of the funds for the maintenance of labour faster than the increase of population," he said. The reason was, he explained, that "from
the nature of population, an increase of labourers cannot be brought
into the market, in consequence of a particular demand, till after the
lapse of sixteen or eighteen years. . . ." (II, p. 312) During such a
lengthy interim wages may be so high that further investment is deterred
and capital becomes redundant.

On the grounds that Say's Law did not hold, Malthus then made
his case for the landlords: Their unproductive consumption was essential to prevent general gluts. Because the "rapid accumulation of capital," which promoted general gluts, was essentially "a rapid conversion

of unproductive into productive labour," it followed that a glut could be prevented by slowing down the conversion process. "It is absolutely necessary that a country with great powers of production should possess a body of unproductive consumers." (II, p. 421) (Malthus used Smith's definitions: "Unproductive labor" included those who produced services, not goods; and "unproductive consumption" was the purchase of the services performed by unproductive workers.)

Who could best indulge in unproductive consumption? Such consumption, said Malthus, is "not consistent with the actual habits of the generality of capitalists. The great object of their lives is to save a fortune. . . ." (II, p. 423) They alone will not afford an adequate market for the services of the unproductive. As for workers, however desirable it might be for them to be better off, an increase in their wages would not help because higher wages reduce profits and impair the motive to accumulate. (II, p. 430) The only "considerable class of other consumers" is the landlords: "the landlords . . . stand preeminent." (II, p. 424) By purchasing the services of menial servants, artists, and others, they save the country from stagnation. They curb too rapid an accumulation of capital and, at the same time, protect the capitalists from themselves by ensuring a favorable rate of profit.

Ricardo did not see any difficulty in refuting Malthus's propositions. Upon rereading Malthus's *Principles,* he wrote to his friend and follower, John R. McCulloch, "I am even less pleased with it than I was at first. There is hardly a page which does not contain some fallacy." (letter of August 2, 1820, VIII, p. 215) He proceeded to make extensive critical notes on the book but they were not published because Malthus's work had "not excited much interest, and these dry . . . comments . . . will excite still less." (letter to McCulloch, November 23, 1820, VIII, p. 298) [2]

Ricardo did not dispute the evidence of temporary gluts; he simply argued that Say's Law was supportable as a general proposition, because there was no long-term tendency toward stagnation in a capitalist, com-

---

[2] As it turned out, Ricardo was wrong; the *Notes* were rediscovered and published over a century later. Moreover, both Malthus's *Principles* and the *Notes* did excite great interest, especially when it became recognized that the Malthus-Ricardo controversy was a prelude to the Keynesian revolution that shook economics in the 1930s. Jacob H. Hollander and T. E. Gregory's edited version of Ricardo's *Notes on Malthus' "Principles of Political Economy"* was published by Johns Hopkins Press (Baltimore) in 1928; in the Sraffa and Dobbs edition of Ricardo's *Works,* the *Notes* appear in volume II.

petitive system. He dismissed Malthus's claim that the postwar depression, which was especially serious during 1819, was sufficient proof of a *general* glut; the crisis was only a temporary one, due to miscalculations:

> The difficulty of finding employment for Capital . . . proceeds from the prejudices and obstinacy with which men persevere in their old employments,—they expect daily a change for the better, and therefore continue to produce commodities for which there is no adequate demand. With abundance of capital and a low price of labour there cannot fail to be some employments which would yield good profits. . . . Men err in their productions, there is no deficiency of demand. (letter to Malthus, October 9, 1820, VIII, p. 277)

Answering Malthus's charge of a lack of effective demand, Ricardo said that "Demand is only limited by the will and power to purchase." "Whoever has commodities," he said, "has the power to consume." (II, p. 306) As for the "will" to consume, it "exists wherever the power to consume is." (II, p. 311) If as Malthus had postulated a large amount of goods was produced and their value fell with respect to wages, workers would have the power to consume a greater amount than before and would do so: "the labourers would be glad to consume conveniences and luxuries if they could get them. . . ." (II, p. 312) Savings, Ricardo pointed out, could not diminish aggregate demand because the funds were simply transferred to others—a different class of consumers to be sure—but they did not disappear. Furthermore, Malthus was inconsistent on the lack of aggregate demand. He wrote in *Principles,* "It is stated by Adam Smith, and it must allowed to be stated justly, that the produce which is annually saved is as regularly consumed as that which is annually spent, but that it is consumed by a different set of people." (II, p. 15) This inconsistency was quickly noted by Ricardo.

Ricardo, surprisingly, did not protest Malthus's argument that high wages in the short run could reduce profits and choke off the incentive to accumulate capital. "Who denies this proposition?" he said. (II, p. 310) This was the exception that he had already foreseen—and explained—in his *Principles*. Ricardo believed that if a glut occurred that caused unemployment, it would only be temporary; the situation would take care of itself. He could not conceive a situation where both capital and labor were unemployed at the same time. "It can never happen," he wrote to McCulloch. (VIII, p. 181) What he meant was that if it did "happen," wages would fall, capitalists would again hire productive labor, and the glut would disappear.

Ricardo had only disdain for Malthus's praise of unproductive consumers. On the basis of Say's Law they were not needed for full production; on the basis of Smith's analysis, since they only consumed goods, they were a drag on the process of capital accumulation. On this point both men agreed, but Malthus applauded the effect whereas Ricardo denounced it. Ricardo likened such consumption, in one place, to a fire that destroyed inventories (II, p. 421), and in another to an "earthquake which overthrows my house and buries my property." (II, p. 436) Assuming that Say's Law was operative in the long run, the dynamic, expanding process of capital accumulation that increasingly converted unproductive into productive labor (as the capitalists increased their hiring) was for Ricardo the only road to economic progress. Malthus's attack on the "bad effects" of capital accumulation, wrote Ricardo to McCulloch, was the "most objectionable" chapter in his whole book. (VIII, p. 181)

Malthus could not accept these conclusions. He found objectionable the belief that capitalists could act without considering the economic role of the landlords and yet promote the best interests of society as a whole. In an article written in 1827, he said, "a notion has been actively propagated . . . that the manufacturing and commercial classes are more important and beneficial to the state than the classes engaged in agriculture. . . . Nothing can be more fallacious, more unphilosophical, more mischievous, than these opinions." In his expanded *Essay on Population,* he said, "The countries which . . . unite great landed resources with a prosperous state of commerce and manufactures, *and in which the commercial part of the population never essentially exceeds the agricultural part,* are eminently secure from sudden reverses." He added, in obvious criticism of Ricardo's stationary state, that "there is no reason to say that they might not go on increasing in riches and population for hundreds, nay, almost thousands of years." (*Essay,* 6th ed., 1826, p. 382, italics added.)

In the end, Malthus's fears that too rapid a growth of capitalism would disrupt the landlord-dominated society he admired led him to contradict the implications of his own theory. After all, if a large non-capitalist body of consumers was necessary to prevent gluts, would it not be desirable to have many proprietors with moderate holdings rather than a few large landlords, since a more equal distribution of income favored more consumption? If so, would it not be in the public interest to break up large estates by abolishing the system of primogeniture?

Malthus admitted that "a very large proprietor, surrounded by very poor peasants, presents a distribution of property most unfavorable to effectual demand" (*Principles,* 2nd ed., p. 373) and a more equitable distribution of real property would create more consumption. But his allegiance to the large landlord prevailed, and he concluded that the law of primogeniture should be maintained:

> It is an historical truth which cannot for a moment be disputed, that the first formation, and subsequent preservation and improvement of our present constitution, and of the liberties and privileges which have so long distinguished Englishmen, are mainly due to a landed aristocracy. (*Principles,* 2nd ed., p. 380)

Thus he acknowledged again the basic noneconomic values that had governed his analysis from his very first statements in the *Essay on Population.*

It was Ricardo's ideas, however, rather than Malthus's, that made more sense to a nation undergoing a fundamental industrial transformation under capitalist direction. Nor were inconsistencies in Ricardo's logic apparent. As Keynes was to lament a hundred years later in his *General Theory of Employment, Interest, and Money* (p. 32), Ricardo won the day: "[He] conquered England as completely as the Holy Inquisition conquered Spain."

Notes to Chapter iv

References to Ricardo are from *The Works and Correspondence of David Ricardo,* edited by Piero Sraffa in collaboration with M. H. Dobb, 9 vols. (London, Cambridge University Press, 1952). For a general review of Ricardo's theories, see Mark Blaug, *Ricardian Economics* (New Haven, Conn., Yale University Press, 1958), and Oswald St. Clair, *A Key to Ricardo* (New York, Kelley, 1965).

Malthus's first edition of *An Essay on the Principle of Population* appears in Thomas Robert Malthus, *On Population,* ed. by Gertrude Himmelfarb (New York, Modern Library, 1960), pp. 1–143. References in the text other than those to the first edition are to the reprint from the last (i.e., the sixth) edition, with a biography and introduction by G. T. Bettany (London, Ward, Lock, 1890). The second and subsequent editions carried a different subtitle than the first. In the first edition, the subtitle was . . . *as it affects the Future Improvement of Society with Remarks* on the *Speculations of Mr. Godwin, M. Condorcet, and other writers.* The *Essay* was published anonymously, although Malthus was soon identified as the author. Later editions carried the subtitle . . . *or, A View of its Past and Present Effects on Human Happiness; with an Inquiry into our Prospects Respecting the Future Removal or Mitigation of the Evils Which It Occasions.*

The opening quotation on rent is from Thomas Robert Malthus, *An Inquiry into the Nature and Progress of Rent, and the Principles by which it is Regulated* (1815), A Reprint of Economic Tracts, ed. by Jacob H. Hollander (Baltimore, Johns Hopkins Press, 1903). Quotations from Malthus's *Principles* are from Rev. T. R. Malthus, *Principles of Political Economy, considered with a View to their Practical Application* (London, Murray, 1820). A second edition of Malthus's *Principles* appeared posthumously in 1836; it was reprinted by Kelley in 1951.

The standard biography of Malthus is James Bonar's *Malthus and His Work* (London, Allen and Unwin, 1924). John Maynard Keynes' biography of Malthus appears in his *Essays in Biography* (London, Macmillan, 1933).

British classical economics is an omnibus term, covering the work of a number of economists, some with significantly different theoretical approaches. (Few of the "classicists," for example, fully accepted Ricardo's theory of value.) The school's leading writers, after Smith, were Jeremy Bentham, Malthus, Ricardo, James Mill and his son John Stuart Mill, Nassau Senior, and John E. Cairnes. J. B. Say, the French economist, is usually considered an adherent.

Other writers (such as Robert Torrens, who independently developed the theory of comparative advantage, and Edward West, who independently discovered the differential theory of rent) also contributed specific theories, and still others (such as John Ramsey McCulloch, Thomas De Quincey, and Henry Fawcett) expounded the new economics in textbooks.

Although James Mill claimed that he and McCulloch were the only true disciples of Ricardo, his theoretical system was nevertheless a focal point for the "classicists." The most important point that united them, however, was their nearly unanimous advocacy (Malthus excepted) of *laissez-faire.*

Classical economic policy is examined by Lionel Robbins in *The Theory of Economic Policy in English Political Economy* (London, Macmillan, 1952) and by Warren J. Samuels in *The Classical Theory of Economic Policy* (Cleveland, World, 1966).

I

For a brief discussion of the relationship of Malthus's population theory to his later theory of gluts, see Notes, section IV, below. The quotation on ratios is from the first edition, p. 13.

Ricardo's monetary theory, which grew out of the bullion controversy of the early nineteenth century, greatly influenced his contemporaries and later members of the classical school; but it was by no means unanimously accepted, even by those who supported the bullionist position that England should resume converting its paper into gold at the earliest possible opportunity. Ricardo generally neglected short-run monetary relationships, such as the effect of the supply of money on interest rates, and the relationship of business confidence to liquidity (i.e., on velocity). Others thought these relationships important. Henry Thornton (1760–1815) in his *Enquiry into the Nature and Effects of the Paper Credit of Great Britain* (1802), for example, was much more perceptive in his analysis of these matters. For a discussion of the theories and policies of this period, see Jacob Viner's *Studies in the Theory of International Trade* and Schumpeter's *History of Economic Analysis,* III, ch. 7.

II

The English Corn Laws, which attempted to ensure a supply of cereal grains sufficient for the population, contained a sliding scale of duties; the tariff on imported grains fell as the domestic price of corn rose. The Act of 1791 provided only a nominal duty of 6*d.* when the domestic price was 54*s.* or more, a moderate duty of 2*s.* 6*d.* when the domestic price was between 54*s.* and 50*s.*, and a duty of 24*s.* 3*d.* should the domestic price fall to or below 50*s.* During the war with France, soaring freight charges together with rising domestic price levels caused grain prices to rise sharply. Corn prices in gold increased from 86*s.* to 100*s.* 3*d.* per quarter from 1809 to 1813, and corn imports were essentially duty free.

Fearing that prices would collapse when the war ended, landlords urged Parliament to raise the duties on corn in order to protect British agriculture. In 1814, the domestic price did in fact fall to 55*s.* 8*d.* Although manufacturing interests fought the proposal to raise the scale of import duties, arguing that they would be injured if food prices were kept artificially high, the landlords won. The Act of 1815 raised the price above which wheat could be imported duty free to 80*s.* per quarter.

The impact of events upon theoretical innovation was clearly evident in the simultaneous appearance of the theory of differential rent in no less than five pamphlets, by four different authors. Within one month, the following documents were published in England:

3 February 1815, Malthus, *Inquiry into Rent*
10 February 1815, Malthus, *Grounds of an Opinion*
13 February 1815, [West], *Essay on the Application of Capital to Land*
24 February 1815, Torrens, *Essay on the External Corn Trade*
24 February 1815, Ricardo, *Essay on Profits*

These dates, reported by Sraffa, are taken "mainly from publishers' advertisements in the newspapers." (IV, pp. 4–5)

Of course, the idea was not invented on the spot. Malthus had been working on it for some time; nor was it new to West and Ricardo. The theory itself went back to Petty and Smith, and one of the clearest statements of it was made by James Anderson (1739–1808), the Scottish author of *An Enquiry into the Nature of the Corn Laws* (1777).

The differential rent theory is an excellent example of the hypothesis that economists' interpretations of events in accordance with their attitudes and values affect the development of economic theory.

III

A. The supply-and-demand approach to value had first been expounded, among those who claimed to be Adam Smith's followers, by Jean-Baptiste Say in his *Traité d'économie politique,* published in 1803. (The English edition, translated by C. R. Prinsep in 1821 from the fourth edition, was especially popular in the United States.)

Despite Say's praise of Smith, he was in fact quite critical. Unlike Smith (and the Physiocrats, whom he specifically attacked), he made utility the foundation of the valuation process, although he did not use the concept of marginal utility. Production, he wrote, "is to reproduce existing materials under another form, which may give them a utility they did not before possess, or merely enlarge one they may have before presented. So that, in fact, there is creation, not of matter, but of utility; and this I call *production of wealth.*" (vol. I, p. 5) He criticized Smith's distinction between productive and unproductive labor by claiming that even though the latter produce services, or "immaterial products" that cannot be accumulated, their labor is still productive because those services satisfy wants.

Say said that utility underlies the demand for goods; "It is not our business here to enquire, wherein these wants originate; we, must take them as existing *data,* and reason upon them accordingly." (II, pp. 4–5) Supply depends on the willingness of the owner of a good or service to sell it. The cost of production of a good, or "the price, or difficulty of acquirement" (II, p. 15), in relation to its selling price affects the seller's inclination to sell. He was one of the first to develop an explicit, quasimathematical, albeit crude, equilibrium analysis of price:

Demand and supply are the opposite extremes of the beam, whence depend the scales of dearness and cheapness; the price is the point of equilibrium, where the momentum of the one ceases, and that of the other begins. . . .
. . . the rise in price is in direct ratio to the demand, and inverse ratio to the supply (II, pp. 15–16)

His explanation of value also applied to the productive services of "industry" (i.e., labor and the entrepreneurs), capital, and land. For every product, the "whole amount of productive agency employed in its completion . . . is always paid for ultimately out of the value of the product." (II, p. 71) Moreover, what is true of a particular commodity is also true for the entire community. Although it appears that only the individual entrepreneur makes a net revenue, his expenses are incomes for others. Thus the "aggregate of individual revenue, the total revenue of the community, is equal to the gross produce of its land, capital, and industry." (II, p. 76)

Just as he disputed Malthus's similar theory Ricardo would have none of Say's analysis. In Chapter XX of his *Principles,* "Value and Riches," he restated his position that labor is basic to exchange values, and that these are not determined by demand (or utility) and supply. He offered several arguments against Say's analysis. One was that price did not measure utility. (I, p. 283) Another was that rent was not a true cost, as Say thought it was: "If all rent were relinquished by landlords, I am of opinion, that the commodities produced on the land would be no cheaper. . . ." (I, p. 284) Also, the introduction of machinery, by reducing labor requirements, would cause the value of the product to fall proportionately (I, p. 286); changes in the relative abundance of the commodity were not relevant to the fall. If Ricardo had given some attention to the process by which the fall in price occurred, he would have been less inclined to dismiss "relative abundance" so casually.

B. For a discussion of Ricardian value theory, see George J. Stigler's "The Ricardian Theory of Value and Distribution," "Sraffa's 'Ricardo,'" and "Ricardo and the 93 Per Cent Labor Theory of Value" in his *Essays in the History of Economics* (Chicago and London, University of Chicago Press, 1965). A well-known, sympathetic treatment of Ricardo occurs in Alfred Marshall's *Principles of Economics,* 9th (Variorum) ed., with annotations by C. W. Guillebaud (London, Macmillan, 1961), Appendix I.

In addition to the exceptions discussed in the text, Ricardo's labor theory of value did not explain the value of goods in international trade. His analysis, which was original and fundamental to subsequent trade theory, was based on a theory of comparative advantage. This theory stated that each country engaging in trade would specialize in the production of those trade goods which it could produce most efficiently. To use a simplified version of Ricardo's example, if England exchanges a certain amount of cloth for a quantity of Portuguese wine, she gains—if the cloth traded requires less labor than

the production of English wine would. For example, if cloth production requires the labor of 100 men, and if wine production would require the labor of 120, she saves the labor of 20 men by exchanging her cloth for foreign wine. If the production of Portuguese wine requires 80 men and the production of Portuguese cloth 90, Portugal gains by devoting her labor to wine. The exchange is advantageous to both sides even though Portugal has an absolute advantage in the production of each commodity; both parties gain in the amount of commodities obtained relative to those exported.

In terms of Ricardo's analytical apparatus, trade increases "riches," not value. The aggregate amount of labor (direct and embodied) employed in each country is the same as it was before trade, but since each country now has more consumption goods, each is better off. Although trade affects the domestic allocation of resources, it will not affect the rate of profit unless the imported commodities affect the wage rate. If, for example, the imported goods are cheaper wage-goods, then money wages will fall and profits will rise.

Although Ricardo did not attempt to explain how the specific ratio at which goods exchange is determined —the question John Stuart Mill examined—he pointed out that it was *not* the amount of labor involved that controlled the ratio. England, by concentrating on cloth, exchanged the labor of 100 men for the produce of 80. The reason for the failure of the labor theory to hold in this instance was, according to Ricardo, the lack of mobility of capital from one country to another.

This assumption was curious in

two respects. First, it violated the principle of profit maximization. A capitalist, said Ricardo, would settle for a low rate of profit in his own country rather than invest abroad at a higher rate because of a "natural disinclination . . . to quit the country of his birth and connexions" for "a strange government and new laws." He admitted that these feelings might be "fancied or real." (I, p. 136) Second, it was a remarkably nationalist theory for one who believed so wholeheartedly in the advantages of free trade. Free commerce, said Ricardo, "by increasing the general mass of productions . . . diffuses general benefit, and binds together by one common tie of interest and intercourse, the universal society of nations throughout the civilized world." (I, p. 134) Unlike John Stuart Mill, however, he was not ready to advocate the outflow of capital from the developed to the less developed nations, even if profit rates there were higher. Loyalty to one's native land (which checks the outflow of capital to "a more advantageous employment" elsewhere), he said, "I should be sorry to see weakened." (I, pp. 136–137)

IV

Malthus's 1827 statement on the social role of capitalists, which appeared in the British *Quarterly Review,* is quoted in Mark Blaug, *Ricardian Economics,* p. 96. Space does not permit consideration of the many issues raised by glut controversy, but at least four deserve some mention.

1. The role of landlords in maintaining high levels of consumption and full employment had been a favorite argument of the Physiocrats; it was their influence that Say had

protested in his *Traité d'économie politique.* In Great Britain, the Physiocratic stress on consumption had been taken up by Lord Lauderdale (James Maitland), who lived from 1759 to 1839 and who wrote *Inquiry into the Nature and Origin of Public Wealth* (1804). Lauderdale criticized Smith on the grounds that parsimony, unless it was offset either by private or public expenditures, would diminish aggregate demand. He attacked especially the sinking funds that had been set up to repay the public debt, claiming that too rapid debt retirement would put funds in hands of those who would not spend it. William Spence, another writer influenced in part by Physiocratic views, also condemned parsimony on similar grounds in his *Britain Independent of Commerce* (1807). It was this pamphlet that James Mill denounced in his *Commerce Defended,* in which he developed his formulation of Say's Law.

For an analysis of this early history, see Joseph J. Spengler, "The Physiocrats and Say's Law of Markets," *Journal of Political Economy* (September/December 1945), LIII, reprinted in Spengler and Allen, *Essays in Economic Thought,* pp. 161ff. See also R. L. Meek, "Physiocracy and Classicism in England," *Economic Journal* (March 1951). Morton Paglin, in his *Malthus & Lauderdale: The Anti-Ricardian Tradition* (New York, Kelley, 1961), compares the glut theories of Malthus and Lauderdale and points out that many of Malthus's ideas had been well expressed earlier by others. (See especially p. 118.)

2. Malthus did not seriously challenge the assumption of Say's Law that money was neutral and not an

obstacle to full employment. The key to progress, he said, was the rate of savings, and "no political economist of the present day can by savings mean mere hoarding. . . . (II, p. 16) According to Malthus, there could be too much savings, but this problem was not due to the circulating medium. In one place (II, pp. 316–317) he did hint that money might have significant uses other than as a medium of exchange, but this was no more than an aside.

3. Among the inconsistencies in Malthus's analysis of gluts was the apparently contradictory position on effective demand in his *Essay on Population* and his *Principles*. In the former, he wrote that population pressed against available food supplies; if more food were available, population would spring forward to consume it. In the latter, he argued that productive resources could remain unused because there was no demand for them. This contradiction persisted even in the last edition of the *Essay*, which was prepared in 1826, after *Principles* had been published.

Spengler attempts to reconcile the two arguments in his article "Malthus's Total Population Theory: A Restatement and Reappraisal," *Canadian Journal of Economics and Political Science* (February/May 1945), vol. xi, reprinted in Spengler and Allen, *op. cit.*, pp. 349ff. In general, he proposes that Malthus came to believe that with industrialization lack of effective demand acted as a third type of check on population— in addition to the positive and preventive checks—but an undesirable one (*ibid.*, p. 359) because it led to a smaller population and a lower standard of living. Nonetheless, he

was reluctant to oppose industrialization, especially in his later writings, since he believed that the combination of the two classes, the landlords and capitalists, in the proper proportion, was the best hope of society.

Paglin, who also discusses this problem (*ibid.*, pp. 132–150), feels that Malthus's two theories cannot be combined except via the restrictive assumption that the *Essay* is a long-run and the *Principles* a short-run analysis and that such a combination involves a further inconsistency since in the *Essay* Malthus denied the need for institutional reform, while in the *Principles* he felt compelled to advocate it.

4. After Ricardo had so thoroughly disposed of Malthus's errors, it is ironic that he should suddenly and without warning confound his closest supporters with an admission that capital investment may, under certain conditions, create unemployment after all. In the third edition of his *Principles* (1821), he introduced a new chapter, "On Machinery," in which he stated that "the substitution of machinery for human labour is often very injurious to the interests of the class of labourers." (I, p. 388) The introduction of machinery, he explains, is a substitution of fixed for circulating capital; when the latter is diminished the "population will become redundant." If the aggregate amount of savings and investment were increasing so that a gradual conversion of circulating to fixed capital did not reduce the absolute amount of subsistence available for workers, then unemployment would not occur. But this did not impair the principle that a sudden increase in fixed capital investment could cause unemployment.

McCulloch reacted quickly to Ricardo's about-face, saying "Little did I expect after reading your triumphant answer to the arguments of Mr. Malthus [i.e., *Notes on Malthus*] that you were so soon to shake hands with him, and to give up all. . . ." This change of mind would, he said, induce people to believe that "Political Economy was a thing of fudge, a fabric without a foundation." (VIII, p. 382)

Ricardo's belated recognition of what was later acknowledged as an obvious characteristic of the industrial revolution—rising amounts of capital per worker—is somewhat astonishing. Explaining it theoretically would have required a considerably more complex analytical apparatus than he had constructed. The writer who developed that apparatus within the framework of the labor theory of value was Karl Marx.

Chapter v

CLASSICAL ECONOMICS
AND DISTRIBUTIVE JUSTICE:

John Stuart Mill

> The laws and conditions of the production of wealth partake of
> the character of physical truths. There is nothing optional or
> arbitrary in them . . . .
>   It is not so with the Distribution of Wealth. That is a matter
> of human institution only. The things once there, mankind,
> individually or collectively, can do with them as they like.
>
> John Stuart Mill, *Principles of Political Economy*

One of the outstanding intellectual figures of Great Britain in the
nineteenth century, John Stuart Mill (1806–73) was a philosopher,
logician, political scientist, and political economist. In breadth of knowledge and sensitivity to the realities of social and ideological conflicts, he
had few equals. He attempted to encompass within a single frame of
analysis the discordant events of his times. His *Principles of Political
Economy, with Some of Their Applications to Social Philosophy,* which
reflected his broad interest in economics, was immediately accepted as
an authoritative expression of a mature science of economics, solid in
theory and representative of the highest aspirations of British society.
Published in 1848, it went through seven editions and dominated the
teaching of economics in English-speaking countries for many years
after his death in 1873.

Although his economics was essentially Ricardian, Mill's objective
was to apply theory to practical problems, which Ricardo had often
quickly passed over. In doing so he modified Ricardian theory and at
the same time infused his book with many of the ethical values he as

105

philosopher supported. Mill was well aware of the logical distinction between theory and policy and was in fact one of the first economists in England to point out that economic analysis dealt with the means to wealth and not the ends of behavior. Yet he justified value judgments in economics on the grounds that the application of scientific principles to practical problems required them; political economy was "inseparably intertwined with many other branches of social philosophy." He wrote:

> Except on matters of mere details, there are perhaps no practical questions, even among those which approach nearest to the character of pure economical questions, which admit of being decided on economical premises alone. ("Preface," *Principles, Collected Works,* II, p. xci)

Mill's own values were eloquently expressed in *On Liberty, Utilitarianism,* and many other writings. Primarily, he sought to strengthen individual expression and promote the common good by education and institutional reform. He was no revolutionary, and he did not support state intervention except in a limited way. He accepted a society based on private property and individual competition: "The object to be principally aimed at," he said, "is not the subversion of the system of individual property, but the improvement of it, and the full participation of every member of the community in its benefits." (II, p. 214)

Yet Mill doubted whether such reforms would be enough. He disliked the competitive system in terms of tis cultivation of undesirable qualities, and he questioned the desirability of further economic growth on the grounds that true individualism did not require the unlimited accumulation of material goods. He never fully resolved his own contradictory attitudes toward the materialist society whose economics he so carefully analyzed and the ethical goals to which he believed society should aspire.

I

No writer was better prepared to reflect the conflicting economic and political philosophy of his times than Mill. From his first rigorous education in the intellectual heritage of the western man and early exposure to theories of reason and utility as guides to social welfare to his absorption of the contrary trends of romanticism, humanitarianism, and socialism during his middle years, he was a product of the divergent forces of his time.

Under the stern tutelage of his father, young Mill began the study of Greek at the age of three and was soon reading Herodotus, Xenophon, and Plato in the original. By the age of eight he had begun the study of Latin, and by the age of twelve had gone on to history, literature, government, philosophy, and mathematics. At thirteen he began his studies of political economy, with Ricardo's *Principles,* which had just been published, as a text. His father would expound the new economics on daily walks, and John Stuart would give him written analyses of their conversations the next day. These summaries were later used as notes from which James Mill wrote his own *Elements of Political Economy* in 1821. John Stuart also read Ricardo's works on the bullion controversy, and finally *The Wealth of Nations,* following his father's urging to apply Ricardo's "superior lights" to "Smith's more superficial views of political economy."

James Mill spared no effort educating his son, for he hoped to demonstrate that proper education would produce the perfectly rational man. His guide and mentor in this regard was Jeremy Bentham, who had himself been a youthful genius and who was then emerging as one of Britain's leading advocates of governmental and legal reform. Bentham believed that his theories, based on a proper understanding and application of the criterion of utility, would lead to the improvement of man and his institutions. Not tradition or natural law, but the maximization of utility, rationally considered, and the minimization of pain, should guide government policy. Reviving doctrines of hedonism, Bentham claimed that the two sovereign motives of pleasure and pain not only explained man's behavior but should be used as a standard of right and wrong. He believed that utility could be measured and summed and "the greatest happiness for the greatest number" determined rationally. Furthermore, given a proper education, the reasoning man would understand this, know what reforms were necessary, and introduce them.

James Mill, who met Bentham in 1808, found these ideas to his liking; he saw their promise for society as a whole and their relevance to the education of his son. He became the organizational manager for the reform of British society in accordance with the principle of happiness. Because he realized the importance of Ricardo's economics to the new radicalism, he urged him to write his *Principles* and enter Parliament. As for John Stuart, he was being groomed for leadership in the next generation.

In 1820, John Stuart Mill was sent abroad for further education. He stayed at the home of Sir Samuel Bentham, Jeremy's brother, in

France, and met Jean-Baptiste Say. Upon his return, he first read law with John Austin and then obtained an appointment, through his father, as a clerk in the office of the Examiner of India Correspondence in India House (a division of the East India Company), where he served from 1823 to 1858. It was at this time that he helped found the Utilitarian Society, named by him. The members of the society promoted what came to be called philosophic radicalism, which was a combination of the political reformism of Bentham, theories of economic competition based on Ricardo's political economics, and an emphasis on birth control and voluntary restriction of the growth of population, a form of neo-Malthusianism. Essentially they believed that truly representative government, complete freedom of discussion, and education which promoted the use of reason would ultimately maximize human welfare.

The inevitable reaction to his father's dominance came in 1826. Although there was never a complete break between them, he experienced a "mental crisis." When he asked himself if obtaining every object he sought would bring him happiness, "an irrepressible self-consciousness distinctly answered, 'No.'" Gradually he turned to an exploration of new ideas, reading sympathetically for the first time the writings of critics of Benthamism such as Carlyle and poets like Wordsworth and Coleridge. The romantic movement in England captured his attention with its cult of "feeling" and its anti-intellectual reliance on duty, loyalty, and tradition.

Mill's exposure to these ideas enabled him to regain his feet. He did not, in the last analysis, abandon the old utilitarianism. Rather, he raised it to a higher level. The "cultivation of feelings" occupied a prominent place in his revised science of pleasure. However, in the case of Carlyle and the German metaphysics of intuitive knowledge, he did not yield at all. He remained convinced that ideas were the result of observation and experimentation, although he admitted that historical analysis must play a much larger role in the social sciences than either Bentham or his father had been willing to allow. He was encouraged in this belief by the French sociologist Auguste Comte, with whom he corresponded. He expressed these newly worked out ideas in *A System of Logic* in 1843, a work recognized as a major contribution to the philosophy and methodology of the social sciences and firmly in the empirical tradition of Locke and Hume. The importance he gave to historical processes reflected an independence of a sort from pure

Benthamism. In economics proper, however, he still found justifiable the abstract deductive method of Ricardo and his father.

Mill also became exposed to socialist criticisms of the subservient and impoverished position of labor in industrial society and to proposals for the reform of social and economic institutions in the interest of humanitarianism. Among the socialist writings that attracted him were those of Saint-Simon, Robert Owen, Fourier, and other pre-Marxist socialists—those whom Marx called Utopian.[1] In general, these writers urged educational reforms and the formation of labor organizations and cooperative associations as a step toward restoring an individualism they believed to have been destroyed by industrialization. One of the most enthusiastic supporters of these ideas was Mrs. Harriet Taylor, whom Mill first met in 1830, and whom he married in 1851, several years after her husband died. Although she herself died seven years later, Mill attributed to her the ideas of moral improvement and the passion for justice and social reformism with which he became identified. He later wrote that while he did not learn the "purely scientific part" of economics from her, she was responsible for the general outlook of his *Principles of Political Economy,* which distinguished it from all previous books on the subject. This book, which appeared in 1848 was political economics in its broadest sense. It was Harriet Taylor, said Mill, who convinced him of the real distinction between the laws of production, which were natural laws, and those of distribution, which depend on the human will and hence could be modified. She was responsible for the chapter (in *Principles*) "The Probable Future of the Labouring Classes." The essay *On Liberty,* he said, was literally their joint production.

In 1865, Mill consented to enter Parliament as a delegate from Westminster, but with the proviso that he would not campaign and that he would not attend to the local business of his constituency if elected. He was elected but served only one term. His views, which were generally too advanced to command a following even within the Liberal Party, included advocacy of women's suffrage, a new Reform Bill, Irish rights, rights of free assembly, and the rights of Negroes in Jamaica. In his last years, he was active in the Land Tenure Reform Association, which had as one of its major goals the taxation of unearned income from land.

[1] For a brief discussion of the views of these early socialists, see the Notes to Chapter vi, Part II.

II

Mill was, at the same time, a pure theorist in economics, a historical analyst, and a social reformer. Methodologically, he was more or less successful in keeping these roles separate. In practice, the divisions between them often broke down, to the confusion of his audience.

In his essay "On the Definition of Political Economy; and on the Method of Investigation Proper to It" and later in *A System of Logic* (1843), Mill described the methodology of his economic analysis and its limitations. Following the tradition of British empiricism, he assumed that knowledge came only through the senses and was organized by the human mind into meaningful categories. In scientific reasoning in general, he said, there are two methods: induction, by which one reasons from specific experience to a general conclusion, and "a mixed method of induction and ratiocination." The first method he called a posteriori, the second a priori. In *Logic,* he called the first method the inverse deductive, or historical, method and the second the concrete deductive method.

Mill claimed that political economy as an abstract science required the a priori method since social experimentation was not feasible. He was careful to draw the line, however, between theoretical conclusions and the behavior of the real world. Because social phenomena are highly complex and subject to a variety of influences, the effects of economic forces are always subject to modification. The laws of political economy are true "without qualification" in cases that are purely hypothetical; they are true in actual cases only if proper allowances are made for other influences. To illustrate this, he used the principle of maximization of wealth on which economic theory was based. Political economy, he wrote in "On the Definition of Political Economy,"

> . . . does not treat of the whole of man's nature as modified by the social state, nor of the whole conduct of man in society. It is concerned with him solely as a being who desires to possess wealth, and who is capable of judging of the comparative efficacy of means for obtaining that end. It predicts only such of the phenomena of the social state as take place in consequence of the pursuit of wealth. (IV, p. 321)

But, he added, there are other motives for human behavior; no economist is "so absurd" to think otherwise. Actions stemming from these other motives will necessarily cause behavior different from that predicted by the maximization principle. In this way, Mill made "the economic man" a hypothetical character and created a "noneconomic man" to go with him. "With respect to those parts of human conduct of which wealth is not even the principal object, to these Political Economy does not pretend that its conclusions are applicable." In the case of predictions of real events, economics will give only an "approximation." "This approximation is then to be corrected by making proper allowance for the effects of any impulses of a different description." (*ibid.*, IV, p. 323) Like Comte, Mill believed that the noneconomic disturbances were themselves subject to laws, which in time could be understood and used to narrow the area of unpredictability.

Through his *Principles,* Mill took the view that the abstractions of political economy had a finality not to be doubted. He wrote of the absolute necessity of not sacrificing "strict scientific reasoning" to practical applications or to hopes of popularity (Preface, II, p. xcii). Consequently, he saw no need to challenge his interpretation of theory, or even to test it. On the basis of this assumption, he wrote the following passage, which amused later generations of students who had been exposed to the marginal revolution in the theory of value that had begun in Mill's lifetime:

> Happily, there is nothing in the laws of Value which remains for the present or any future writer to clear up; the theory of the subject is complete: the only difficulty to be overcome is that of so stating it as to solve by anticipation the chief perplexities which occur in applying it. (III, p. 456)

In addition to the hypothetical theory of pure economics and the noneconomic variables that affected its application, Mill distinguished an analytically separate field of value judgments. These dealt with the ends of behavior, and he was well aware that behavioral goals are unscientific. One cannot prove scientifically which behavioral goals are more desirable. That question is in the domain of ethics, not science. It relates to what ought to be done, not what is or will be, said Mill, and it is therefore generically different from scientific propositions.

Despite this, he himself attempted to justify a "scientific" approach to ethics on the basis of utility. His value judgments, in fact, dominate his *Principles of Political Economy.* He expressed them openly, perhaps on the grounds that he was, after all, writing on applications of social philosophy.

Mill began with Bentham's utilitarian theory of ethics whereby the single, overriding goal of behavior for members of society was the maximization of utility—"the greatest happiness for the greatest number." This social philosophy contained many deficiencies, of which Mill himself became painfully aware during his mental crisis, and he soon amended his beliefs to allow for different qualities of utility and the "cultivation of feelings," which were the higher qualities. But this concept had certain disturbing aspects. As different qualities could not be aggregated, any overall index of social utility would be ambiguous. Moreover, there would be no necessary relationship between such an index—even if it could be constructed—and the production of wealth. The key assumption of classical economics that goods and utility were positively related would have to be discarded.

Mill was not wholly ready to discard the idea that goods increased utility because he believed that a certain minimum standard of living was necessary for everyone. One of his objectives was to abolish poverty, an objective that he argued could be accomplished within a generation. Moreover, as he wrote in his essay on de Tocqueville, "The spirit of commerce and industry is one of the greatest instruments, not only of civilization in the narrowest, but of improvement in the widest sense." The higher qualities of utility could be reached only from a sufficiently well-developed economic base.

Mill's striving for higher goals and his deprecation of the indefinite accumulation of commodities was reflected in many of the passages of his *Principles*. He wrote:

> In England, it is not the desire of wealth that needs to be taught, but the use of wealth, and appreciation of the objects of desire which wealth cannot purchase, or for attaining which it is not required. Every real improvement in the character of the English, whether it consist in giving them higher aspirations, or only a juster estimate of the value of their present objects of desire, must necessarily moderate the ardour of their devotion to the pursuit of wealth. (II, p. 105)

The same point of view was strongly expressed in his analysis of the stationary state. Mill disputed those who dreaded its eventual attainment, specifically McCulloch, who thought that the "test of prosperity is high profits," and Adam Smith, who believed that the conditions of the people in a stationary situation must be "pinched and stinted." Said Mill:

> I cannot . . . regard the stationary state of capital and wealth with the unaffected aversion so generally manifested towards it by

political economists of the old school. . . . I confess I am not charmed with the ideal of life held out by those who think that the normal state of human beings is that of struggling to get on. . . . In the meantime, those who do not accept the present very early state of human improvement as its ultimate type, may be excused for being comparatively indifferent to the kind of economical progress which excites the congratulations of ordinary politicians; the mere increase of production and accumulation. (III, pp. 753–755)

Among the higher human objectives, if not the highest, for Mill, was the achievement of full individuality. He believed in the idea of an independent, adult human being, male or female, able and willing to exert his or her will as he or she saw fit. Moreover, economic development was not necessarily consonant with individualism in this sense. In the first place, industrial growth could produce population and environmental problems that would destroy the dignity of the individual. In the following passage, Mill reveals himself as one of the first modern ecologists.

There is room in the world, no doubt, and even in old countries, for a great increase of population, supposing the arts of life to go on improving, and capital to increase. But even if innocuous, I confess I see very little reason for desiring it. . . . A world from which solitude is extirpated, is a very poor ideal.

Nor is there much satisfaction in contemplating the world with nothing left to the spontaneous activity of nature; with every rood of land brought into cultivation, which is capable of growing food for human beings; every flowery waste or natural pasture ploughed up, all quadrupeds or birds which are not domesticated for man's use exterminated as his rivals for food, every hedgerow or superflous tree rooted out, and scarcely a place left where a wild shrub or flower could grow without being eradicated as a weed in the name of improved agriculture. If the earth must lose that great portion of its pleasantness which it owes to things that the unlimited increase of wealth and population would extirpate from it, for the mere purpose of enabling it to support a larger, but not a better or a happier population, I sincerely hope, for the sake of posterity, that they will be content to be stationary, long before necessity compels them to it. (III, p. 756)

In addition, the spirit of commercialism could be detrimental to the spirit of freedom and creativity. The rise to political power of the masses often created a new tyranny, a "tyranny of the majority," which lowered tastes and spread conformity. In his review of de Tocqueville's analysis of the leveling effects of democracy in the United States, Mill argued that it was not primarily the nature of governmental institutions that generated "the hypocrisy of luxury," superficial values, and the conformity of bourgeois opinion: These were the result of the growth of industry and wealth and the spread of commercialization not only in America but, increasingly, in England as well. The growth of commercial society created a middle class that imposed its values on everyone: "the most serious danger to the future prospects of mankind is in the unbalanced influence of the commercial spirit."

Finally, Mill stressed the production rather than the consumption of wealth: If pain could not be avoided, he said, at least individuals should be compensated for it. The production of goods required the expenditure of labor in the form of physical and mental exertion, and abstinence, defined as the sacrifice of present for future consumption— by oneself, one's children, or others for whom one is willing to make such sacrifices. Both types of disutility should be paid for, and the payment should be roughly proportional to the sacrifice involved. This principle was the basis of his theory of justice. If persons were not adequately compensated, then the system of remuneration was unjust.

In general, Mill assumed that abstainers were adequately compensated in an industrial society. The gravest charge that could be made against the existing industrial system in England was its toleration of the unjust position of the working classes. Output was so distributed, he said, that the largest amounts went to

> those who have never worked at all, the next largest to those whose work is almost nominal, and so in a descending scale, the remuneration dwindling as the work grows harder and more disagreeable, until the most fatiguing and exhausting bodily labour cannot count with certainty on being able to earn even the necessaries of life. . . .
> (II, p. 207)

In the same passage, he gave his verdict on the present state of society:

> If . . . the choice were to be made between Communism with all its chances, and the present state of society with all its sufferings and injustices; if the institution of private property necessarily carried with it as a consequence, that the produce of labour should be apportioned as we now see it, almost in an inverse ratio to the labour . . . all the difficulties, great or small of Communism would be but as dust in the balance. (*ibid.*)

This statement caused consternation among Mill's followers when it first appeared in the third edition of his *Principles* in 1852, but he kept it in the remaining editions and continued to write about his sympathies for socialism and communism. The forms of social organization he favored were the associative, cooperative varieties of Robert Owen and Fourier, who sought as their ideal the independent workers who joined together to operate their own establishments. (Mill criticized strongly any form of centralized socialism as inconsistent with true individualism.)

Mill's value judgments governed the direction of his economic analysis. He believed that a nation should strive to increase its output as much as necessary to provide an adequate standard of living for its people, but straining for ever-greater production could be destructive of higher ideals, including that of true individualism. The primary goal of distribution was to bring compensation into line with the disutilities incurred in production.

III

The high level of national income in England was, according to Mill the result of the laws of production, which, like "physical truths," could not be altered. However, this did not mean that any nation would automatically travel the road of economic progress. The laws he was talking about were hypothetical, relevant only when they were not offset by contrary actions and wrong public policies. Mill believed that the industrialized nations which had achieved a favorable economic position could not assume that their gains would continue or even that they would be able to hold onto their present status. One of Mill's fears with regard to production was that a high population growth rate would undermine the country's economic surplus.

According to Mill, they hypothetical laws governing the production of wealth were rooted in the "nature of things," in technology as well as in human nature. He began his study of productivity with an analysis, largely Ricardian, of land, labor, and capital and the conditions under which they could be increased.

First, he said, the quantity of natural resources (land) is fixed but their quality (productivity) can be improved by technology. Given a static technology, the continued application of labor and capital will yield diminishing returns. However, it is unlikely that even the introduction of new technology will in the long run offset the increasing difficulty of producing agricultural goods for a constantly growing population.

As for labor, he stressed the importance of its skills, intelligence, energy, and moral qualities to its productivity. He made a special point of human capital investment. Rearing children, he said requires the "expense of much labour to some person or persons. . . . To the community at large, the labour and expense of rearing its infant population form a part of the outlay which is a condition of production." Part of this outlay is not for strictly economic purposes:

> . . . technical or industrial education of the community . . . is really, and in general solely, undergone for the sake of a greater or more valuable produce thereby attained, and in order that a remuneration, equivalent or more than equivalent, may be reaped by the learner, besides an adequate remuneration for the labour of the teacher, when a teacher has been employed. (II, pp. 40–41)

Mill considered the costs of education part of the cost of maintaining a productive society, and he included among those costs not only expenditures for the education of manual workers, but also the expenses incurred in training inventors, managers, and "savants, or speculative thinkers" whose "theoretic discoveries" extended man's power to control nature, perhaps not immediately, but ultimately.

Like Smith, Mill discussed the importance to productivity of the division of labor—he preferred the phrase "the cooperation or the combination of labor"—but he emphasized the role of machinery, the fixed capital used with labor. He also recognized that the introduction of expensive machinery required larger firms and the formation of joint-stock companies in order to assemble the requisite capital. Mill saw certain disadvantages in this form of business organization, particularly the possibility that the hired managers might not be too efficient. But unlike Smith he believed that on balance a corporate type of organization was desirable. Efficiency, he felt, could be maintained by recruiting better-trained managers and by such pecuniary inducements as profit-sharing.

Mill accepted the Malthusian proposition that the population (and hence the supply of labor) could be increased indefinitely if there were sufficient food supplies. He made one amendment to Malthus's and Ricardo's proposition that population was perfectly elastic when wages were at the subsistence level, however. There was not, he said, a physical minimum toward which wages would tend in the long run but rather a moral minimum related to the fact that workers could become used to "subsisting" at a higher level of income. If the economic position of the workers temporarily improved and if they came to regard the new comforts as indispensable, then a new minimum wage, sufficient to maintain this higher subsistence level, would come into being. The curve of the labor supply (assuming that the demand for labor increases over time) would then be upward-rising rather than horizontal as Ricardo had said. Mill did not hold out much hope, however, that laborers would restrict the size of their families.[2]

In general, Mill accepted Smith and Ricardo's theory of capital. What distinguished capital from other goods was the fact that it employed labor productively. Mill's four fundamental propositions concerning capital were (1) that the amount of industry was limited by capital, (2) that capital came from savings, (3) that capital was consumed, and (4) that the demand for commodities was not a demand for labor. In other words, output will increase in proportion to the savings invested in productive labor. (The fourth proposition that the demand for commodities is not a demand for labor did not deny that consumer demand guided the employment of capital in different industries; it merely reasserted, paradoxically, that savings, not consumption, paid labor's wages.)

Mill saw no limits to the growth of capital and hence output, short of the stationary state. However, he noted several possible interruptions in the process of capital investment, none of them serious. He criticized the critics of Say's Law and thus supported Ricardo's position in the glut controversy. Savings did not reduce purchasing power; investing them channeled it to others. Unproductive consumption was not necessary to maintain aggregate demand; it merely reduced the pool of productive labor. On the other hand, Mill, like Ricardo, admitted that

[2] Mill's crusade for limiting the size of families runs through all his work. He believed that it would probably be possible to abolish poverty within a generation. Not only did he urge public education for all in population principles; he sought also to mobilize the power of public opinion to restrain man's sexual drives—"a public opinion by which intemperance and improvidence of every kind would be held discreditable, and the improvidence which overstocks the labour market would be severely condemned, as an offence against the common weal." (II, p. 375) It is ironic that Mill, who had elsewhere condemned the stultifying effects of public opinion, would here deliberately cultivate it as an instrument of economic development. Mill's pioneering stand on women's rights gave him a further argument against overpopulation: "It is seldom by the choice of the wife that families are too numerous; on her devolves (along with all the physical suffering and at least a full share of the privations) the whole of the intolerable domestic drudgery resulting from the excess. To be relieved from it would be hailed as a blessing by multitudes of women who now never venture to urge such a claim, but who would urge it, if supported by the moral feelings of the community." (II, p. 372)

temporary gluts were possible. Since the production of goods does not necessarily create an immediate demand for them, there may be times when individuals prefer holding money to spending it on consumption goods. In such periods, goods will remain unsold and capital will be unemployed (II, p. 65). Mill did not dispute the occurrence of these "commercial crises." However he blamed them on the overextension and contraction of credit, not on the inherent characteristics of the production process.

Mill also smoothed over the Ricardian heresy that the conversion of circulating into fixed capital might cause technological unemployment. With Ricardo, Mill admitted the possibility: "All attempts to make out that the labouring classes as a collective body *cannot* suffer temporarily by the introduction of machinery, or by the sinking of capital in permanent improvements, are . . . necessarily fallacious." (II, p. 96). But he concluded with Ricardo's argument that as such changes are made slowly and as there is always a growth in aggregate savings over time, such unemployment rarely occurs: "I do not believe that as things are actually transacted, improvements in production are often, if ever, injurious, even temporarily, to the labouring classes in the aggregate." (II, p. 97) Moreover, he said, because such improvements must either reduce prices to consumers or increase profits, society ultimately gains. He quickly pointed out, however, that the gains could accrue to future generations, not the current one. If there were any injury through unemployment to the existing generation, governments had "the obligation of alleviating, and if possible, preventing" it. (II, p. 99)

The supply of savings was unlimited so long as the rate of profit was high enough to compensate for abstinence. Two factors governed the rate of saving, said Mill. One was the size of the fund out of which savings could be made, and the other was the strength of disposition to save. The "fund" was equivalent to the social surplus—i.e., the net revenues of society in the form of profits and rents. The disposition to save was a psychological propensity related to the rate of return on capital. Although Mill noted the technical fact that saving involved sacrificing present goods for future goods—"abstinence" in the terminology of his contemporary Nassau Senior—he was more concerned with the factors that governed the strength of the disposition to abstain from present consumption, particularly the moral and social attitudes of the individual. Provident motives, he believed, often stemmed from a concern for others, for the security of one's children or the advancement of private and public causes. But he also recognized less admirable motives for abstinence, such as the quest for power through wealth, the wish to move up the social ladder, and the desire for the prestige of being able to retire from work. These factors, in addition to the Englishman's "extreme incapacity . . . for personal enjoyment"—attributed to the Puritan heritage (II, p. 171)—strengthened the disposition to save. To Mill, England was characterized by the availability of a large net revenue for savings and strong motives to save. Despite low profit rates, he did not foresee any limit to the future supply of capital.

Mill's laws of production led with rigorous Ricardian logic to his principles of distribution. Rents to landlords depended on the law of diminishing returns in agriculture because rent was the differential surplus between the costs of production on supramarginal land and the price-determining costs on the least fertile lands under cultivation. Wages depended on the ratio between the size of the labor force and the amount of capital. In the short run, this wage might be above, equal to, or below the subsistence level, but in the long run it depended on the "strength of the checks by which the too rapid increase of population is restrained." (III, p. 696) Profits on capital were what remained of society's output after rents and wages were paid. These conclusions with respect to distribution, said Mill, were universal, independent of the existence of a market system:

> If we examine, on what the pecuniary value of labour, and the pecuniary value of the use of land, depend, we shall find that it is on the very same causes by which we found that wages and rent would be regulated if there were no money and no exchange of commodities. (III, p. 695)

The same is true of profits.

Having arrived at this Ricardian formulation of distribution theory, Mill was prepared to investigate the "influence of the progress of society on production and distribution" (the title of Book IV of his *Principles*). Savings and capital investment would continue he predicted, until the economy reached a stationary state. This stationary state would occur when an expanding population required the cultivation of lands of such inferior quality that the profits, after rents and wages, were too low to make further investment attractive. As Mill defined it, "there is in every country some rate of profit, below which persons in general will not find sufficient motive to save for the mere purpose of growing richer, or of leaving others better off than themselves. (III, p. 737)

He spelled out four factors that governed the speed of the movement toward a stationary state: (1) the rate of increase in capital, (2) the rate of growth of population, (3) the supply of fertile land, and (4) the rate of technological change in agriculture. With the rate of savings (1) and the supply of fertile land (3) given, the attainment of the stationary state rested upon the relative strength of the two conflicting forces, the rate of growth of the population and the rate of technological improvement in agriculture. To the extent that the former exceeded the latter the advent of the stationary state would be hastened; a consistently higher rate of technological change could, however, postpone the end of economic development.

Although these forces were universal, Mill was especially concerned about the position of England: Was she poised on the brink of the stationary state? As we have seen, Mill did not believe that such a state, if it did come, would be a disaster, but rather, it would be an opportunity for greater development of the individual and the "Art of Living." Nevertheless he did not urge the economy toward it.

Mill believed that England had already achieved a level of income that was more than high enough to supply the minimum needs of her people, but the surplus could easily be dissipated by taking the wrong path, namely, by allowing the population to grow too rapidly. The reason for England's currently favorable position was first that technological changes in agriculture had been proceeding at a faster rate than population growth. In the previous "fifteen or twenty years," said Mill, there had been a "strong impulse in agricultural improvement." (III, p. 713) Moreover, four additional factors had tended to offset a falling rate of profit. One was commercial crises that reduced capital: There had been a "waste of capital in periods of overtrading and rash speculation, and the commercial revulsions by which such times are always followed." (III, p. 741) However, subsequent periods of economic growth quickly replenished the supply. The second was the great improvements in industrial techniques, which had reduced costs and made more goods available (a direct gain for the economy as a whole). A third factor was the repeal of the Corn Laws, which had also lowered the price of food. The fourth and last factor was an "overflow of capital into colonies or foreign countries, to seek higher profits than can be obtained at home." Mill believed this "to have been for many years one of the principal causes by which the decline of profits in England has been arrested." (III, p. 746) To the extent that the outflow of capital spurred the production of food in fertile foreign lands for export to England, it would buoy profits at home.

In Mill's opinion, England was a capital-surplus nation, and in such countries "the rate of profit is habitually within, as it were, a hand's breadth of the minimum, and the country therefore on the very verge of the stationary state." (III, p. 738) This did not mean that the stationary state would necessarily be reached *soon,* but it *could* be attained quickly. The worst that could happen would be an uncontrolled population explosion that would eat up the surplus. But if population growth could be held in bounds, then society could begin to attack its ills and use its surplus for social and economic reform.

IV

In capital-surplus nations the primary issue was no longer production but distribution: "It is only in the backward countries of the world that increased production is still an important object; in those most advanced, what is economically needed is a better distribution . . . ." (III, p. 755) By distribution, Mill did not mean the share of the aggregate output devoted to wages, rents, and profits, but the distribution of income to individuals as compensation for their efforts and abstinence. What was at stake here was the principles governing economic value.

In his analysis of value, Mill modified Ricardo's labor theory so thoroughly that not much of it remained. Although he minimized the extent to which he had deviated from Ricardo's original position, Mill's shift was significant in that he was able to incorporate many of the criticisms advanced during the nearly a third of a century that had elapsed since Ricardo's first edition. In addition, he introduced certain theoretical innovations of his own, although, characteristically, he did not emphasize his own originality.

In Mill's analysis of exchange value, commodities were divided into three classes: those whose supply could not be increased; those whose supply could be increased indefinitely without a rise in costs, and those whose supply could be increased only with rising costs. In the case of the first type, it was the relationship of supply and demand that determined price; in the case of the second, it was the cost of production; and in the case of the third, it was the cost of production in the most unfavorable existing circumstances. This classification roughly paralleled Ricardo's: The first group included unreproducible goods such as works of art, commodities produced under monopoly conditions, goods entering international trade, and commodities whose supplies had not been adjusted to market demands through factor mobility; the second included reproducible, manufactured goods in the long run; and the third included agricultural goods subject to the law of diminishing returns due to a limited amount of available fertile land.

Although he always spoke respectfully of Ricardo, Mill broke with his labor theory of value in two ways. First, he acknowledged that if all industries employed labor and capital in the same proportion, and if wage and profit rates were the same everywhere, then the prices of commodities would be proportionate to the amount of labor required for their production as Ricardo had indicated (i.e., for all commodities in group two and for the marginal outputs of group three). But, said Mill, where any one or more of these conditions does not hold, then firms, under competition in the long run, will sell their commodities at prices equal to money costs of production; but such costs would not be proportionate to the quantities of labor embodied in production.

Second, Mill extended the analysis of costs beyond money wages and the going rate of profit to the "real" costs of production—the workers' exertion and discomfort when working and the capitalists' abstinence from consumption when saving. This real-cost analysis had its roots in Smith's theory of the disutility (the "toil and trouble") of labor and Benthamite hedonism rather than in Ricardo's theory of labor (in man-hours) as an objective cause of value. Mill's shift to the subjective approach to costs had the philosophical advantage of giving the capitalist an equal role (along with the worker) in determining a good's economic value. This both Smith and Ricardo had failed to do, as various socialists (including Marx) were not slow to notice.

Whatever injustices there might be in the existing system of distribution, they were not, according to Mill, due to exploitation of the worker under a system of competition and private property. Yet he sometimes expressed views that contained hints of a labor theory of value. In his chapter on profits, for example, Mill stated flatly: "The cause of profit is, that labour produces more than is required for its support." (II, p. 411) Furthermore, "the reason why capital yields a profit, is because food, clothing, materials, and tools, last longer than the time which was required to produce them." (*ibid.*) Since the capitalist advances these goods to workers on the condition that he receive the whole of what they produce, this means that the workers "in addition to reproducing their own necessaries and instruments, have a portion of their time remaining, to work for the capitalists." (*ibid*). The idea that a worker spends part of his time working for himself and part working for the capitalist was exactly the proposition Marx advanced in *Capital.* (Marx would also have agreed with Mill that profit arises from conditions of production, not from the conditions of exchange; he would have disagreed with the proposition that there could be profits whether or not there was an exchange economy.)

Mill's rejection of profit as a form of exploitation was based on his acceptance of the institution of private property. Given the legitimacy of the ownership by capitalists of the goods advanced to labor, their profits too became legitimate as a reward for the abstinence (saving) required to purchase the means of production. If the workers themselves, said Mill, had accumulated property through saving, they would not need to divide their product with anyone. But where workers did not have materials, machinery, and provisions of their own and used those advanced by others, the output must be shared; and the "terms of cooperation between present labour and the fruits of past labour and savings, are subject for adjustment between the two parties. Each is necessary to the other." (II, p. 216)

Although there were loopholes and inconsistencies in his argument, Mill's grounds for a "better distribution" were that personal incomes should be related to real costs. He recognized that this was not always possible.

Mill's assumption of a relationship between real costs and economic values in a competitive society did not apply to goods in the first category, whose values were determined by supply and demand alone. In the cases of nonreproducible goods and of reproducible goods in the market at any given time, costs did not control prices. Monopolistic prices, Mill agreed, were exploitative, and he enlarged to some extent on the usual monopoly analysis of contemporary British writers. (He evidently was unaware of the work of Augustin Cournot, the French economist, on duopoly, published in 1839.) Mill pointed out, first, that where there were only several large companies in an industry it would be erroneous to assume that competition would keep prices low. "Where competitors are so few, they always end by agreeing not to compete." (II, p. 142) Moreover, in retail trade, custom, habit, ignorance, or search costs often allowed different prices for the same good to exist in the market at the same time. Here Mill anticipated later theories of monopolistic competition.

In the case of international trade, Mill, like Ricardo, believed that the law of costs did not apply because of the immobility between nations of labor, capital, and of course land. In an early essay, "Of the Laws of Interchange between Nations," written in 1829 and published in his 1844 *Essays on Some Unsettled Questions in Political Economy,* he sought (as Ricardo had not) to determine the specific price ratio of commodities in international trade; in doing so he showed that he understood the concept of demand as a schedule or function. Using the example of two countries each with one commodity to exchange (he later expanded his analysis to three countries), Mill stated that the terms of trade depended on the relative strength of the demand which each country had for the other's products. In a disequilibrium situation where the value of one country's imports was less than the amount the other country was willing to buy, a fall in the price ratio would increase the quantity imported and at the same time make its exports of goods to the other country less attractive. Equilibrium would be reached when the price ratio was such that the quantities exchanged exactly paid for each other. In examining the possible combinations, Mill indicated different types of demand schedules, which reflected the behavior of total revenue as price changed, types later referred to as elastic, unitary, and inelastic. He recognized, along with Ricardo, that a country would gain in "riches" as a result of trade; he did not attempt, however, to measure the gains.

In the case of the reproducible goods sold in a competitive market (commodity categories two and three), prices tended to reflect real costs, except rents. Rents were price-determined, as Ricardo had claimed, and hence unearned. Said Mill, the natural progress of society makes the landlords "grow richer, as it were in their sleep, without working, risking, or economizing." (III, pp. 819–820)

Profits were payments to capitalists for their abstinence, risks, and the wages of superintendence. Although "the rate of necessary remuneration for abstinence . . . differs widely in different states of societies and civilization," (II, p. 402) capitalists' savings at any one time and place reflect the "comparative value placed . . . upon the present and future . . . ." (*ibid.*)

In the case of wages, the situation was more complex, and Mill's position was somewhat ambiguous. Although in his discussion of socialism he had made the point that wages were not directly proportional to disutilities, he tended to modify his position when discussing labor markets in detail.

In general, Mill did *not* claim that workers would be inadequately paid in labor markets where competition existed and where workers had sufficient knowledge of the market: ". . . it is a mistake to suppose that competition merely keeps down wages. It is equally the means by which they are kept up." (II, pp. 356) He repeated his argument in reviewing socialist ideas. While he agreed with many of them, he said, "I utterly dissent from . . . their declamations against competition." In the labor market, competition "is a source not of low but of high wages, wherever the competition *for* labour exceeds the competition *of* labour . . . ." (III, p. 794)

Yet Mill noted several exceptions. He made a special point of refuting Adam Smith's theory of net advantages with respect to occupations where the work is especially disagreeable. Smith had argued that such jobs had to pay a higher wage in order to attract workers, while in the agreeable and desirable employments which workers naturally sought out, wages would be lower. Mill found this "altoghether a false view of the state of facts . . . . The really exhausting and the really repulsive labours, instead of being better paid than others, are almost invariably paid the worst of all . . . ." "The hardship and the earnings, instead of being directly proportional . . . are generally in an inverse ratio to one another." (II, p. 383) The reason was that the workers in these jobs, who were most likely to be degraded and uneducated, had no other choice.

The lack of correspondence between earnings and exertion was also shown in Mill's analysis of "natural monopolies" of labor, or what John Eliott Cairnes later called labor's "non-competing groups." There were, said Mill, different grades of labor, both manual and professional, so completely separate that each one constituted a different population and was unaffected by wage levels in other groups. This separation of groups, said Mill, is "almost the equivalent to an hereditary distinction of caste; each employment being chiefly recruited from the children of those already employed in it." (II, p. 387) He identified three types of manual laborers (artisans, skilled and unskilled workers) in addition to the "liberal professions" which were "mostly supplied by the sons of either the professional, or the idle classes." (*ibid.*) Mill claimed that the professions were generally overstocked. Among manual workers, the wages of artisans were higher "than is justifiable" in comparison with the two lower classes, primarily because the "artizans are a more prudent class, and do not marry so early or so inconsiderately." (II, p. 388) The remedy for low wages among the others was to limit the size of their families.

Late in his career, Mill acknowledged that there might be a deficiency in the labor market mechanism even under competitive conditions. He explicitly abandoned the wage-fund theory in 1869 when he wrote a sympathetic review in the *Fortnightly Review* of William Thornton's book *On Labour: Its Wrongful Claims and Rightful Duties, its Actual Present and Possible Future.* Thornton had argued that supply-and-demand analysis could not explain wages under certain conditions, that the level of the wage fund was not fixed, and that workers tended to have an inferior bargaining position. Mill rejected the argument against the applicability of the theory of supply and demand, but he did accept the possibility that the wage-fund could, under certain circumstances, vary. He admitted that the wage-fund was not always the same because the total receipts that the employer keeps for himself and family, over and above depreciation, other business costs, and the necessaries for his family, are variable. If wage rates are higher, he may keep less of the business receipts for himself and purchase the same amount of labor as before. The ultimate, upper limit to the wage level is the point at which the employer would be ruined, "not the inexorable limits of the wages-fund." Mill went on to say, "The doctrine hitherto taught by all or most economists (including myself), which denied it to be possible that trade combinations can raise wages . . . is deprived of its scientific foundation, and must be thrown aside." ("Thornton on Labour and Its Claims," (V, pp. 645–646) Mill also accepted the possibility that employers may have a advantage in wage negotiations; because they could hold out longer in a labor dispute, they could depress wages below the competitive level.

Mill's recantation of the wage-fund doctrine caused consternation and discussion among many economists. Mill himself did not modify his original statements of the theory in the next (1871) edition of his *Principles,* the last during his lifetime, except to mention in the Preface that there had been instructive discussion on the subject "but the results, in the author's opinion, are not yet ripe for incorporation in a general treatise on Political Economy." (II, p. xciv)

Fortunately for his theories Mill did not explore the ramifications of his abandonment of the wage-fund doctrine. It undermined his theory that wages were brought into a proper relationship with disutilities through competition, and it opened the door for unions to raise wages without reducing the funds available for other workers. Worse yet, it unhinged the whole structure of the classical theory of distribution. If the theory of the determination of wages was uncertain, so was the theory of profits which depended on it. And as the theory of economic growth depended on the rate of profit, the central classical theme of the necessary course of economic development was suddenly left hanging.

V

The source of the injustices of the existing system of the distribution of income, according to Mill, lay in the maldistribution of the ownership of property. If appropriate reforms were made, he believed, then the market system of competition, property rights, and individual responsibility would be superior to any form of socialism or communism.

Mill's rule governing the just distribution of property was that persons should receive "the fruits of their own labor and abstinence." (II, p. 208) Income (and hence property) would then reflect proportionately individual differences in exertion and abstinence; moreover, such proportionate returns would furnish the needed rewards and incentives to production.

To revise the laws of property so that ownership represented the fruits of labor and abstinence was a formidable task. Mill recognized that, in the past, fortunes had been acquired through conquest, violence, and fraud; but he was unwilling to disturb unjust claims if the injustice had occurred long ago. As for those who inherited wealth, however, he found their claims unsupportable on the basis of equity. Why should they have income from the exertion and savings of others, simply because of inherited wealth? He consequently recommended a heavy inheritance tax, although he would permit a modest amount of the deceased's property to remain with his heirs. To him, the most difficult problem in relating property to effort was in the case of land ownership since, by definition, rents were unearned. He did not actually recommend the abolition of property in land, however. He was willing to concede that if the landlord improved the land, his claim of ownership should be accepted, subject to the proviso that all land rights are tentative and depend on the "general interests of the community." (II, p. 231) If land was appropriated by the state however, landlords should be recompensed. If a landlord did not improve his land, then political economy could have nothing to say in his defense. (II, p. 228) One specific proposal that Mill favored was a tax on gains from rising land values as a result of population growth. He recommended that such a tax be imposed not immediately, but at some future, specified date, so that landlords would have fair warning.

Mill analyzed a number of forms of economic organization from the standpoint of justice and the encouragement of individualism. He believed that peasant proprietorships had much to commend them, because they fostered the spirit of individual independence, a trait he valued highly. They enabled owners to reap the rewards of their own effort and frugality, and they promoted prudence in restricting the size of families. Nonetheless, Mill did not actually recommend the "diffusion" of landed property (except in Ireland, where the agricultural situation was so exploitative and backward that proprietorships would be a definite improvement). He believed that large establishments with hired labor and tenant-capitalists were more efficient than small enterprises and hence should be encouraged.

The existence and efficiency of the large joint-stock companies, which hired large numbers of workers, also raised the similar issue of the degree of independence that workers could win in an industrial society. In the chapter in his *Principles* "On the Probable Futurity of the Labouring Classes," Mill condemned the typical dependency of hired workers on employers and urged workers' participation in governing their own affairs through associations, profit-sharing, and cooperatives. Whether cooperatives could compete successfully with joint-stock companies was questionable, however, because technological aggressiveness and innovation were less likely in group endeavors than in organizations run by private capitalists. (III, p. 793) Mill had several suggestions for stimulating the productivity of cooperative enterprises, but they appeared to be more in the nature of pious hopes than businesslike propositions.

The role of government in Mill's program for reform was essential yet carefully restricted. As a minimum, governments should protect individuals' personal freedoms and their rights to the acquisition and exchange of property, insofar as these rights were the result of effort and frugality. Mill opposed absolutely any governmental interference with domestic or international markets in the form of price or wage controls or tariffs, except in the case of infant industries (which might be protected for a limited period to permit them to gain their feet. He also opposed monopoly grants (except patents and copyrights), laws against workmen's combinations (if they were voluntary), and restraints on freedom of speech and the press.

There were other areas in which governmental intervention was optional. Mill's argument here was that in certain cases the good accomplished would outweigh the inherent disadvantages. The disadvantages were that governments had to use force to make an individual act against his own interests, tended to be less efficient than private groups motivated by personal gain, and undermined individual self-reliance. Thus, *"Laissez-faire . . .* should be the general practice: every departure from it, unless required by some great good, is a certain evil." (III, p. 945)

Whether a particular governmental policy was a "greater good" remained for individuals themselves to determine. For the "greater good," Mill himself recommended compulsory elementary education (to the extent that it was not provided by private institutions), government protection of children, laws regulating hours of work, government sponsorship of scientific research and professorships, and colonization. He also supported regulation of nautral resources, public works, and restrictions on certain types of contracts (such as selling oneself into slavery) and on bequests.

Although Mill was generally cautious and reluctant to expand the functions of government, he pointed to one argument often used by political economists against government expenditures that was no longer valid. In countries like England where the stock of capital was large and profits low, it was no longer true, he said, that government expenditures would impoverish the country; new savings could quickly replenish the amounts drawn from accumulated capital. He even admitted that "this view of things greatly weakens, in a wealthy and industrious country, the force of the economical argument against the expenditure of public money for really valuable, even though industriously unproductive, purposes." (III, p. 748) However, he did not place a high priority on massive government spending for any purpose, except possibly for education. The road to justice and the higher aspirations of mankind was not to be paved with government spending.

Notes to Chapter v

I

References in the text to Mill's *Principles of Political Economy with Some of Their Applications to Social Philosophy* are from volumes II and III of the *Collected Works of John Stuart Mill* (Toronto, University of Toronto Press, 1965). V. W. Bladen prepared the introduction, and J. M. Robson edited the text. Mill's *Essays on Some Unsettled Questions on Political Economy*, first published in

1844, is included in volume IV, with an introduction by Lord Robbins. Although some volumes are still in preparation, this collection will be of inestimable value to scholars, who have long felt the need for fully collated and accurate texts of Mill's extensive writings. Related to this enterprise, and of value to those interested in keeping abreast of current work on Mill, is *The Mill News Letter.* Edited by J. M. Robson, it has been published regularly since 1965 by the University of Toronto Press.

References to Mill's "De Tocqueville on Democracy in America" (1843), "On Liberty" (1859), and "Utilitarianism" (1863) are from Marshall Cohen, ed., *The Philosophy of John Stuart Hill: Ethical, Political and Religious* (New York, Modern Library, 1961). The edition used here of Mill's *Autobiography* (1873) is edited by Harold Laski (London, Oxford University Press, 1924). The quotation on logic is from Mill's *System of Logic, Ratiocinative and Inductive: being a Connected View of the Principles of Evidence and the Methods of Scientific Investigation,* 8th ed. (New York, Harper & Brothers, 1874). Mill's *Considerations on Representative Government* (1861) is included in John Stuart Mill, *Utilitarianism, Liberty, and Representative Government,* with an Introduction by A. D. Lindsay (New York, Dutton, 1951).

Bibliographical references to Mill are extensive, befitting his important role in the history of thought in so many fields. For authoritative, general works in areas outside economics, see R. P. Anschutz, *The Philosophy of J. S. Mill* (London, Oxford University Press, 1953); Leslie Stephen, *The English Utilitarians* (London,

Duckworth, 1900), vol. III; John M. Robson, *The Improvement of Mankind: The Social and Political Thought of J. S. Mill* (Toronto, University of Toronto Press, 1968).

Biographical information concerning Mill is found in Michael St. John Packe, *The Life of John Stuart Mill* (London, Martin Secker & Warburg, 1954). See also F. A. Hayek, *John Stuart Mill and Harriet Taylor* (London, Routledge & Kegan Paul, 1951). For a useful and important analysis of the intellectual background in which John Stuart Mill was raised, see Elie Halevy, *The Growth of Philosophic Radicalism,* tr. by Mary Morris [1928] (Boston, Beacon Press, 1966).

Bentham's influence on John Stuart Mill looms large. Even though Mill later reacted against Benthamite sectarianism and attempted to place the ethics of utility in a different perspective, he did not doubt the connection between liberalism, individualism, utility (in some form), and experimentalism as the source of knowledge.

Jeremy Bentham (1748–1832) dedicated himself to exposing the inadequacies of governmental institutions and the abuses of law. He spared no one who stood against the rational application of the principles of utility to government policies. He was under thirty when, in *Fragment on Government* (1776), he attacked the highly prestigious *Commentaries* on British law of William Blackstone. In *Defense of Usury* (1787) he found fault with Adam Smith's strictures against the profligate and spendthrift and his advocacy of restrictions on the interest rate, for he believed that every man was a true judge of his own self-interests and should be allowed the freedom to follow these interests without government interference.

Bentham's premise was the principle of hedonistic calculus: "Nature has placed mankind under the governance of two sovereign masters, pain and pleasure. It is for them alone to point out what we ought to do, as well as to determine what we shall do." (*An Introduction to the Principles of Morals and Legislation,* 1789) Bentham made no distinction between cause-and-effect analysis, morals, and government actions. In his view, individuals acted to maximize utility and minimize pain; this was also what they should do. As governments and institutions, more often than not, were guided by erroneous doctrines such as natural law or the need to promote the national character, which blinded them to the principle of maximum utility, they should be reformed.

Although Bentham was concerned with policy, not theory, his analysis of utility led him to approximate the concept of diminishing marginal utility—a formulation in the utility tradition of Hutcheson and Pufendorf that Smith had abandoned but that foreshadowed postclassical writers. It is somewhat ironic that Bentham considered himself the "spiritual father" of James Mill, who was in turn the "spiritual father" of Ricardo, when Ricardo, thus his "spiritual grandson," rejected so completely the utility approach to economic value. But Ricardo was a Benthamite to the extent that he accepted the principle of utility as the basis of governmental reforms.

Bentham believed in the measurement and interpersonal comparison of utility: Only with such an objective comparison of utilities could a science of legislation be constructed. There were several elements in his "calculus" of pleasure and pain: intensity, duration, certainty or uncertainty, propinquity or distance, fecundity (the probability that one kind of sensation would not be followed by an opposite kind), and finally extent (the number of individuals affected). Using these dimensions of utility, the degree to which a proposed policy would promote the greatest happiness for the greatest number could be calculated by a kind of moral arithemetic.

The principle of diminishing marginal utility led Bentham to recognize that maximization of utility in society could best be promoted by equalizing income. As the utility derived from an addition to wealth was less for those with high incomes than for persons with low incomes, a transfer of funds from the wealthy to the poor would raise the aggregate utility of society. But Bentham backed away from accepting the equalization of income as essential to governmental reform. Such a course, he said, would conflict with the principle of property, and only when property is respected and protected will individuals devote their energies to production. If property were equally divided, "everything would be speedily destroyed. . . . If the condition of the industrious were not better than condition of the idle, there should be no reason for being industrious." The willingness to sacrifice the equality implications of their theory on the altar of expediency characterized all utilitarians, including John Stuart Mill; for this reason some socialists condemned their arguments as hypocritical.

The governmental policies advocated by Mill fit the Benthamite theoretical framework. Bentham stated that the rules of government were usually unnecessary because individuals knew their own self-interests better than the governments, and pernicious because governmental restraints caused pain and not pleasure. Moreover government actions required revenues, and hence taxes, and taxes were coercive by definition because they were a payment made without a *quid pro quo.* On the other hand, Bentham did not believe in a natural harmony of interests, but rather that the government was responsible for laying down the ground rules for individuals' pursuit of maximum utility. Each proposal for intervention, therefore, should be examined separately. Bentham himself admitted the desirability of many exceptions to the rule of *laissez-faire,* some more drastic than even John Stuart Mill was willing to allow. (Mill rejected price-fixing, for example, whereas Bentham was willing to have governments set maximum prices and provide for grain storage, on the grounds that the "uncoerced and unenlightened propensities and powers of individuals are not adequate" to ensure adequate provisions against the possibility of a scarcity. (Quoted by T. W. Hutchison in "Bentham as an Economist," reprinted in Spengler and Allen, *Essays in Economic Theory,* p. 343.)

Bentham's works pertinent to economics are collected by W. Stark in Jeremy Bentham, *Economic Writings* (London, Allen & Unwin, 1952–54), 3 vols. Mill's relationship to Bentham is discussed by Jacob Viner in "Bentham and J. S. Mill: The Utilitarian Background," *American Economic Review,* vol. xxxix (March 1949), pp. 360–382.

II

Mill's economic methodology was generally accepted by his contemporaries and followers, although there were some variations in emphasis. To him the science of economics consisted of deductive conclusions concerning wealth that could not be tested empirically. Applying these conclusions to matters of public policy, however, entailed a consideration of other social objectives. Like medicine, economics had both a theoretical and a practical side. It was in one way science, and in another an art involving, in Mill's words, considerations of social philosophy. Value judgments affected the art, not the science.

Essentially the same view were held by Nassau Senior (1790–1864) in his later years. Senior held the Drummond chair of political economy at Oxford from 1825 to 1830 and again from 1847 to 1852. At first, dividing political economy into a deductive science with a practical branch, he held that the practical applications of economics were as certain and as universal as the theory. In his *Outline of the Science of Political Economy* (1836), however, he changed his mind and stated that other factors must be considered in putting economic theories into practice. He limited economics to pure theory and distinguished it from the science of legislation, which was concerned with human happiness. Wealth was only one of the elements a legislator had to weigh in making decisions. Senior himself was a lawyer as well as an economist and moved freely from one role to the other; in general, he advocated *laissez-faire* policies.

The line between the science and art of economics was sharply drawn by John Elliott Cairnes (1823–75), an Irish economist and a close follower of Mill who taught at University College, London. In his *Essays in Political Economy, Theoretical and Applied* (London, Macmillan, 1873), he wrote:

> . . . *laissez-faire* falls to the ground as a scientific doctrine. . . . let us remember that it is a practical rule and not a doctrine of science; a rule in the main sound but like most other sound practical rules, liable to numerous exceptions; above all, a rule which must never for a moment be allowed to stand in the way of the candid consideration of any promising proposal of social and industrial reform. (p. 251)

Henry Sidgwick (1838–1900), in 1883 a professor of moral philosophy at Cambridge University—which still did not have a chair of political economy—took a different position in his *Principles of Political Economy,* emphasizing the art rather than the science of economics. This tended to confuse the issue. By admitting that the art included not only theory but ethical judgments, he returned economics to the fold of moral philosophy from which it had sprung in the days of Hutcheson and Smith.

For a general discussion of these issues, see T. W. Hutchison, *"Positive" Economics and Policy Objectives* (London, Allen & Unwin, 1964), especially ch. 1.

III

Mill's assumptions concerning the physical laws of production and the modifiable laws of distribution governed the organization of material in his *Principles.* He put the discussions of production and distribution in Book I and Book II respectively. In Book IV, he continued the analysis of distribution in a growing economy. His placement of the discussion of exchange and economic value in Book III was quite controversial; the normal procedure would have been to begin with an analysis of value and apply the resultant theory to both production and distribution. Mill rejected this with uncharacteristic sharpness. Such a procedure, he said, would be "not only a logical, but a practical blunder." (III, p. 455) Exchange and the laws of value could be analyzed scientifically only in a competitive situation. On the other hand, the laws of production were universal and "would be the same as they are, if the arrangement of society did not depend on Exchange, or did not admit of it." (*ibid.*) The mode of economic organization did not matter. In the case of distribution, economic value was significant, but again only in a competitive system. At the conclusion of Book II (on value), Mill reiterated his belief that the laws governing the determination of distributive shares in a barter economy were the same as those in a money economy.

Few economists supported Mill's arrangement of materials; yet it suited his purpose. It emphasized the laws of production and distributive *shares* (as opposed to patterns of property ownership), which were universal, and deemphasized economic motives: The amount of saving was greatly affected by noneconomic attitudes (i.e., frugality); the level of wages depended on attitudes toward limiting family size (prudence). In Book IV, in which Mill discussed growth models, value played no role; the analysis was a mechanistic development of different assumptions concerning real variables. Given the law of diminishing returns in agriculture and the Malthusian population principle, the end result of classical economics was always a stationary state. Despite Mill's orderly presentation of growth models, it is hard to see how Alfred Marshall could have called them "profound." (See Alfred Marshall, *Principles of Economics,* 9th (Variorum) ed., London and New York, Macmillan, 1961, Appendix J, vol. I, p. 824.)

Mill's exposition of production and distribution, of course, is essentially Ricardian. He maintained the characteristic distinction between productive and unproductive labor, although he had reservations concerning the undesirability of both unproductive labor and consumption. Mill's belief in the capital surplus generated by the British economy accounted for his moderate attitude. Although he considered certain luxury goods such as "gold lace, pine apples, or champagne" unproductive consumption items, he did not unilaterally condemn such consumption, as long as the basic wants of the populace were met. As he put it, "it would be a great error to regret the large proportion of the annual produce, which in an opulent country goes to supply unproductive consumption. . . . The things to be regretted . . . are the prodigious inequality with which this surplus is distributed . . ." (II, p. 54)

Mill's ideas on capital have long stirred controversy. See A. C. Pigou, "Mill and the Wages Fund," *Economic Journal* (June 1949), vol. 59, pp. 171–180; Harry G. Johnson, "Demand for Commodities Is *Not* Demand for Labor," *Economic Journal* (December 1949), vol. 59, pp. 531–536. His change of heart about the wage-fund was a devastating blow to classical theory. Cairnes attempted to reinstate the validity of the concept in *Some Leading Principles of Political Economy Newly Expounded* (1874). In the United States, Francis A. Walker in *The Wages Question* (1876) bitterly attacked the wage-fund theory, while Frank A. Taussig, in *Wages and Capital* (1896), attempted to revive it.

Mill's position on Say's Law was defended by a number of writers after Keynes' attack on the principle in the 1930s. See Gary S. Becker and William Baumol, "The Classical Monetary Theory: The Outcome of the Discussion," *Economica* (November 1952), vol. XIX, pp. 355–376.

Because he supported the Malthusian theory of population, Mill has often been accused of reviving a doctrine that at the time was on the way out. (See, for example, Mark Blaug, *Ricardian Economics, A Historical Study,* New Haven, Conn., Yale University Press, 1958, especially pp. 117–120.) His contemporaries had stressed the great advances in agricultural techniques that had eased the pressure on the food supply. Mill admitted this and was willing to agree that a statistical check on the behavior of food prices over a period of time would give some indication of what the outcome had been in the race between technology in agriculture and population. (See III, p. 714).

But he saw no reason to assume that the past rapid rate of technological change would continue indefinitely. Neither he nor his contemporaries could guarantee future increases in productivity sufficient to offset the increase in population. It was only natural, therefore, for him to emphasize preventive checks to population growth as a means to a higher standard of living for British workers.

IV

Mill's switch from a labor theory of value to a supply-and-demand-analysis in which costs governed the values of reproducible goods in the long run has been both condemned and praised by later economists. Generally, the early marginal-utility theorists condemned Mill on the grounds that he neglected demand. Alfred Marshall, the neoclassical economist who sought to bridge the gap between classical economics and later theories of utility valuation, believed that Mill's theory of value needed only a more careful restatement and a few additions to be perfectly acceptable. (See his *Principles of Economics*, Appendix I, especially pp. 819–820.) In *History of Economic Analysis* (p. 603), Schumpeter concurs and praises Mill for building a halfway house to modern theory. Lord Robbins called Mill's early essay on international values and reciprocal demand "surely one of the most powerful contributions ever made to the evolution of economic analysis." ("Introduction," *Essays on Economics and Society, Works,* IV, p. ix). George J. Stigler, in "The Nature and Role of Originality in Scientific Progress," *Economica* (November 1955), vol. XXII, reprinted in *Essays in the History of*

Economics (Chicago, University of Chicago Press, 1965), pp. 7ff., praises Mill's original treatment of the economics of the firm, joint costs, alternative costs, and noncompeting groups, as well as his general supply-and-demand analysis and his treatment of Say's Law.

Most writers agree, however, that the most significant of Mill's technical contributions was in the area of international economics. For a general discussion of his position on the subject, see Jacob Viner, *Studies in the Theory of International Trade* (New York, Harper & Row, 1937). Mill's treatment was classical in the sense that he believed the solution to the problems of international trade lay in the way import/export price-ratios, or the terms of trade, were determined. In contrast, modern theorists emphasize the underlying factor endowments governing trade relationships among countries and the importance of income effects as well as price ratios. Mill gave some recognition to the latter when he examined the effect of an import duty that would raise the price of a commodity in the importing country and reduce it in the exporting country. The latter, he noted, would now find its exports insufficient to purchase its previous level of imports; gold would flow out of the country and prices would fall. Its income would also fall; i.e., its addition to "riches" in the Ricardian sense would be less. The country collecting the import duty, on the other hand would increase its income. (Mill's analysis found little favor with ideological free-traders.)

Mill's recognition of the limitations of supply-and-demand analysis with respect to labor markets was a result of his openmindedness regarding factual evidence, his willingness to respect the diverse noneconomic influences on behavior, and a humanitarian concern for the poor that made their problems worth studying. It was also inspired, in part, by the criticisms of traditional theory advanced by Thornton, Long, and others. Mill in turn had a direct effect on Marshall's later, sympathetic treatment of labor markets.

V

Mill's advocacy of reform of the institutions of property, his praise for certain socialist principles in many works, especially those written after 1852, and his own statement in his *Autobiography* that he and his wife would probably classify themselves as socialists raised the question of the extent to which Mill had abandoned the economics of unbounded individualism and become in fact a socialist.

Sidney Webb, one of the British Fabian Socialists, later claimed that Mill had definitely entered the fold. This remark was made after Mill's three "Chapters on Socialism," which again reflected his sympathy with certain socialist views, were published posthumously in 1879. Mill consistently opposed any form of centralized, governmental-run society, but

he did espouse consumers' and producers' cooperatives and associations of workers, a relatively mild form of socialism. His brand of individualism was not consistent with the rule of the masses. In certain respects he feared the setting of behavioral standards by the majority, as much as he criticized a distribution of income that did not reflect subjective costs. Also underlying his work was the undemocratic idea that the educated were superior—politically—to the uneducated. Although he consistently advocated political representation for workers (and women), he added a number of provisos: A voter should have to pass a literacy test, a voter should pay a direct tax, a voter should not receive relief, and a better-educated voter should have more than one vote. (See his *Representative Government*, ch. VIII, "Of the Extension of the Suffrage.")

Controversy over the nature of Mill's socialism is still alive however. See *The Mill News Letter*, especially James B. Bennett, "Mill, Francis W. Newman, and Socialism: Mill's Two Argumentative Voices" (Fall 1966), vol. II, no. 1, pp. 2–7; L. E. Fredman and B. L. J. Gordon, "John Stuart Mill and Socialism" (Fall 1967), vol. III, no. 1, pp. 3–7; Pedro Schwartz, "John Stuart Mill and Socialism" (Fall 1968), vol. IV, no. 1, pp. 11–15.

Chapter vi

CAPITALISM

AS AN EXPLOITATIVE

AND TRANSITORY SYSTEM:

The Economics of Karl Marx

The reader will bear in mind that the production of surplus-value, or the extraction of surplus-labour, is the specific end and aim, the sum and substance, of capitalist production . . . .

Karl Marx, *Capital*

Those economists who, like Ricardo, regard the capitalist mode of production as absolute, feel nevertheless, that this mode of production creates its own limits. . . . But the main point in their horror over the falling rate of profit is the feeling, that capitalist production meets in the development of productive forces a barrier, which has nothing to do with the production of wealth as such . . . .
. . . *The real barrier of capitalist production is capital itself.*

ibid.

In the history of economic theory, Karl Marx holds a unique and paradoxical position. For decades his theories were either ignored or dismissed by non-Marxists as erroneous. But as socialist movements began to win political power in many parts of the world, long after his death, and as the Great Depression of the 1930s and then the Keynesian revolution thrust into relief the limitations of *laissez-faire* capitalism, interest in Marx's economics revived and intensified. This interest was whetted also by the discovery that Marx had much to say about contemporary problems such as the economics of growth.

Despite belated recognition of his theoretical insights, non-Marxist and Marxist economists are still divided by their views on the nature of capitalism. To the former, private ownership of the means of production and profit maximization under competition promote individual welfare and an optimum rate of growth. To the latter, capitalism is a system of labor exploitation that generates contradictory economic forces incompatible with its continued existence. To Marx himself, capitalism was a transitional stage in economic development that would eventually give way to socialism and freedom from exploitation.

The issue of whether capitalism is exploitative and transitory illustrates strikingly the nature of controversy in economics. Using a particular set of analytical tools or precise verification procedures cannot resolve such disputes "scientifically." Marx used the same analytical tools as Ricardo, but he came up with different conclusions. Modern economists use tools similar to Marx's concept of "expanded reproduction," but their conclusions are not necessarily Marxian. The impasse in the dispute over Marxian economics arises from differences in judgment concerning the type of problems to be analyzed, the scope of inquiry, and methodology.

In this chapter, we shall first examine the value judgments, range of inquiry, and methodology that set Marx apart from non-Marxists, whether they are classical, neoclassical, or modern Keynesian. We shall deal in sections two and three with his interpretation of the labor theory of value, and in sections four and five with his view of the theory of capitalist accumulation and that of crisis and capitalist breakdown.

I

The foundation of Marx's analysis of capitalism reflected a unique intellectual background that included German Hegelian philosophy, French and English socialism, and British classical political economy. He integrates his new theory of society with concepts and relationships drawn from these diverse sources. His work was also influenced by his experiences as a political activist.

Born in Trier of upper-middle-class parents, Karl Marx (1818–83) studied at the Universities of Bonn and Berlin, where he absorbed the philosophical ideas of Georg W. F. Hegel. Becoming dissatisfied with the interpretations of Hegel's theories at Berlin, he left for the University of Jena, where he found an atmosphere more to his liking. He received his doctorate in philosophy there in 1841 after writing a dissertation on the atomistic philosophy of Democritus and Epicurius. At this point he seemed ready for an academic career, but when a teaching position failed to materialize he turned to journalism. He soon became editor of the *Rheinische Zeitung,* a paper that ran into censorship problems with the reactionary Prussian regime. In 1843, now married to Jenny von Westphalen, the daughter of a German baron, Marx left for Paris, where he took part in the intense political, socialist, and philosophical discussions that made it the haven of political exiles.

In that period from 1843 to 1845 Marx completed the transition from a Hegelian philosophy to a materialist interpretation of history and began for the first time to study political economy. It was this new interest that led him to Friedrich Engels (1820–95), who became his lifelong friend, collaborator, and frequent benefactor. Engels, a Rhinelander, had represented his father's manufacturing business in Manchester, England. His stay there had given him an opportunity both to observe British industry and to learn something of classical political economy. In 1845, Marx and Engels collaborated in publishing *The Holy Family,* in which they stated their differences with Hegelian idealist philosophy. In 1845, Engels published *The Condition of the Working Classes in England,* a work drawn in part from his personal observation of the new industrialism. Marx's first work in economics, *The Poverty of Philosophy,* appeared in 1847. A reply to Pierre-Joseph Proudhon's *The Philosophy of Poverty,* it revealed Marx's acquaintanceship with British economists, including the Ricardian socialists.

Meanwhile, the long arm of the Prussian government had forced Marx to leave Paris. He moved to Brussels just before the outbreak of the German and French Revolution of 1848. The *Communist Manifesto,* prepared by Marx and Engels for the Communist League convention in London in December 1847, became (although not immediately) the basic philosophical document of the communist movement and a guide to political action. Despite its call for "workingmen of the world to unite," and despite the fact that it was written with an eye to stimulating the current revolutionary unrest in Europe, the *Manifesto* had little immediate impact except on a few, mainly German, activists. It was written in German, and the first English translation, in 1850, attracted only a limited audience. (A second translation appeared in the United States in 1872, and a third in England in 1888.)

In 1848, Marx returned to Paris and went on to Cologne, where he became editor of the *Neue Rheinische Zeitung.* Revolutionary activity in that city was reaching a peak, but again he was forced to leave. In

1850, after the ferment caused by the revolutions and counterrevolutions of the previous two years had ebbed, Marx went to London, where he remained for the rest of his life. Although his politically active days were for the most part over, he kept in touch with revolutionary leaders and in 1864 took part in the establishment of the International Workingmen's Association (later known as the First International). That organization finally split over the irreconcilable ideologies and personal antagonisms of Marx and Mikhail Bakunin (1814–76), the Russian-born anarchist.

From 1850 on, Marx devoted himself to economics. He spent his days largely in the British Museum, where he absorbed the writings of economists and studied the growing mass of facts on labor and working conditions supplied by government reports and commissions. In 1859, he published his *Zur Kritik der politische Öckonomie* (*Introduction to the Critique of Political Economy*) and then began his major attempt to reconstruct economics, *Das Kapital*. Marx never completed his plan of work. Only the first volume, *Capitalist Production*, published in 1867, appeared during his lifetime. (He died in 1883 while preparing a third German edition of the first volume.) By the time of his death, Marx had worked out certain essential portions of the remaining volumes, but they were by no means complete. Engels, who had ended his business ventures in 1869 to work more closely with Marx, took on the role of editor and published volume two of *Capital* in 1885 and volume three in 1894, one year before he himself died. These two volumes (necessarily incomplete and raising the question of Engels' interpretation of Marx's notes) were subtitled, respectively, *The Process of Capitalist Circulation* and *The Process of Capitalist Production as a Whole*. After Engels' death, Karl Kautsky undertook the task of editing and publishing what Marx had originally planned as book four of *Capital*. This work appeared, also in German, under the title *Theories of Surplus Value* in three volumes from 1904 to 1910.

From Hegelian principles, Marx developed his own theory of society and social change. Hegel's philosophy had been idealist and essentially conservative. He emphasized the interrelatedness of all aspects of a culture; any one event could be understood only in terms of the whole culture and its history. Concerned with the development of civilization, he believed that social evolution in the last analysis reflected the gradual realization of the Absolute Idea, a metaphysical entity, in the social structure and its culture. He also posited a theory of social change: What exists, exists only in the process of becoming something else. The dialectic of Hegel was the law of change, a process of conflict between opposites, the thesis and antithesis, which resolve into a synthesis, which is something new, both embodying and destroying the old. Even though what is is always in the process of becoming something else, Hegel believed that social institutions at any moment in time are nonetheless the logical products of rational development. Therefore, what is, is desirable.

Marx converted Hegel's theories into a materialist and revolutionary philosophy. He accepted the interrelatedness of social phenomena and the idea of change through conflict, but he rejected Hegel's idealist conception of social evolution. Following the lead of the Left Hegelians, he inverted the theory that the Absolute Idea was the prime mover of society and assigned that role to the material world. Developing these concepts in his own way, Marx said that the real foundation of society was the economic mode of production; it furnished the ultimate grounds for the social and political superstructure. He stated his position in the preface to *A Contribution to the Critique of Political Economy:*

> In the social production of their lives, men enter into certain definite relationships, indispensible to them and independent of their will: these are the relationships of production, which correspond to a specific stage in the development of their material productive forces. The sum total of these relationships of production constitutes the economic structure of society, the real foundation upon which the juridical and political superstructure rises, and to which specific forms of social consciousness correspond. It is the mode of production in material life that determines the general process of men's social, political, and intellectual life. It is not men's consciousness that determines their being; on the contrary, it is their social being that determines their consciousness.

As the mode of production changes, so the "entire immense super-structure is more or less rapidly transformed."

On the other hand, Marx liked Hegel's dialectical process of social change. The relationships between changes in the mode of production and elements of the noneconomic superstructure of society came about, said Marx, through conflict, especially the class struggle. Although changes in the "mode of production" could be major or minor, he was primarily interested in the major ones, the ones that revolutionized society. Two major transformations had already occurred: the development of feudal society and the development of capitalism from feudalism. As feudalism became obsolete, it was the bourgeoisie, or the middle classes, that fought to establish a new society. But with the growth of capitalism, there came a new mode of production that required wage-earners; thus a new class emerged, the proletariat, a class in conflict with the owners and controllers of capital. When this new class became conscious of its mission, according to Marx, it would transform capitalism into socialism.

Marx's theory of classes was an integral part of the process of social change. In the *Communist Manifesto* he stated at the very beginning, "The history of all society that has existed hitherto is the history of class struggles." By classes, he meant economic classes whose functions were determined by their relationship to the mode of production. He spoke generally in broad terms: the bourgeoisie, the workers. But he recognized subgroups: the small businessmen who were disappearing in the face of competition from the larger, more powerful capitalists; the *Lumpenproletariat,* the workers who were worn out and had been discarded during capitalism's technological advance. In his economic analysis of capitalism, Marx sought to show how the conflict among classes, each of them with a different role in the productive process, reflected the contradictory nature of the productive system.

Marx's theories of the primacy of economic modes of production, of historical change, and of classes directly affected his approach to economic analysis. First, he studied capitalism as a unique historical system, one that had a beginning and would have an end. During the period of capitalism, there were also changes, in its own institutions. The specific historical facts of development were extremely important to Marx, as the wealth of empirical information in *Capital* attests. For example, he spelled out in great detail the struggles over the passage of the ten-hour law in Great Britain and the Parliamentary investigations of the effects of the introduction of machinery on employment. To Marx, the rise of trade unions in response to conflicts over wages and jobs was not an exogenous factor, as non-Marxist economists often assumed, but part and parcel of the process of economic development. In short, he propounded a theory to explain economic history. Unlike later marginalists, he was not interested in using statistical or historical information to verify universal economic principles. His concern was the historical development of capitalism itself. In this sense, the scope of his analysis was limited. The objective of his "scientific socialism" was to analyze the "laws of motion" which would lead to an eventual breakdown of capitalism and the coming of socialism, not the economics of a socialist society. As the latter did not exist when he wrote, it could not be scientifically analyzed.

A second general characteristic of Marx's approach to economics is his assumption that members of a social class will generally act more or less in accordance with the interests of that class, whether they realize that they are doing so or not. On the other hand, a particular individual may transcend his class position. Marx wrote in the Preface to the first edition of *Capital,* vol. 1,

> I paint the capitalist and the landlord in no sense *couleur de rose.* But here individuals are dealt with only in so far as they are the personifications of economic categories, embodiments of particular class-relations and class-interests. My stand-point, from which the evolution of the economic formation of society is viewed as a process of natural history, can less than any other make the individual responsible for relations whose creature he socially remains, however much he may subjectively raise himself above them. (I, p. 15) [1]

His belief that individuals' actions are conditioned by class interests caused Marx to be suspicious of attempts to analyze human behavior on the basis of a universal principle of utility. Although he wrote the first volume of *Capital* before the marginal-utility revolution of the 1870s, Jeremy Bentham had already laid down the principle of utility as a universal guide to economic action. Marx's criticism of Bentham was scathing:

> To know what is useful for a dog, one must study dog-nature. This nature itself is not to be deduced from the principle of utility. Applying this to man, he that would criticize all human acts, movements, relations, etc., by the principle of utility, must first deal with human nature in general, and then with human nature as modified in each historical epoch. Bentham makes short work of it. With the dryest näiveté he takes the modern shopkeeper, especially the English shopkeeper, as his normal man. (I, p. 668, n. 2)

To Marx, the overriding feature of capitalism was not a striving for maximum utility but the drive by capitalists to produce surplus value (profit) and to reinvest it, in a constantly expanding process that he called accumulation. As he saw it, the urge to invest was almost compulsive. He admitted that in the capitalist's breast there is a "Faustian conflict between the passion for accumulation, and the desire for enjoyment" (I, p. 651) but he believed that the desire for accumulation would win out: "Accumulation for accumulation's sake: by this formula classical economy expressed the historical mission of the bourgeoi-

---

[1] Unless otherwise noted, all volume and page references are to *Capital.*

sie. . . ." (I, p. 652) In a terse passage, Marx said, "To put it mathematically: the rate of accumulation is the independent not the dependent variable." (I, p. 679)

To explain the historical process Marx employed a variety of "dynamic" devices. First, he claimed that the institutions within which economic activity was carried out, and which modern economists accepted as given and as outside the scope of inquiry, could and would change in response to the historical process. He argued that the general nature of such changes could be predicted, although he was reluctant to date specific developments or to identify the details of the new institutions that would emerge. (It would have been inconsistent with the Hegelian dialectical process to do so.) In addition, he treated specifically economic factors, such as cost functions, the degree of monopoly, and the supplies of factors, as variables that would change in predictable ways. For example, continued capital accumulation, he said, would lead to monopoly control and a breakdown of competition. Finally, he introduced new theoretical tools that, although primitive by modern standards, were dynamic in the modern, technical meaning of the word. An event in one period $(t + 1)$ could be predicted from events in the previous period (t) if conditions in t were rigorously defined and there were no extraneous forces at work. (Marx used this approach in volume two of *Capital,* in his discussion of interindustry relationships and capital accumulation.)

In sum, Marx's objective was to analyze capitalism dynamically at different levels of abstraction. He attempted to explain the behavior of specific economic variables within hypothetical limits, then changes in the behavior of economic parameters, and finally the historical changes in the social and economic institutions of capitalism itself. In this sense, his scope of analysis was far broader than that of any other major economist or social scientist of his century.

Finally, throughout his adult career, Marx advocated changes in the existing order. In his early days in Paris, he wrote in his *Theses on Feuerbach,* no. XI, "The philosophers have only *interpreted* the world, in various ways; the point, however, is to *change* it." In the *Communist Manifesto* he urged workers to unite to overthrow capitalism. In his most serious work, *Capital,* he attempted to give socialist leaders, and anyone else who would listen, grounds for supporting the rise to power of the working classes—"to shorten and lessen the birth-pangs of the new society." However, policy avowals, even the avowal of revolution, do not necessarily indicate a lack of scientific objectivity in building and testing theoretical models. From the time of Locke and Petty on, economists attacked policies they believed disastrous and advocated reforms they believed desirable. They, as well as Marx, assumed that their economic analyses were sound in the sense of being efficient guides to action, for to be successful in advancing a particular policy it is necessary to understand what the "objective" situation is, what forces can or cannot be controlled, and what sort of reaction there is likely to be. The more scientific knowledge there is of a subject, the more efficiently goals in that area can be achieved.

Nonetheless, there was a profound difference between the policy goals of Marx and the goals of orthodox economists from the Physiocrats and the British classical economists to the Keynesians. The non-Marxists generally directed their demands for policy changes to the existing government, viewing it as the agency through which existing social institutions, including private property, could be modified. Marx, however, wanted to abolish private property rights to the means of production because he believed that they inhibited the full utilization and development of productive forces by creating an unjust distribution of income. The capitalist state, in the last analysis, was the defender of private property and could scarcely be expected to undermine itself. Workers should nonetheless attempt to win concessions through political action whenever possible, even though the ultimate goal might be far away. Gains such as the shorter workday were worthwhile in themselves; at the same time political activity within the ranks of labor strengthened worker organizations and increased labor's understanding of the political process.

The historical uniqueness of capitalism, the invalidity of assuming that the principle of utility governs free choice in a class society, the necessity of attempting to explain institutional changes, and the need to abolish private property before a rational reorganization of society could take place were four basic conclusions that Marx drew from his philosophic and socialist principles. It is these conclusions that by and large separate Marx and the non-Marxists.

II

Using the framework of his theory of a historical materialist approach to capitalism, Marx developed his economic analysis of value and of the system's laws of motion. He took his economic models primarily from the British classical economists, and above all from Ricardo.

A student of the history of economic thought, he saw the line of theoretical development that culminated with Ricardo and gave it a name, classical economics. In his *Contribution to the Critique of Political Economy* in 1859, he described the determination of value by labor time time as the result "of a century and a half of critical study by the classical school of political economy which dates from William Petty in England and Boisguillebert in France and closes with Ricardo in the former country and Sismondi in the latter." (p. 56) In Ricardo, "political economy reached its climax." Marx claimed that the development of political economy had paralleled the development of capitalism itself and that only with capitalism had a truly scientific analysis become possible. This was because only markets gave an objective independence to transactions.

Although he recognized that some economic categories were applicable to any society, Marx taught that concepts and economic relationships must in the end represent reality. As economic reality changes, so must the categories used to describe it. The labor theory of value of Ricardo was, he believed, the best analysis of exchange value under capitalism. In his hands it became a theory of exploitation. If the value of goods was determined by the amount of labor embodied in them, and if workers were paid less than that value, then the difference, the "surplus value," was being appropriated by the capitalists. The ratio of this surplus value to wages was a measure of the exploitation of labor.

Marx's labor theory was essentially a critique of private ownership of the means of production. He did not deny that capital goods were of use or that improved machinery could enhance the output of commodities. But capital goods, factories, and machines, were themselves the products of labor. It was their ownership by nonworkers—capitalists and landlords—that enabled such persons to appropriate surplus value. The exploitation of labor was therefore the result of a particular system of property and the legal institutions that supported it.

In joining the issue of ownership with the labor theory of value, Marx drew on socialist controversies over the theory of private property that went back to Locke, Hume, and Bentham. In the seventeenth century Locke had used the principle of labor's right to its product to build a political theory of individual rights and freedom and a critique of arbitrary government. As the factory system spread, it was not difficult for its critics to conclude that capitalism had separated the worker from the products of his labor, that a nonproductive class was living off the labor of others, and that workers should be entitled to the fruits of their own efforts. (Of the early critics, nonsocialist Simonde de Sismondi and

Thomas Hodgskin—later called a Ricardian socialist—came closest to Marx's later position by distinguishing the technical and ownership characteristics of capital in a private-enterprise system.) [2]

But by the time the pre-Marxian socialists were advocating the moral right of labor to its full share, the orthodox position on property had already shifted from one based on Lockean natural rights to one based on expediency. Hume used social benefits as a justification of private property because he believed that private property stimulated frugality, prudence and industry. At the same time, he recognized that the institution of property would undoubtedly lead to inequalities of income and wealth. By such inequalities, he pointed out, "we rob the poor of more satisfaction than we add to the rich, and . . . the slight gratification of a frivolous vanity in one individual, frequently costs more than bread to many families, and even provinces." He would have liked to see the inequalities reduced, but in such a way that the system of private property was preserved.

Bentham and Mill came to the same conclusion, but based their arguments on the principle of utility and not on natural rights. Bentham admitted that a more equal distribution of property would increase aggregate utility, but he rejected any policy that would abrogate property rights: If property were equally divided without further ado, "everything would be speedily destroyed." John Stuart Mill may have considered property reforms expedient, but he too backed away from eliminating the system of private property. He argued that on balance there would probably be a greater maximization of utility if those who owned property were allowed to operate in and collect the profits from its operation than if a system of communal ownership were adopted.

Marx objected to this argument. Utility had nothing to do with the existence of a class that controlled the instruments of production and the political power it wielded. Marx held firmly to the labor theory of value because he believed that, properly interpreted, it revealed the true social relationships that lay behind transactions in the marketplace he condemned. Those economists concerned only with the "superficialities" of supply and demand were, he said, guilty of a "fetishism of commodities" (by which he meant they attributed to commodities an existence independent of social-class relationships). Marx objected to the fact that the system of distribution in classical theory was not

[2] See the Notes to Chapter vi, Part II, for a discussion of these early socialist writers and forerunners.

integrated with the social structure. He scorned the classical linkage between capital and profit, land and rent, and labor and wages as meaningless. Capital was not the sum of the produced means of production, but the "means of production monopolized by a certain part of society. . . ." (III, p. 948) It was not the fertility of the soil that determined rent, but the economic laws regulating market values. Labor creates value, but this has "nothing to do with the distribution of this value among the different categories." (III, p. 958) Marx stressed the unity of the social system, which made its distribution relationships the result of the class structure of the ownership of the means of production. Because of the nature of these property relationships, according to Marx, the system was exploitative by definition.

III

Marx used the labor theory to explain exchange value in a capitalist economy, a procedure that had a number of limitations. Like Smith and Ricardo, he excluded final services (i. e., immaterial goods) from his analysis. He also excluded goods produced for one's own use and goods produced by inefficient or outmoded methods; he was interested only in goods that had an objective (market) exchange value. Like his classical predecessors, he said that such goods had a use value, or utility; but that utility did not determine exchange. It (utility) was not a homogeneous substance or an attribute common to various goods.

Marx's objective was to investigate the exchange values of commodities in a long-run competitive equilibrium. His theoretical model was similar to Ricardo's. The exchange value of a good was determined by the amount of labor required to produce it relative to the amounts of labor needed to produce other goods with which it could be compared. Only "socially necessary" labor counted, that is, only the amount of labor-time "required to produce an article under the normal conditions of production, and with the average degree of skill and intensity prevailing at the time." Labor-time was a homogeneous, abstract measure. Continuing to follow Ricardo, Marx converted the labor-time of skilled workers to unskilled labor-time by using a multiplier equal to the ratio of their wages. (He rejected disutility as the common element in labor on the grounds that it was a subjective measure.)

The amount of homogeneous units of labor-time embodied in a good consisted of c, the constant capital, v, the variable capital, and s, the surplus value. The first was the labor-time embodied in raw materials and the amount of capital goods used up in the production process; variable capital was paid labor, and surplus value was the amount of unpaid labor-time contributed by the worker. By Marx's account, when the capitalist invests his capital ($c + v$) in production, he makes his profits (s) by employing workers for more time than it takes for them to earn their wages. If the output equivalent of the wage in value terms is, say, five man-hours, the capitalist gains a surplus value (i.e., he profits) from every hour he keeps the worker employed beyond five hours. In a ten-hour workday, the worker does five hours of unpaid labor, the value of which is appropriated by the capitalist. The conflicts over the length of the working day, which was a burning issue in England in Marx's time, were readily explainable with this theory. The ratio of unpaid and paid labor, s/v, Marx called the rate of exploitation. The capitalist gained by extending the workday; he could also gain by speeding up the work so that the worker earned his keep in less time. A longer workday thus meant an absolute increase in the rate of exploitation; improved productivity meant a relative increase.

In sum, Marx's definitional equations were:

$$C = c + v$$
$$M = c + v + s$$
$$M = C + s$$
$$s' = s/v$$

where C is capital, M is the value of the output, and s' is the rate of exploitation. The capitalist who turns over his capital in a production process will obtain M, an amount greater than his initial capital by s.

There are three technical peculiarities of this model that may be unapparent to modern students of economics unfamiliar with the labor theory of value. The first is the relationship of value to riches, or abundance, in Ricardo's terminology. On a nonaggregative basis, the labor theory is straightforward. The relative amounts of labor-time required to produce two goods, L_a and L_b, measure their relative scarcity and hence their exchange values, M_a/M_b. But the labor theory is not a measure of aggregate output. The sum of all M's (excluding raw materials in constant capital to prevent double counting) is the sum of the inputs of active and embodied labor ($C + V + S$), but it is not a measure of aggregate output. With output omitted from the equations, there can be no measure of productivity. Hypothetically, if the productivity of all inputs were increased—by raising the level of technology and improving the skills of the labor force—the net incomes of labor and capital

$(V + S)$ could both be increased; but the aggregate value would remain the same. Both Marx and Ricardo were fully aware of the implications of this aspect of the labor theory. As Chapter iii showed, Smith's labor-commanded theory of value was an attempt to measure output; but it created other problems and Ricardo at least dropped it. The shift from analyzing inputs to analyzing outputs came primarily with the marginal revolution in economics and the development of index-number theory in statistics.

The second unique feature of Marx's model was his definition of profits and the profit rate. Surplus value was more than simply a return on capital. It specifically included profits in the narrow sense, interest payments, a portion of ground rents, "wages of management," and special services (such as advertising and personal selling) purchased by the capitalists. Marx was more interested in the aggregate surplus than in the ways by which capitalists fought among themselves over its division. (This subject, which he reserved for volume three of *Capital,* was less important because it did not affect the development of capitalism except in one regard: The capitalists' struggles among themselves for surplus value tended to produce larger, more powerful firms.)

Marx's formula for the rate of profit was unique. He defined it as $P' = \dfrac{S}{C} = \dfrac{s}{c + v}$, the ratio of surplus value to constant and variable capital. However, the denominator $(c + v)$ represented not a stock, but a flow in inputs over a period of time. Converting his rate of profits to the more usual return on stock is not difficult, but the procedure is cumbersome. Chapter 4, "The Effect of Turn-over on the Rate of Profit," in volume three of *Capital,* discusses the effect of different turnover rates of constant-capital inputs on the rate of profit. One would also have to relate the depreciation of fixed capital to the value of the fixed-capital stock to obtain a measure of the rate of profit in the modern sense.

The third unique aspect of Marx's labor theory of value is its inadequacy as an explanation of prices. Marx showed in volume three that prices will differ from values when the ratio of constant to variable capital (c/v), which he called the organic composition of capital, differed among industries. Competition for capital would equalize the rate of profit; but it would not affect the composition of capital, which was the result of technical considerations. If commodities sold at a price equal to their labor values but were produced with different organic ratios, then profit rates would not be equal; if profit rates were equal, but the capital composition differed, then the prices of goods would not equal their values. If $q =$ the organic ratio, then Marx's rate of profit can be written:

$$P' = \frac{\dfrac{s}{v}}{\dfrac{c}{v} + \dfrac{v}{v}}$$

$$= \frac{s'}{q + 1}$$

Assuming that the rate of exploitation, s', remains the same, the rate of profits will vary inversely with changes in q. For example, assume that there are two industries, each with a total capital of 100. In one industry (A) the organic composition of capital is lower than in the other. If the rate at which surplus value is produced is the same (100 percent), the profits in each case will equal the amount of variable capital; but the *rate* of profit in the first industry will be higher than in the second, as Table 2 shows.

Table 2

The Divergence of Prices from Values in the Marxian System

Industry	Constant Capital	Variable Capital	Surplus Value	Total Value	Rate of Profit	Price After Equalization
A	50	50	50	150	50%	140
B	70	30	30	130	30%	140
TOTAL	120	80	80	280	40%	—

When there is competition, different rates of profit cannot exist. In the case of the two industries just described, the average rate of profit would be 40 percent. Industry A would retain 40 of its 50 units of surplus value and give 10 to industry B, raising its profits to 40 units also. The price of the goods produced by each industry would be 140, instead of 150 and 130. Where organic ratios differ, therefore, the tendency toward a uniform rate of profit will cause prices to differ from values.

When this analysis appeared in volume three of *Capital* (which was published posthumously), Marx was criticized for supporting a cost-of-production theory of prices (one based on costs plus an average rate of profit) and abandoning the labor theory of value of volume one. His supporters, however, argued that he had been aware of the problem from the beginning but that he had not been primarily interested in attempting to explain individual prices as such, and that the aggregate value of goods within the economy was still determined by the amount of labor expended.

But one technical issue was not so easily resolved. If the two industries, A and B, were unrelated, the existence of a set of commodity prices that differed from the goods' values did not create any additional problems for Marxian theory. But if one industry produced goods that were purchased by the other—if B were a capital-goods industry whose products were purchased by A—then transforming values into prices would require cumbersome calculations. (If the products of industry B have a higher price, the constant capital of A will be more than the 50 indicated by C_A. Taking the new amount into account requires recalculating the rates of profit, which in turn requires a further adjustment of the value of A, and so on.

IV

The accumulation of capital was the overriding objective of capitalist society. Marx's analysis of the accumulating economy sought to explain the historical development of capitalism, especially the British system, and to demonstrate its economic effects on both the capitalists and the workers. For analytical purposes, he distinguished between simple reproduction and accumulation. In the first case, the capitalist consumes all the surplus value he receives; new savings and investment are zero. (Workers' incomes are considered too low to permit savings in any case.) In the second case, the capitalist constantly extends his capital.

Marx also distinguished between primitive and capitalist accumulation. Primitive accumulation precedes the development of the capitalist mode of production and is therefore its starting point. In European and British history especially, this period (of primitive accumulation) included both the agrarian revolution and the commercial revolution. It was characterized by a build-up of private wealth in the hands of merchants and master manufacturers on the one hand, and the expropriation of laborers from the land on the other. The historical process said Marx, was one in which force was "midwife" for the new society of capitalism that wrenched peasants and yeomen from the soil, turning them into a propertyless class dependent on the free labor market. The discovery of gold, the use of slavery, the colonial system, and even the growth of the public debt—which made possible the development of banks and a financial system—all contributed to the initial accumulation of investment capital.

In capitalist society, accumulation proceeds by investment of the surplus value that arises from the employment of free labor. As Marx observed the process in Great Britain, he drew several conclusions. Extending Adam Smith's analysis of the division of labor, he argued that as technology improves investments are made in machines and factories, in fixed capital, and in the larger establishments that are needed to take advantage of the lower costs of a greater division of labor. The development of capitalism meant a tendency toward the concentration of capital in particular firms and, at first, toward greater competition among more capitalists. From this competition emerged the stronger capitalists who were able to gain the upper hand over their competitors and centralize the ownership of capital. To the degree that such men are successful, the centralization (in contrast to the concentration) of capital further accelerates the process of accumulation. The larger firms, headed by the successful capitalists, increase their exploitation of new inventions and discoveries and gain competitive advantages that lead to the expropriation of smaller firms.

These tendencies, which Marx believed were a basic feature of capitalistic development, tended in turn to cause the rate of profit to decline. Capitalists would fight to get a competitive advantage by introducing more, and more productive, capital goods—innovations which, in modern terms, were labor-saving and capital-using. In contrast to other economists of his day, Marx emphasized the increasingly longer lifespans of these fixed-capital assets. The effect was to raise the proportion of constant to variable capital, that is, q, capital's organic composition. As this ratio rises, the rate of profit must decline, if s', the rate of exploitation, remains the same. To repeat the previous definitional equation,

$$P' = \frac{s}{c + v} = \frac{s'}{q + 1}$$

The tendency toward a declining rate of profit was one of the most significant results of capitalist accumulation. Its implications for the business cycle and the breakdown hypothesis will be examined later. At this point, however, three characteristics of the tendency should be noted. First, according to Marx, the mass of profit need not decline even if the rate does. With no change in the rate of exploitation, profit will vary directly with wages (variable capital); even if the difference between the two is a smaller percentage of total capital, so long as it grows absolutely the mass of profits will also rise. Second, the formula for P is expressed in terms of value, not output. Profits in terms of commodities may continue to rise, despite a fall in the amount of surplus value, because of rising productivity. In short, a falling rate of profit could easily be consistent with an improvement in the real economic position of the capitalists as a class. But to Marx this possibility was irrelevant to the compulsive drive of the capitalist to accumulate and to convert more surplus value into more material commodities.

The third characteristic of capitalist accumulation is the seeming contradiction between greater investment in constant capital relative to variable capital when surplus value arises only from variable capital. To Marx, the individual capitalist gained a relative advantage by lowering his costs through a higher capital/labor ratio. As other capitalists followed suit, however, a new equilibrium situation would be reached in which the rate of profit was lower all-around. Although the evidence is not clear, Marx seemed to believe that the rate of profit does not tend to drop gradually, but rather to vary from one cycle to another. New production techniques tend to be introduced in bunches.

In addition to producing a decline in the rate of profit and increasing the centralization of capital, capitalist accumulation also tended to increase the misery of labor; this was an "absolute general law of capitalist accumulation." (I, p. 707) Considerable controversy has arisen over Marx's definition of this law: For example, he tells us at one point that "in proportion as capital accumulates, the lot of the labourer, *be his payment high or low,* must grow worse." (I, p. 709, italics added) In the very next passage, he points to the accumulation of wealth at one pole and "at the same time accumulation of misery, agony of toil, slavery, ignorance, brutality, mental degradation, at the opposite pole." One explanation of how misery could increase despite high wages is that Marx was referring not simply to employed workers but to the industrial-reserve army, the castoffs of industrial change. He included in this army the unemployed, "pauper children and orphans," and unemployables, chiefly those unable to adjust to new jobs, those who were too old, the disabled, and the entire "sphere of pauperism," which is a "dead-weight" on society.

A second interpretation is that by "increasing misery" Marx meant the subjective pain of submission to the capitalist system (i.e., to exploitation). The means of production, he said in a lengthy passage, are the "means of domination [and] they mutilate the laborer into a fragment of a man; degrade him . . . , destroy every remnant of charm in his work. . . ." (I, p. 708) The worker's alienation from control of his work and product during his lifetime becomes the "misery" of capitalism.

For the employed workers, however, the law of "increasing misery" is probably more accurately interpreted as declining relative wages (i.e., as a rising rate of exploitation), with real wages constant or even rising in the long run.[3] Marx clearly accepted a modified version of the subsistence theory of wages of Smith and Ricardo. Labor, he said, will have a minimum value equal to the value of those commodities "without the daily supply of which the laborer cannot renew his vital energies. . . ." (I, p. 192) As technological change increases productivity, the value of wage-goods falls and the worker can earn them in less time. The ratio of surplus to variable capital rises, causing the share of wages in total income to fall. Such a fall would of course tend to counterbalance a decline in the rate of profits.

With this approach to wages, Marx did not mean that subsistence wages could not be modified. In the short run, when the rate of capital investment was high, wages would be bid upward. Unlike the classical writers, however, Marx put no stock in the Malthusian theory that an increase in population would eventually reduce wages to the subsistence level again. He believed that the industrial-reserve army, fed by the technologically displaced, would perform the function of keeping wages low. During booms, when the reserve army was depleted wages might rise; but depressions would reduce wages again and enlarge the reserve army so that it could serve its function of regulating wages in the next cycle. In the long run, "subsistence" wages might even increase. Marx pointed to the "historical and moral element" in the value of labor power. The "so-called necessary wants" are a product of historical development and depend "on the degree of civilization of a country." (I, p. 190)

V

Marx stated in the first volume of *Capital* that the process of capitalist accumulation, which led to centralization of the means of production on the one hand and misery for the masses on the other, would

[3] It was principally in the *Communist Manifesto* that Marx pointed to a fall in real wages as a result of capitalist accumulation.

produce a revolutionary explosion in which the "capitalist integument" would be "burst asunder," and the expropriators expropriated. (I, pp. 836–837) Thus the transitory system of capitalism would come to a dramatic end as a result of its own contradictions.

Actually he recognized that the process was more complex, and in the later volumes of *Capital* especially he sought to elaborate those complexities. Even without the apocalyptic vision of a final conflict, Marx's critique was serious enough. The "internal contradictions" of capitalism created difficulties in sustaining accumulation, which brought on business crises. Although these tendencies might be temporarily counteracted, they would sooner or later reassert themselves as more serious obstacles.

Marx's argument took several directions, and later Marxist economists and others influenced by him have themselves disagreed as to which line of reasoning should be followed. His explanation of capitalism's limited lifespan that is most directly related to the position of the classical economists is the theory of the declining rate of profit, although he saw socialism rather than the stationary state as the end of the developmental process. A second explanation, more compatible with his own theory of the increasing concentration of wealth and income at one pole and misery at the other, emphasizes underconsumption as the underlying cause of business crises and the inability of the system ever to resolve the growing conflict over the distribution of income. A third theory of Marx concerns not the eventual collapse of capitalism, but the "anarchical" characteristics of it that make business crises possible. This theory, sometimes called the disproportionality theory of crises, is the one we shall discuss first. Although, ironically, Marx did not consider it as important as his other theories in explaining cycles, modern economists find it a major contribution to aggregative analysis.

The specific analytical tool that Marx developed for his "disproportionate" theory was an aggregative economic model of interindustry relationships. Giving credit to Quesnay, whose *Tableau Économique* he considered a prototype, he sought to analyze the aggregate flows of goods and money not among the productive, proprietary, and sterile classes (as Quesnay had done), but among the capitalists and workers in two major divisions of the economy, the industries that produce the means of production and those that produce the means of consumption. His objective was to examine the relationships governing the aggregate flows of commodities and money outlays for consumption and capital investment, for the reproduction as well as the accumulation of the social capital of the economy. Presenting this analysis in volume two of *Capital,* he distinguished between the economic position of the individual capitalist, who could realize a profit by selling commodities in the market, and capitalists as a whole. In the latter case the conversion of surplus value into capital is affected by the division of the entire social product between wages, constant capital, and surplus value, as well as by the market for particular products. The movement of total social capital is, in Marx's words, "not only a reproduction of value, but also of material, and is, therefore, as much conditioned on the relative proportions of the elements of value of the total social product as on its use-value, its material substance." (II, p. 456)

Marx illustrated his point by dividing the total production of society into two sections: department I, which produced the means of production (i.e., fixed-capital goods and raw materials), and department II, which produced consumer goods. (His further division of II into a wage-goods sector and a luxury-consumer-goods sector will not be considered here.) In each department, the aggregate value of the output (O) was equal to the value of its constant and variable capital and the surplus value produced.

$$(1) \quad \text{I. } c_1 + v_1 + s_1 = O_1$$

$$(2) \quad \text{II. } c_2 + v_2 + s_2 = O_2$$

In the case of simple reproduction, where there was no net investment or saving, for capitalists to realize their initial capital ($c_1 + c_2 + v_1 + v_2$) from product sales, certain conditions would have to hold. First, the output of department I would have to equal the constant capital consumed in both departments. Second, the aggregate amount of consumption outlays by workers and capitalists would have to equal the aggregate output of department II. Thus,

$$(3) \quad c_1 + c_2 = O_1, \text{ and}$$

$$(4) \quad v_1 + v_2 + s_1 + s_2 = O_2$$

Substituting equation 3 in 1, or 4 in 2, meant that the economy would be in equilibrium when

$$(5) \quad v_1 + s_1 = c_2$$

That is, there would have to be an exchange between the two departments. The capital goods of department I would have to be traded for consumer goods equal in value to the wages and surplus value of department II for an equilibrium position to be maintained. Marx believed that even in the case of simple reproduction this might not occur. In tracing the circular flows of money and goods through the economy, he showed, for example, that the amount of money accumulated for depreciation allowances might be larger or smaller than the assets actually used up in production, thus throwing the economy out of balance. There were no automatic forces that would ensure the attainment of equilibrium.

In the case of capital accumulation, equation 5 would not hold. Using an assumed rate of savings from surplus value in several simple models, Marx worked out arithmetically the implications of capital accumulation over a few years. He assumed that accumulation would both increase the production of constant capital and require the purchase of additional labor from the industrial-reserve army.

Although this analysis of the process of capital accumulation was an original growth model, Marx's purpose was not to show how growth could continue indefinitely. Rather he drew the conclusion that the conditions needed to maintain equilibrium were so restrictive that they brought with them "the possibility of crises, since a balance is an accident under the crude conditions of this production." (II, p. 578) Nonetheless, the disproportionality theory could not explain the basic cause of crises; it dealt with the circulation of capital. To Marx, the fundamental contradictions of capitalism went deeper, to the sphere of production itself.

The tendency for a fall in the rate of profit to cause business cycles and the transitory nature of capitalism were a constant theme in Marx's writings. A particularly clear statement occurs in volume three of *Capital:*

> . . . so far as the rate of self-expansion of the total capital, the rate of profit, is the incentive of capitalist production . . . its fall checks the formation of new independent capitals and thus seems to threaten the development of the process of capitalist production. It promotes overproduction, speculation, crises, surplus-capital along with surplus-population. . . . this peculiar barrier testifies to the finiteness and the historical, merely transitory character of capitalist production. (III, p. 283)

Despite the clarity of the passage, however, the precise way by which the decline in the rate of profit led to business crises of increasing severity is open to dispute. In the first place, Marx recognized that a decline in the profit rate did not mean that the mass of surplus value would decline. In fact, he pointed out how the "two-faced" law also led capitalists to accelerate their capital accumulation in order to offset the decline. Of course, from Marx's point of view, such an acceleration of investment in constant capital relative to variable capital would cause the profit rate to fall even more. Second, he pointed out six factors that tended to counterbalance the declining rate of profit: (III, ch. XIV)

1. An increase in the rate of surplus value as a result of longer workdays, greater exploitiation of labor, or a reduction in the prices of commodities workers buy. "Whatever tends to promote the production of relative surplus-value by mere improvements in methods, for instance in agriculture, without altering the magnitude of the invested capital" would have the effect of raising the rate of exploitation.

2. A fall in the level of wages.

3. Technological changes that lowered the price of constant capital vis-a-vis variable capital.

4. A high rate of technological change. According to Marx, this produced a "surplus population," which could have several effects. Wages would fall, and there might be an "imperfect subordination of labor to capital in certain lines of activity." (III, p. 277) In industries that could not be readily mechanized the organic composition of capital would remain relatively low. Moreover, new lines of production, "especially for the production of luxuries," started with variable capital as the predominate element and only by degrees went through the historical process of increasing the proportion of constant capital.

5. Foreign trade. Marx accepted the classical view that foreign trade increased "abundance" by increasing the amount of goods per unit of labor. "To the extent that foreign trade cheapens partly the elements of constant capital, partly the necessities of life for which the variable capital is exchanged, it tends to raise the rate of profit by raising the rate of surplus-value and lowering the value of the constant capital." (III, p. 278)

6. Lower interest rates. Although they did not affect the rate of profit as previously defined, Marx noted that the rate of profit to the active directors of large capitalist enterprises such as the railroads could be kept from falling by paying lower rates of interest to investors and by increased borrowings from this source. Interest rates, he believed, were in general lower than the rate of return to industrial capitalists.

Marx did not believe that these factors would be sufficient to keep the rate of profit from falling. In the short run, the behavior of wages especially would have a direct effect on the rate of profit. During the upswings of the business cycles, wages would begin to rise as the industrial reserve army was depleted by expanding employment, and the rate of profit would begin to fall. To the extent that capitalists were able to introduce new labor-saving capital to reduce the demand for labor and dampen the rise in wages, they might be able to keep the rate of profit from falling. But this could not go on forever because it was precisely the substitution of capital for labor that underlay the fall of profits in the first place.

To the extent that this process reoccurred in each cycle (Marx spoke in terms of a decennial cycle), the average organic capital ratio would be racheted higher. Thus there would be a long-run tendency for the rate of profit to fall. At some point, if one were to follow the classical argument, the rate of profit would become too low to stimulate further investment. At this point, a final breakdown of the system could result, although there would be no reason to assume that the end would be cataclysmic.

The theory of the declining rate of profit has been considered at variance with Marx's other theory of "the poverty and restricted consumption of the masses" as the "last" cause of "all real crises." (III, p. 568) The reason, as noted above, is that with technical progress the constant rate of exploitation assumed by the formula for the profit rate would mean secularly rising wages, while constant real wages would raise the rate of surplus value and offset a decline in the profit rate. "Poverty" and a declining rate of profit could not occur together, except perhaps where the organic capital ratio rises faster than the rate of exploitation. But even in this case the level of real wages need not necessarily fall and might even rise.

Marx in his theory of "poverty" as a cause of the business cycle was not a crude underconsumptionist. In a passage explicitly directed toward Rodbertus' belief that crises occurred because wages were less than total output, he argued that "crises are precisely always preceded by a period in which wages rise generally and the working class actually get a larger share of the annual product intended for consumption." (II, p. 476)

If "poverty" does not mean absolute poverty, and if crises can occur when the aggregate purchasing power of labor is increasing, then what remains of Marx's underconsumption argument? The answer seems to be that both much and little remain. As far as the precise sequence of events during a business cycle that lead to a crisis are concerned, it tells us far less than his theory of falling profit rates. However as a description of the underlying problems of capitalism as he saw it, the theory of "restricted consumption" was fundamental. The decrease in the relative importance of wages meant an increasing disparity between the expansion of productive capacity on the one hand and the inability of the system to promote the welfare of those worked on the other. In the last analysis this, to Marx, was the system's greatest contradiction.

VI

Marx failed to prove his case that capitalism was transitory; the very fact that political action would be necessary to bring the system of private property to an end put the matter beyond the reach of economic analysis. Nor did he prove that business cycles would necessarily become more severe, except in the sense that the difficulty in sustaining production associated with the long-run tendency of the rate of profit to fall, together with a greater disparity in income, would make the economy more susceptible to periodic contractions.

What Marx accomplished in economic analysis, however, was to reopen the discussion of business cycles in market economies closed by the classical theorists, to introduce dynamic processes into economic reasoning, and to make a beginning in aggregative analyses of income, consumption, savings, and investment. From a modern technical viewpoint, the labor theory of value, with its inadequate handling of input-output relationships, made a precise analysis of the effect of technological change on the distribution of income as impossible for Marx as it had been for John Stuart Mill; and the lack of a systematic analysis of aggregate demand hindered his integration of interindustry analysis with his theory of underconsumption. However, although his analytical tools had serious limitations, Marx raised questions about the nature and development of capitalism that did not easily go away.

Notes to Chapter vi, Part I

It is remarkable that Marx was so little appreciated by English-speaking economists prior to the 1930s. He was well acquainted with the work of John Stuart Mill, but Mill knew nothing of him. Alfred Marshall dismissed Marx after a few references; but he was obviously unaware of Marx's theories since he uncritically (and erroneously) linked them with those of Rodbertus. (See *Principles of Economics,* 9th (Variorum) ed., New York, Macmillan, 1961, vol. I, pp. 587–588, 632n, 816, 817n.) John Maynard Keynes, in his *Essays in Persuasion,* called Marx's *Capital* "an obsolete economic textbook . . . not only scientifically erroneous but without interest or application for the modern world." (p. 300)

On the continent, the situation was different. Eugen von Böhm-Bawerk, a leading Austrian economist, published the first major critique of Marx's analysis, *Karl Marx and the Close of his System,* in 1896 (it was translated into English in 1898), immediately following the publication of the third volume of *Capital.* While Böhm-Bawerk found Marx inconsistent, a Russian, non-Marxist economist, Mikhail Tugan-Baranowsky (1865–1919) took the "disproportionate" theory of *Capital,* vol. II, and developed it into one of the first non-Marxist theories of the business cycle. Also before World War I, Ladislaus von Bortkiewicz, a German mathematician and economist, was the first to offer a solution to the Marxian problem of the transformation of values into prices. German economists, especially in the period before Hitler, were well acquainted with Marx's work.

Perhaps no prominent non-Marxian, European economist was more influenced by his work than Joseph A. Schumpeter, whose *Theory of Economic Development* (1911) bore several Marxian characteristics, even though his formal explanation of equilibrium was Walrasian. He himself became known later as "the bourgeois Marx." His theory of innovation and imitation as a basic cause of business cycles was antici-

pated by Marx, who noted how individual capitalists may get a headstart on competitors by making use of inventions before they are generally introduced. (*Capital,* III, p. 274) Schumpeter's *Business Cycles* (1939, two volumes) attempted an interpretation of economic history in terms of his own dynamic theory, an attempt similar to Marx's. And like Marx, Schumpeter was a thorough student of the development of economic thought. His *History of Economic Analysis,* a critical investigation, was published posthumously in 1954. Schumpeter was generous in his recognition of Marx's accomplishments, even though he found fault with his theoretical constructions. In *Capitalism, Socialism, and Democracy* (New York, Harper & Row, 1942), he said:

> . . . there is one truly great achievement to be set against Marx's theoretical misdemeanours . . . the idea of a theory, not merely of an indefinite number of disjointed individual patterns or of the logic of economic quantities in general, but of the *actual* sequence of these patterns or of the economic process as it goes on under its own steam, in *historic* time, producing at every instant that state which will of itself determine the next one. (p. 43)

With the Great Depression of the 1930s attitudes toward Marx's economic theories in English-speaking countries changed and a number of sympathetic works appeared. In Great Britain, Maurice Dobb wrote *Political Economy and Capitalism* (London, Routledge & Kegan Paul, 1937); a little later, in the United States, Paul M. Sweezy published *The Theory of Capitalist Develop-*

ment: *Principles of Marxian Political Economy* (New York, Oxford University Press, 1942). For a more recent interpretation of Marx's economics, see Paul Baran and Paul M. Sweezy's *Monopoly Capital: An Essay on the American Economic and Social Order* (New York, Monthly Review, 1966.)

Keynesian economics kindled an interest in Marx despite Keynes' own distaste for him. The first Keynesian to treat Marx seriously was Joan Robinson, one of Keynes' students, who wrote *An Essay on Marxian Economics* (London, Macmillan, and New York, St. Martin's Press, 1942.) She has also written "Marx, Marshall and Keynes," *Collected Economic Papers*, II (Oxford, Blackwell, 1960), and an "Introduction to Rosa Luxemburg" (the German World War I Marxist) in a reprint of the latter's *The Accumulation of Capital* (1951). Mrs. Robinson has been concerned with showing that Marx was essentially a precursor of Keynes. An American Keynesian, Lawrence R. Klein, also found places in Marx's work where he anticipated modern macro analysis. (See his *The Keynesian Revolution*, New York, Macmillan, 1947.) For a recent collection of articles on various phases of Marxian economics, see David Horowitz, *Marx and Modern Economics* (New York and London, Modern Reader Paperbacks, 1968).

I

An old but good biography of Marx is Franz Mehring's *Karl Marx: The Story of His Life*, trans. by Edward Fitzgerald (New York, Covici Friede, 1935). A recent account of Marx's early years is provided by David McLellan in *Marx Before*

Marxism (New York, Harper & Row, 1970).

The editions of Marx's writings referred to in the text are as follows:

A Contribution to the Critique of Political Economy, trans. from the second edition by N. I. Stone (Chicago, Kerr, 1904);

Capital, A Critique of Political Economy, trans. from the third German edition by Samuel Moore and Edward Aveling, ed. by Frederick Engels (New York, Modern Library, from Kerr's 1906 edition), vol. I.

Capital, A Critique of Political Economy, trans. from the second German edition by Ernest Untermann, ed. by Frederick Engels (Chicago, Kerr, 1907), vol. II, *The Process of Circulation of Capital*.

Capital, A Critique of Political Economy, trans. from the first German edition by Ernest Untermann, ed. by Frederick Engels (Chicago, Kerr, 1909), vol. III, *The Process of Capitalist Production as a Whole*.

Another important economic work is Marx's *Theories of Surplus Value*, trans. by G. A. Bonner and Emile Burns (New York, International Publishers, 1952). "Wage-Labor and Capital," in Marx and Engels' *The Essentials of Marx* (New York, Vangard Press, 1926), was an earlier statement by Marx based on lectures given in 1847.

For a statement of the Marxian theory of history, see Frederick Engels' "On Historical Materialism," which was written in English. This and other related works can be found in *Karl Marx and Frederick Engels, Basic Writings on Politics and Philosophy*, ed. by Lewis S. Feuer (Garden City, N. Y., Doubleday, 1959). For a non-Marxist's evaluation of his theory, see M. M. Bober's *Karl Marx's Interpretation of History* (Cambridge, Mass., Harvard University Press, 1948).

The discovery and publication in the 1920s (in English in 1959) of the *Economic and Philosophic Manuscripts* that Marx had written in 1844 created a new interest in his earlier views. These writings reveal a humanistic sensitivity to the alienation caused by industrial life. The worker produces goods that have an existence beyond his control, a life that, in fact, "confronts him as something hostile and alien." (Karl Marx, *The Economic & Philosophic Manuscripts of 1844,* ed. by Dirk J. Struik, New York, International Publishers, 1964, p. 108.) The end to alienation comes when the worker directly controls his own activities and finds self-realization in them. Recent debate over the manuscripts has centered on whether Marx abandoned these views in his later work. Although Marx's economic analysis came later and was necessarily more technical, there is no strong evidence that he did. (See McLellan, *op. cit.,* especially chs. 7 and 8.)

II

Socialist thought concerning exploitation and private property as developed by some of Marx's forerunners and contemporaries is discussed in Part II of the Notes. Marx and Engels drew a sharp distinction between themselves and the "utopian" socialists, as they called them, on two grounds: (1) that the latter were making a moral judgment about the evils of capitalism, whereas they were investigating the contradictions of capitalism scientifically, and (2),

a more important point, they (Marx and Engels) did not believe that the evils of capitalism could be eliminated by moral reform. (See Marx and Engels, "The Communist Manifesto," and Engels, "Socialism: Utopian and Scientific," both reprinted in Feuer, *op. cit.*)

The shifts in the theory of property from Locke to Hume, Bentham, and Mill have been discussed in earlier chapters. The quotations from Hume and Bentham on p. 147 are from the discussion in Lionel Robbins' *The Theory of Economic Policy in English Classical Political Economy* (London, Macmillan, 1852), pp. 52 and 63 respectively.

The importance of Marx's doctrine of "fetishism," contained in *Capital,* vol. I, ch. I, sec. 4, cannot be underestimated. It is a key to understanding the Marxian system precisely because it raises the question of the relationship of economic behavior to the underlying social structure and the historical character of production. For this reason, Marxists emphasize its importance (see, for example, Sweezy, *op. cit.,* pp. 34–40), while critics give it hardly a line (see Murray Wolfson, *A Reappraisal of Marxian Economics,* New York, Columbia University Press, 1966, p. 44).

Marx's reluctance to examine a situation outside its historical context is well known. He justified his aggregative model of simple reproduction, which because of its assumption of zero investment was inconsistent with capitalist society, on the grounds that the accumulation process contained within it the simple reproduction model. (II, p. 456) In criticizing those who claimed a machine was only a complex tool, he wrote, "From the economical standpoint this explanation is worth nothing, *because the historical element is wanting."* (I, p. 406, italics added.) Marx's general economic method was to insist that a logical process was a historical one.

III

The limitations of the labor theory of value as an explanation of prices have been reviewed in Chapter 4. The particular problems in Marx's formulation are (1) the calculation of profit as affected by the turnover of capital and (2) the transformation of values into prices. The first problem, which presents no serious difficulties, is examined in detail by Leo Rogin in *The Meaning and Validity of Economic Theory: A Historical Approach* (New York, Harper & Brothers, 1956), ch. 9.

The transformation problem has received considerable attention. One of the first to develop the argument beyond the point where Marx left it was Ladislaus von Bortkiewicz in "Value and Price in the Marxian System," reprinted in *International Economic Papers* (1952), no. 2 and originally published in German in 1906 and 1907. Sweezy in general follows Bortkiewicz, *op. cit.*, ch. vii. For several post-World War II interpretations see articles in the *Economic Journal* by J. Winternitz (June 1948), K. May (December 1948), and Ronald Meek (March 1956). The major issue in these writings is whether the transformation of values into prices can be accomplished in such a way that the sum of the prices based on an average rate of profit equals the sum of the values at the same time that total profit equals total surplus value.

IV

The controversy over Marx's theory of increasing misery as a result of capitalist development is thoroughly examined by Thomas Sowell in "Marx's 'Increasing Misery' Doctrine," *American Economic Review* (December 1960), pp. 111–120. This article also appears in Ingrid H. Rima, ed., *Readings in the History of Economic Theory* (New York, Holt, Rinehart & Winston, 1970), pp. 109–116. Sowell's argument is that Marx, up through the time he wrote the *Communist Manifesto* in 1848, probably believed that real wages would decline under capitalism but that by the time he wrote the first volume of *Capital* in 1867 he no longer held that view. He now felt that rising real wages were not only possible under capitalism, but likely. To claim that Marx's work later had to be "revised" to account for the historical tendency of wages to rise is therefore erroneous, according to Sowell.

V

In his analysis of business cycles and the long-run development of capitalism Marx did not bring together in any summary or integrated way the various forces that he believed to be at work. As noted, the last two volumes of *Capital,* in which much of this subject is discussed, were published posthumously. The one chapter where Marx attempted to examine the effects of both underconsumption and falling profit rates on the business cycle was Chapter XV in volume three, entitled "Unraveling the Internal Contradictions of the Law." (The "law" was the tendency of the profit rate to fall.) Although Marx further criticizes underconsumption as a specific cause of cycles, he clearly brings out the long-run tendency toward a disparity between capitalism's productive capacity and its ability to utilize it because of a restrictive distribution structure. (III, pp. 312–313)

The importance of this controversy, however, recedes somewhat if an assumption which Marx sometimes, but not always, made (that the rate of surplus value remains the same) is dropped. Real wages, then, could still rise as increasing investment raised the organic capital ratio; at the same time the rate of exploitation could also increase. As Marx pointed out, this would tend to offset the fall in the rate of profit. As modern writers have shown, whether this offset would be sufficient to actually keep the profit rate from falling depends on the relative changes in s', the rate of exploitation, and in q, the organic capital ratio. For a mathematical description of the relationship, see Irma Adelman, *Theories of Economic Growth and Development* (Stanford, Calif., Stanford University Press, 1961), p. 82.

Notes to Chapter vi, Part II:

Some Socialist Forerunners and Contemporaries of Marx

Sismondi (1773–1842)

Jean Charles Leonard Simonde de Sismondi, born in Switzerland, was both an economist and a historian, but not a socialist. Nonetheless many of his ideas influenced Marx. Sismondi's first work in economics, *De la richesse commerciale (On Commercial Wealth)*, published in 1803, was a sympathetic exposition of the views of Adam Smith. But his later writings in economics reflected a different point of view, and he charged that the Ricardians had improperly neglected important facts in forming their theories. A statement of his changed economic views first appeared in "Political Economy," a lengthy article prepared for Brewster's *Edinburgh Encyclopedia* in 1818 and then elaborated into a treatise, *Nouveau principes d'économie politique (New Principles of Political Economy)*, the first edition of which came out in 1819, and the second edition in 1827.

Sismondi claimed that Ricardian economics ignored discrepancies between facts and theory, and he stressed the need to study facts and institutions through observation and the reading of history. In particular, he said, he had been strongly moved by the commercial crisis that swept Europe and "the cruel suffering of wage earners in manufacturing, which he had witnessed in Italy, Switzerland, and France and which through public reports, had been shown to be equally severe in England, Germany, and Belgium."

(*Nouveau principes,* 2nd ed., p. xxii.) He disagreed with Say's Law on the grounds that unemployment in the real world flatly contradicted the theoretical abstractions of full employment. Sismondi was at first hostile to Malthus because he considered his population theory an overdrawn abstraction; later, he recognized that Malthus's glut theories were similar to his own. Because he felt that abstract theorizing could not only create misleading analyses but lead to erroneous policies, Sismondi criticized the policy of *laissez faire et laissez passer.* He was the first to apply the term "orthodox" to the leading economists of his day, and he realized that the combination of an orthodox theory and policy produced an ideology that was difficult to attack with any success. In the second edition of *New Principles,* he complained that even though events had more than substantiated his earlier criticisms, he had not received approval from the most respected economists, because, he added, he was attacking "an orthodoxy, an enterprise as dangerous in philosophy as in religion." (*ibid.,* p. 1)

Sismondi's concern with individual and social welfare was expressed in connection with two types of problems—economic crises and poverty —both arising from the growth of the new industrial system. Business crises, he claimed, were characteristic of the new, factory-based industrial system, which required greater amounts of fixed capital, and competition for profits. The desire of businessmen to improve their profit position led them to undercut their rivals and induced their competitors to do likewise in order to survive. The result was an overproduction of

goods in one industry that, combined with similar effects in other industries, gave rise to a general crisis.

Sismondi stressed the lack of balance between production and consumption. He used a rudimentary dynamic approach, claiming that the annual production of one year was purchased with the income of the previous year. Time, he said, was needed to reallocate resources, and during the period of transition maladjustments could lead to crises and unemployment before a new equilibrium was reached.

In his analysis of the poverty of the wage-earner, Sismondi said the growth of the factory system had created two classes, the rich and the poor. He was the first modern writer to use the word *proletarii,* a name borrowed from the Romans, to designate the factory workers, a new class in society for whom poverty had, he felt, become the normal state of affairs. The *proletarii* of ancient Rome were useful only as parents of children; like the factory workers of the new industrial system they had no means of providing for their offspring. Sismondi elaborated his analysis by claiming that as the new system grew, the rich became richer and the poor poorer. The cause of this increasing distress was, again, the competitive system under which the businessman, in order to expand production, cut costs by lowering wages and by using women and children, who had the least bargaining power. He laid the foundation of an exploitation theory of wages by stating that profits "are sometimes nothing but the exploitation of the worker. . . . One could almost say that modern society lives at the expense of the proletariat." Sismondi's graphic description of the plight of the worker applied not only to his wages, but his working conditions, health, and hours of work as well.

In Sismondi's writings we also find the idea of an industrial-reserve army. The introduction of labor-saving machinery into industry, said Sismondi, would increase our comforts or our leisure *if* the worker were his own master. But where the workers work for others in a competitive market, the immediate effect is likely to be unemployment for some workers; this in turn depresses the wages of all workers. The net result is diminished consumption of goods and a fall in aggregate demand. Although new machines might lower prices and increase the consumption of certain goods, such as luxuries, new machinery and new products also created problems. Let us desist, he said, from making "abstractions of time and place" and look at the "obstacles and frictions" of the marketplace: Workers may put up with lower wages rather than shift jobs or become unemployed; and since fixed capital cannot be transferred from one use to another, the manufacturer also takes a loss.

To Sismondi this analysis demonstrated the disastrous effects of *laissez-faire* policies on the development of the industrial system. His own reform proposals were consistent with his analysis. He urged governmental measures to assist the poor. One of the first advocates of a welfare state, he also urged legislation to curb lengthy workdays and eliminate child labor. However, he proposed that the state require employers to provide for their workers in their old age and in case of sickness, accidents, or unemployment, rather

than do so directly. Such costs should be considered part of the cost of producing goods. He urged the government to discourage the concentration of wealth by progressive taxes and by eliminating patent laws. He was not a socialist since he did not wish to abolish private property; he did not believe in the unlimited encouragement of industrialization; and he was not a democrat, believing that democracy meant mob rule and tyranny. Rather he believed that a reunion of the worker with property, through peasant proprietorships or small businesses, would restore the proper relationship between the growth of population and income so that the poor would not become poorer.

The First Socialists

Although socialist and communist ideas were of ancient origin,[1] the development of the modern movement began in the nineteenth century. The new socialism was immediately rooted in the French Revolution, which sent ideological shock waves throughout Europe. Accompanying the slogan of liberty, equality, and fraternity were ideas of economic progress, of democratic control, and of the perfectibility of man if social institutions were properly reformed. The early writers believed that the

[1] The word "socialism" was new, however, having been coined almost simultaneously in England and France. In England it was used in an Owenite journal in 1827; in France it was used by Pierre Leroux in 1832, in a journal edited by the Saint-Simonians. In both cases, the word was intended to convey the antithesis of individualism. The first use of the word in the title of a book in English was in Robert Owen's *What Is Socialism?* (1841).

promises of the revolution had not been fulfilled and that new reforms were necessary, but they were little concerned with economic analyses as such.

1. The Count of Saint-Simon (1760–1825), who participated in both the American and French Revolutions, was opposed to idlers and argued that men had different capacities and should be rewarded in accordance with their work. He saw the French Revolution as a conflict between those who worked and those who did not, and he held that industry needed new institutions in order to realize its potential. France should be turned into a workshop, he said; all citizens should have a duty to labor, and the government should be so reorganized that the economically active (workers and employers) would control, enlarge, and direct the productive powers of the nation without interference by those who did not work. Saint-Simon sought abolition of a government that exercised control over men in favor of one that administered things. He advocated an industrial parliament with three chambers—one of engineers, who would be concerned with invention and planning; one of scientists, to examine the plans; and one of leaders of industry and banking, to execute the plans. Individual motivation for industrial development would be provided by appropriate payments from the national product. Saint-Simon did not urge state ownership of property, but reforms that would spur individual activity.

2. Saint-Simon's followers transformed his ideas into a criticism of private property and laid the basis for the keystone of socialist thought, the abolition of private property in industry. Augustin Thierry, Enfantin, and Bazard were among those who reinterpreted and propagandized Saint-Simon's ideas. In the *Doctrine de Saint Simon, Exposition* (1829), they published a criticism of private property as a means by which owners acquire a return in the form of rent or interest similar to a private tax on income produced by others. To the extent that capitalists and landlords worked, they contributed to the national output; but on the basis of their claims as capitalists and landowners they received unearned income and hence exploited those who worked. The entrepreneur's profit was justified by his direction of the enterprise. To the Saint-Simonians, the system of inheritance, which made income an accident of birth, was a particularly obnoxious aspect of private property. They argued that, on the grounds of justice and economic efficiency the state should inherit all wealth so that eventually the instruments of production would be in one central fund. These instruments could then be distributed and employed by persons, or associations of persons, in a manner consistent with their capacities and abilities.

3. A different form of socialism was advocated by Charles Fourier (1772–1837), the French socialist, who attacked vigorously the evils of industrial society and urged the creation of small, communistic communities called phalanxes. Unlike Saint-Simon, he did not promote industrialism, preferring to avoid it altogether. A believer in "associative socialism," he argued that individualism was destroyed by the factory system and by the impersonal competition of the marketplace. However he sought the abolition neither

of property nor of profit. Capital, labor, and management would be joined in each community, and each man would receive a predetermined share of the product. The ultimate goal was to make each worker a co-operative co-owner of the productive property of the community. Fourier claimed that such a scheme would abolish the conflicts between producers and consumers, debtors and creditors, capitalists and labor.

4. Robert Owen (1771–1858) was a British exponent of cooperative communities. Early in life he acquired the New Lanark cotton mills, where he set about showing the world that improving factory conditions and the home life of his workers was consistent with financial success. During the depression after the Napoleonic wars, Owen advocated the establishment of "Villages of Co-operation," where the unemployed could earn the basic necessities instead of having to depend on public relief. Later, he expanded the idea to include cooperative communities, a new form of social organization that would abolish poverty and improve man's character (which he believed was formed by his environment).

Owen laid the basis of his labor theory of exchange in his *Report to the County of Lanark* (1821). Since labor was the cause and the measure of value, he said, goods should be exchanged at a price that reflected the labor they required. This notion was based on the assumption that the amount of labor embodied in goods should equal the amount of labor they commanded; profit and rent were improper, and even immoral, subtractions from the value of goods. To Owen, the profit motive, competition, and metallic money were the roots of all evil.

They induced capitalists to exploit labor, which in turn led to business gluts when workers could not buy all that they had produced. The remedy for this, he said, was for workers to receive the full value of what they produced. Goods should be sold for labor notes, issued in proportion to the labor time required to produce them, rather than metallic money.

Socialists and the First Economic Criticisms

Whereas the first socialists were humanitarians, morally shocked by the conditions of workers under the new factory system with its competitive drive for profits, later socialists (though still pre- or anti-Marxian) began to give more attention to economic analysis. The growing prestige of economists that followed publication of Ricardo's *Principles* in 1817 could not be ignored by those who felt that the new theories supported an oppressive economic system and rationalized attacks on those who sought to reform it.

1. In France, Pierre-Joseph Proudhon (1809–65) was one of the first to attempt to expose the "contradictions" of the economic system, but his contribution to a socialist theory of economics was slight. In fact, he was as critical of previous socialist writers as he was of anyone else, and if he had a theory at all it was the desirability of a competitive economy consisting of independent producers, each of whom negotiated exchanges of his own output, with no help from the state. In short, Proudhon extended *laissez faire* to the extreme of anarchism.

His critique of capitalism, nonetheless, was comprehensive and unsparing. In his first work, *Qu'est-ce que la propriété? (What Is Prop-*

erty?), published in 1840, he answered this question with a phrase that became famous: "Property is theft." Property rights enabled nonworkers to exact a toll of rent, profits, and interest from the labor of others. He described the conflicts between labor and capital, producers and nonproducers, consumers and sellers, in various works, including his *Contradictions économiques, ou la philosophie de misère (Economic Contradictions, or The Philosophy of Poverty)*. Published in 1846, the book was made famous by Marx's scathing reply, *The Poverty of Philosophy*. Proudhon believed that labor alone was productive and that these conflicts had only one solution, the exchange of goods by the producers themselves (i.e., the workers).

Proudhon proposed an exchange bank to issue interest-free notes (i.e., money) to facilitate the circulation of goods. He assumed that the bank would be able to suppress interest charges and make easy loans to workers for investment purposes. Unlike Owen, he did not believe goods should always sell at prices that reflected their labor cost; rather, prices should be negotiated by the parties directly concerned—the buyer and the seller.[2]

2. In England a number of writers, known as Ricardian socialists,[3] began to point out the socialist implications of the labor theory of

[2] See Charles Gide and Charles Rist, *A History of Economic Doctrines From the Time of the Physiocrats to the Present Day*, 2nd English ed. (Boston, Heath, n.d.), especially p. 314–326.

[3] The term Ricardian socialists was first used by Herbert Somerton Foxwell, a British economist, in his introduction to Anton Menger's *Right to the Whole Produce of Labour* (London, Macmillan, 1899).

value. After Ricardo's *Principles* was published in 1817, the idea that political economy had "proven" the exploitation of wage-earners gained headway. If the value of commodities reflected the amount of labor required to produce them, and if capital itself was only stored-up labor, then was it not irrefutably true that profits on capital (which in British terminology meant interest as well as entrepreneurial profits) were a deduction from income that rightfully belonged to labor? The writers who so argued included William Thompson (1785–1833), Thomas Hodgskin (1783–1869), John Gray (1799–1859), and John Francis Bray (1809–95). The differences among them were less important than the similarities. They argued that workers should receive the full fruits of their labor and disagreed mainly over the means of accomplishing this goal. Union organizations, legislation to improve factory conditions, and "cooperation" were remedies most generally advocated. Gray and Bray both advocated national-bank schemes to provide workers with cheap funds for capital. Like Owen, they also believed goods should circulate at prices determined by the amount of labor they required.

3. In Germany, Johann Karl Rodbertus (1805–75) also expressed the belief that workers should receive the "full value" of their labors, but his reasoning was more complex than that of the Ricardian socialists. Rodbertus was responsible for a number of concepts that later made their way into socialist literature.

He did not believe that the value of each commodity was determined by the amount of labor embodied in it; rather, it was the output of the social system that was labor-determined. He stated that since workers received only a subsistence wage, as the productivity of the system increased labor's *share* of the national output in the form of wages would automatically fall. The remainder of the national product he called "rent" (a term similar to Marx's surplus value, as it included profits, interest, and land rents). "Rent" tended to rise with economic growth.

Rodbertus concluded from all this that there would always be a tendency toward gluts, or overproduction of goods under capitalism because workers spent their total income on consumer goods, whereas recipients of other forms of income did not. Rodbertus's underconsumption theory of business depressions was in part a restatement of Sismondi; it was a theory not of business cycles, but of a tendency toward chronic depression.

Chapter vii

SUBJECTIVE ECONOMICS AND THE CONSERVATIVE REACTION:

Menger and the Austrian School

> Goods always have value *to* certain economizing individuals and this value is also *determined* only by these individuals. . . . [T]he quantities of goods employed in the production of a good have neither a necessary nor a directly determining influence on its value.
>
> Carl Menger, *Principles of Economics*

> What characterizes the theories of A. Smith and his followers is the one-sided rationalistic liberalism, not infrequently impetuous effort to do away with what exists . . . .
>
> Menger, *Problems of Economics and Sociology*

> Testing the exact theory of economy by the full empirical method is simply a methodological absurdity, a failure to recognize the bases and presuppositions of exact research.
>
> *ibid.*

> If what I have said is true, the socialist Exploitation theory, as represented by its two most distinguished adherents [Rodbertus and Marx], is not only incorrect, but, in theoretical value, even takes one of the lowest places among interest theories.
>
> Eugen von Böhm-Bawerk, *Capital and Interest*

In Austria-Hungary during the latter part of the nineteenth century there arose a school of economics that became widely known for its unique subjective theory of value, for its highly conservative stance on economic policy, and for its readiness to engage in battle those with

173

contrary views. The Austrian school, as it was called, made its influence felt upon economics in other lands as well. A relatively few but highly articulate exponents of its view forced economists of other persuasions to reexamine their premises and theories. Ironically, the major works of the school's founder, Carl Menger, a professor at the University of Vienna, were two rarely read books published in 1871 and 1883. These were not translated into English until after World War II, over two-thirds of a century later. It was Menger's disciples—particularly Friedrich von Wieser and Eugen von Böhm-Bawerk before World War I—who attracted worldwide attention.

The loss of its home base in Austria with the collapse of the Hapsburg monarchy in 1918 reduced somewhat the effectiveness of the school. Although its younger members eventually went to other countries, such as Great Britain and the United States, the Austrian point of view (which denied the relevance of real costs in the determination of value) did not make much headway against the classical and neoclassical theories dominant in English-speaking countries. The Austrians' lack of enthusiasm for the mathematical aspects of economics and statistical testing also ran counter to the trend of modern economics. And their opposition to the increasing role of governments in the economic life of nations meant that they had no alternative to the main course of events of the twentieth century other than its reversal.

The economics and the message of the Austrian school differed sharply with that of the British classical economists, the Marxists, and the school of historical economics dominant in neighboring Germany during the nineteenth and early twentieth centuries. Menger's revolutionary subjective theory of marginal utility denied the cost theory of value supported by the classicists and Marxists. His exposition of the methodology of economics, his insistence that economic science should be divorced from value judgments, and (at the same time) his hostility to economic reform raised new questions concerning the methods and meaning of economics. One of his followers, Wieser, developed the opportunity-cost concept to replace classical doctrines, and another, Böhm-Bawerk, constructed a theory of capital and interest to replace classical profit theories (which he believed were inadequate and open to Marx's charge of exploitation).

I

Carl Menger (1840–1921) war born in Galicia (which was then under Austrian rule), studied at the Universities of Vienna, Prague, and

Cracow, and then entered the field of journalism, where for the first time he became interested in economics. He later worked for the Austrian civil service, during which time he completed his first book, *Principles of Economics* (*Grundsätze der Volkswirtschaftslehre*). Published in 1871, it contributed to the beginning of the marginal revolution in economics and laid the basis for the subjective economics of the Austrian school. Two years later, Menger obtained an appointment as professor extraordinary at the University of Vienna, but he soon left to become a private tutor to the young Crown Prince Rudolph. For two years, he traveled with the prince throughout Europe; he then returned to the university, this time as an "ordinary" (i.e., full) professor of political economy. His second major work, *Problems of Economics and Sociology* (*Untersuchungen über die Methode der Socialwissenschaften und der politischen Oekonomie insbesondere*),[1] which appeared in 1883, brought his theories to a wider audience. In this work, he attacked the historical approach to economics then characteristic of the leading economists in Germany and gave an ardent defense of his own theoretical method. Gustav Schmoller, the current leader of the German school, reacted swiftly in defense of his position; and the argument over method (known as the *Methodenstreit*) suddenly gained international attention. As followers of each economist also sprang into the dispute, the cleavage between the two points of view was deepened by the fact that both Menger and Schmoller held such commanding positions in the educational establishments of their respective countries that they could virtually close teaching opportunities to those who professed allegiance to the other side. Although the *Methodenstreit* gradually died out, the issues raised were far from resolved. Schmoller eventually admitted the importance of theory: Using both deduction and induction, he said, was as necessary as using the right and left foot in walking. But there was no agreement on either the nature of theory or the purposes of historical research. Only gradually was it recognized that Menger's attack on the German historical school had included a vigorous criticism of British classical economics.

Menger wrote several shorter works on gold and currency problems. He served as a member of the governmental commission established in 1892 to consider resumption of specie payments and solutions for various monetary problems confronting the Austria-Hungarian monarchy. Böhm-Bawerk, then in the Ministry of Finance, was a governmental

---

[1] The literal translation is "Investigations of the Method of the Social Sciences and of Political Economy in Particular."

representative on the same commission. Eventually, Menger was made a life member of the upper chamber of the Austrian Parliament, but he participated in its sessions only infrequently.

Retiring from the University of Vienna in 1903, he turned to the task of enlarging his *Principles of Economics,* which had originally carried the subtitle "First, General Part." But his hopes for a comprehensive statement of his theories were never fulfilled. A second edition, edited by his son, Karl, and published posthumously in 1923, added little to his earlier statements.

Neither Friedrich von Wieser (1851–1926) nor Eugen von Böhm-Bawerk (1851–1914) were students of Menger, although both had studied at the University of Vienna and learned of his theories there. Old friends (Wieser eventually married Böhm-Bawerk's sister), they not only completed their studies at Vienna together but spent several years attending the same universities in Germany during the 1870s. Paradoxically, they participated in seminars held by leading exponents of the "older" German historical school—Karl Knies at Heidelberg, Wilhelm Roscher at Leipzig, and Bruno Hildebrandt at Jena. But they continued to hold to the ideas of Menger, and began to work out elaborations of his propositions.

It was Wieser, during a subsequent period of service with the Austrian government, who developed the alternative cost approach that complemented Menger's theory of subjective value. When his book *Origins and Principal Laws of Economic Value* was published in 1884, Wieser entered upon an academic career that included teaching at the University of Prague and later at Vienna as a successor to Menger. He also wrote other works, including *Natural Value* (1889) and *Social Economics* (published in 1914 and translated into English in 1927), one of the most comprehensive expositions of the doctrines of the Austrian school.

Although Wieser made important contributions to Austrian theory —it was he who introduced the term "marginal utility" (*grenznutzen*)— his interests diverged somewhat from those of other Austrians. He was more concerned with history and the characteristics of institutions, and less convinced that the natural growth of social institutions promoted an efficient allocation of resources. His last work dealt with the sociology of power. Although Weiser seems to have preferred the isolation of the university, where he could concentrate on his own studies, to governmental work, he did serve as Minister of Commerce for two years in Austria during World War I.

Böhm-Bawerk, in contrast, was far more active in governmental affairs and far more ready to engage in polemical exchanges with other economists. An early paper on subjective value that won the approval of Menger helped him to obtain a professorship at the University of Innsbruck, where he remained for eight years. It was during this period that he completed his major work, *Capital and Interest,* which appeared in two volumes. The first volume, *History and Criticism of Interest Theories* (1884), contained his analyses—generally adverse—of all previous interest (and profit) theories. The second volume, *Positive Theory of Capital* (1888), presented his own theory of capital and the laws governing interest rates. However, parts of the second volume were hastily written and contained a number of inconsistencies. Böhm-Bawerk had evidently decided earlier to enter government service and was under pressure to complete his manuscript. He was associated with the Austrian Ministry of Finance from 1889 to 1905 and helped prepare a draft of the law reforming the Austrian system of taxation. In addition he served at three different times as Minister of Finance. During this period he also continued to write extensively, defending his theories and attacking Marxian economics. (He wrote *Karl Marx and the Close of His System* in 1896.) Following his years of government service Böhm-Bawerk became a professor at the University of Vienna, where his seminars attracted students from many countries.

Among the younger Austrians who continued to support Menger's original theories relatively unchanged were Ludwig von Mises (1881–1969) and Friedrich von Hayek (b. 1899). Mises criticized pricing under socialism, believing that rational economic behavior was impossible under nonindividualistic conditions. Hayek's principal contributions were in the field of business cycles. In general, he defended and extended Böhm-Bawerk's theory of capital.

Some other economists prominent for their own contributions to economic analysis but significantly influenced by Austrian theory were Phillip H. Wicksteed (1844–1927), the English "Austrian"; Knut Wicksell (1851–1926), the Swedish economist; and Joseph A. Schumpeter (1883–1950), who as a student had attended Böhm-Bawerk's seminars.

II

The economic approach of the Austrians was very different from that of the British classical writers, Marx, or the historical economists whose views dominated Germany and had begun to spread to other countries. The Austrians were not concerned primarily with promoting economic growth, with institutional change, or with social or class conflicts. Although during this period the Austrian-Hungarian monarchy had to deal with conflicts among the many nationalities under its rule, social unrest, and socialist agitation, the stability of the sociopolitical structure of the nation seemed assured to its political leaders and most members of the academic establishment. The desirability of existing economic and political institutions was seldom questioned and quickly defended when it was attacked.

Menger was explicitly conservative in his value judgments with respect to social change, and his attitudes as expressed in his sociological analyses of institutions became part of the philosophical underpinning of Austrian economics. Although he sought to create a "value-free," exact science of economics, it was only "value-free" within an institutional system he supported. In his *Principles,* he wrote,

> One of the strangest questions ever made the subject of scientific debate is whether rent and interest are justified from an ethical point of view or whether they are "immoral" . . . . But it seems to be that the question of the legal or moral character of these facts is beyond the sphere of our science. (p. 173)

But he added,

> The prices of these goods (the services of land and of capital) are therefore the necessary products of the economic situation under which they arise, and will be more certainly obtained the more developed the legal system of a people and the more upright its public morals. (pp. 173–74)

Menger believed that the existing system of property ownership was an organic part of "the human economy." He argued that property and economy had a common origin. They were not arbitrary inventions, but "rather the only practically possible solution of the problem that is, *in the nature of things,* imposed upon us by the disparity between requirements for, and available quantities of, all economic goods." (*ibid.,* p. 97, italics added.)

In his study on methods (*Problems of Economics and Sociology*), Menger drew on Burke and Savigny's conservative political philosophies to support his view that property was a natural institution. Edmund Burke (1729–97), the British statesman and political writer, had defended the British governmental and legal system as the end product of a lengthy process of historical development that expressed the wisdom of generations. In his *Reflections on the Revolution in France,* published in 1792, Burke had established himself not only in England but throughout Europe, including Germany, as the defender of the monarchical institutions of the *ancien régime.* He believed that the advocates of the rule of reason and the rights of man should bear the responsibility for the downfall of the French regime and the subsequent bloodshed. "The age of chivalry is gone," he lamented. "That of sophisters, economists, and calculators has succeeded."

Menger praised not only Burke but also Friedrich Karl von Savigny (1779–1861), a German jurist who developed a sociology of law that viewed juridical institutions and doctrines as part of a historical and organic whole—an integral part of the national character and soul. Savigny and his followers denied that attempts to reform the law in accordance with rationalistic objectives were desirable or even possible without undermining the viability of the social whole. Man's wisdom and reason would never be adequate for understanding the importance of tradition and the unity of social institutions that had survived the test of time; hence he could never hope to reform them.

This philosophy, which was the direct antithesis of Benthamism, was taken over completely by Menger, who called it an "organic view of social phenomena." Social institutions, he said, are organically related to each other. They are the natural products of the historical development of the whole of society. His favorite term for this process of change was "unintended." Although he admitted that individuals could by joining together effect changes through pragmatic agreements or "positive" legislation, the best social institutions were those that came about as the unintended result of actions of individuals with separate goals: "Language, religion, law, even the state itself, and, to mention a few economic social phenomena, the phenomena of markets, of competition, of money, and numerous other social structures" evolved unintentionally in this way. (*Problems,* p. 146) And although they were not part of the organic structure per se, prices, interest, rents, and profits also tended to come about unintentionally. This was as it should be, for the natural process of evolution reflected a "higher wisdom" than the pragmatic aspirations of men; it had an "inner historical necessity" (*ibid.,* p. 175) and served the welfare of society.

Menger used the organic theory to attack the British classical school ("Adam Smith and his followers") on the grounds that theirs was a pragmatic, and hence inadequate, vision of society. This put them, according to him, in the same camp as the one-sided, rationalist French exponents of the age of enlightenment. Smith "did not know how to value the significance of 'organic' social structures for society in general and economy in particular and therefore was nowhere concerned to preserve them." His writings were characterized by a "not infrequently impetuous effort to do away with what exists, with what is not always sufficiently understood, the just as impetuous urge to create something new in the realm of political institutions—often enough without sufficient knowledge and experience . . . ." (*ibid.*, p. 177) Only the orientation of Burke-Savigny could provide an antidote to the "one-sidedly rationalistic mania for innovation in the field of economy" and prevent "the dissolution of the organically developed economy by means of a partially superficial pragmatism, a pragmatism that contrary to the intention of its representatives inexorably leads to socialism." (*ibid.*)

Although Menger did not raise the issue of socialism in his *Principles* in 1871, the issue began to haunt him and his followers. The proposition that unintended social changes are always best led to the corollary that reformers, whether moderate or radical, disturbed the natural process and set in motion irreversible forces destructive of society itself. Menger sought to preserve the social system of contemporary Austria. Later Austrians, like Mises in *Socialism* (1921), Joseph Schumpeter in *Capitalism, Socialism, and Democracy* (1942), and Hayek in *Road to Serfdom* (1944) seemed to believe that the symptoms of the irreversible process of decay set off by rationalist attempts to control institutional development were already apparent.

The main target of Menger's criticisms in his work on methodology, however, was neither the classical school nor the socialists but the German historical school. At first glance, this seemed paradoxical, as the German writers themselves criticized the classical economists. Wilhelm Roscher, the founder of the German historical school, published in 1843 his argument that economics should be treated from a historical point of view. He explicitly accepted Savigny's assumption that institutions could only be understood in light of the historical development of the entire society. In fact, Roscher claimed he was using the same techniques to study economic institutions that Savigny had used to study jurisprudence.

It was Roscher's emphasis on the historical point of view that led him to deprecate classical theoretical analysis. Thorough empirical investigations, he believed, might eventually reveal general laws relating to the economic development of society, in all its complexity, a subject the classicists had ignored. Bruno Hildebrandt, the second member of the "older" German historical school, also sought laws of economics development and was even more critical of classical theory. History did not justify, he said, acceptance of the university of economic laws, as the British had assumed; nor did the classicists allow for differences in the psychological motivations of individuals or in the customs and traditions among peoples of other economies. The third member of the older school, Karl Knies, was less sanguine about finding laws of economic development and more eclectic in his view as to the adequacy of existing theory. He tended toward a relativistic approach, believing that theory itself was historically determined. Both Hildebrandt and Knies were critics of socialist views.

Although Menger's critique of the historical school was directed particularly against these three German writers, the issue came to a head with Gustav Schmoller (1838–1917), a professor at the University of Berlin who became known as the leader of the "younger" German historical school. Schmoller was far less tolerant of economic theory than the older three; moreover, through the Association for Social Policy (Verein für Sozialpolitik), he and his supporters promoted certain social reforms in Prussia to mitigate the increasing unrest of the working classes. Although no socialist, Schmoller found Menger's position particularly objectionable, reacted quickly to his book, and in general escalated the controversy.

The arguments of the German historical school were disturbing to Menger first because they disparaged theory and second because he disagreed with their particular type of historical research. In many respects, their attitude toward research agitated Menger more. To him, historical research was important in economics only if the researchers, like Savigny, operated on the principle that "the 'subconscious wisdom' which is manifested in the political institutions that came about organically stands high above meddlesome human wisdom." The German writers did not take this view: ". . . nothing was further from the thoughts of the historical school of economists in Germany than the idea of an analogous conservative orientation in the field of economy." (*Problems,* pp. 91, 92) Instead of supporting conservatism, the German approach made social and economic institutions appear relativistic and malleable. They went so far, said Menger (in an implicit reference to Schmoller), that they offered "the rare spectacle of a *historical* school of economists with socialistic tendencies." (*ibid.,* p. 92) To Menger, the false research of the Germans led to a concern with national problems, reformist tendencies, and a "one-sided collectivism," all of which were characteristic of the economics of the British classicists whom they thought they were criticizing.

Both the German and British economists misunderstood the nature of true historical research because, Menger believed, they lacked an appreciation of the requirements of an exact theory of economics. The Germans did not attempt to understand the role of theory, while the British tried but marched in the wrong direction.

To Menger, it was essential to begin with an understanding of the characteristics of economic theory. Theory dealt with the general nature of economic phenomena; it differed from two other subgroups of economic science, the historical and the practical. The former described unique phenomena; the latter included both public and private policies through which appropriate, specific goals could be most "suitably fulfilled." (See *Problems,* Appendix IV.) Menger's doctrine was that theory was derived neither from facts nor from policies, and in this belief lay the key to the Austrian theory.

Menger's basic objective was to create a science of economics with laws that were the equivalent of the laws of nature in the physical and biological sciences. Such laws he termed "exact" and distinguished from "realistic-empirical" generalizations and "pragmatic" guidelines. Exact laws were learned by the process of deduction from fundamental assumptions about the nature of economic activity; they explained, or helped to explain, the real world but they themselves were universal, indisputable, and *not* testable by the world. Reality contained other, noneconomic phenomena; therefore the study of facts by the realistic-empirical method could never uncover exact laws; nor could experiments produce them. "The purpose of the theoretical sciences is understanding of the real world, knowledge of it extending beyond immediate experience, and control of it." (*Problems,* p. 55) Since there could be no precise correspondence between reality and exact propositions because of the noneconomic aspects of all behavior, the validity of the science of economics must reside in its assumptions and the Euclidean process of logical deduction, not in a verification procedure, in prediction, or even in application.

> To want to test the pure theory of economy by experience in its full reality is a process analogous to that of the mathematician who wants to correct the principles of geometry by measuring real objects. . . . (*ibid.,* p. 70)

Menger's approach was not Bacon's "empirical-realistic induction," by which one arrives at generalizations through precise observations and then makes deductions from them. That method he condemned on the grounds that theory requires not facts but the "essence" of facts, facts reduced to their "most general" or "simplest elements." Menger also disputed the assertion that theoretical laws were hypothetical; this too was "empirical-realistic." Such erroneous reasoning, he said, permeated British classical economics and explained why "in the hands of Adam Smith and his followers" even the "most elementary problems have found no solution. . . ." (*ibid.,* p. 27)

Exact laws, according to Menger, were revealed by introspection, "by our laws of thinking." (*ibid.,* p. 60) "Cognition" enabled the theorist to recognize the "simplest elements" of economic life. Moreover, by introspection one arrived at exact laws that were not hypothetical but part of the nature of reality itself and hence absolute. To opponents, this "absoluteness" meant dogmatism; to Menger and the Austrians, however, it meant that the new theories, once they were expounded systematically and in detail, would promote an understanding of economic phenomena that had until then eluded even economists.

III

Menger's innovation in economic theory was that economic values of all goods are determined by the final consumer in accordance with the principle of marginal subjective valuations. The principle became known as the marginal-utility theory of value, although Menger did not use either the word "utility" or the word "marginal" in this way. His theoretical system was significantly different from those of other "co-discoverers" of the marginal-utility principle.

The idea of approaching the problem of determining value from the point of view of demand rather than costs had been expressed in various ways by a number of earlier writers. The first systematic treatment of marginal utility as a determinant of value appeared in 1854 in a work, *Development of the Laws of Human Relationships,* written by the German Hermann Heinrich Gossen. The book found no market whatsoever, but was rediscovered many years later by Jevons. In the early 1870s three works were published (independently and nearly simultaneously) that advanced a similar approach. In 1871, the same year in which Menger's *Principles* appeared, William Stanley Jevons in England proposed a theory of marginal value in *The Theory of Political Econ-*

omy. In 1874, Leon Walras published *Elements of Pure Economics* (*Les élementes d'économie politique purs*). These were the three works that set in motion what came to be known as the marginal revolution in economics.[2]

Although all three writers, as well as Gossen, emphasized marginal utility as a determinant of economic value, there were several significant differences among them in their theories and in their methods. First, both Jevons' and Walras's theories were mathematical, in method, whereas Menger's was not. Menger did not believe that the evaluation process could be quantified because he did not believe that objective standards of subjective value were possible. Second, both Jevons and Walras accepted the utilitarian position on pleasure and pain, a concept foreign to Menger's philosophy. Hedonism, with its implication that consumers rationally calculated the utility of their purchases, did not enter into Menger's theory. Moreover, the choices that individuals made were not translatable into units of pleasure that could be summed for the economy as a whole as a guide to action. Finally, Menger repudiated the concept of a real, subjective cost, while Jevons developed a concept of the increasing marginal disutility of effort, parallel to the law of diminishing marginal utility. Walras, like Menger, did not use the concept of disutility or real costs.

Menger's exposition of his theory of value was elaborate and painstaking. It began with the definition of "useful things" as those things, material or immaterial, that satisfy man's needs in a cause-and-effect relationship. For "things" to become "goods," there must be (1) a human need, (2) a thing with the ability to satisfy it, (3) human knowledge of the source of satisfaction, and (4) the power to direct its use. Consumer goods, which Menger called goods of the first, or lowest, order, satisfied man's needs directly, while other goods did so indirectly. The latter were goods of a higher order. For example, if bread is a good of the first order, the flour and salt that go into it, the labor of the bakers, and the utensils they use are second-order goods. Grain mills and wheat, a step further back in the chain of production, are third-order goods; the fields and the farmers' services are fourth-order goods. The order of a good is not inherent in its physical characteristics, but is due to its position in the chain of causal relationships between it and the satisfaction of a human need.

[2] Jevons' work is discussed in Chapter viii, especially in the Notes (p. 225). Walras's economic theories are considered in Chapter x.

This theory of valuation had three unique characteristics. First, goods of a higher order received their goods-characteristics from and only from goods of a lower order. Second, goods of a higher order had to be used with complementary goods in order to become goods of a lower order. And third, the process of conversion took time. The idea of causality, said Menger, "is inseparable from the idea of time." (*Principles,* p. 67) As goods of a higher order are future goods, the valuation process requires foresight concerning future needs and is therefore uncertain.

Menger distinguished between economic and noneconomic goods. The first were those of which the supply was less than the need; the second were those of which there was more than enough to go around. Commodities in the first group had to be economized and it was this process, he said, that gave rise to value. Value was the subjective perception of the relative worth of scarce goods in meeting needs, "a judgment made by economizing individuals about the importance their command of the things has for the maintenance of their lives and well-being." (*ibid.,* p. 121)

The principle underlying such judgments was related not to the entire supply of goods, but to individual units of each good. With this observation, Menger arrived at the principle of marginal utility. Successive units of goods, within a given period, provide very different degrees of satisfaction. The importance of an additional unit will diminish as the supply of a good increases until a point is reached when a further unit may give no satisfaction at all. Menger generalized further that since a person has many needs, each characterized by diminishing marginal utility, the individual with limited resources will satisfy each need partially, so that the marginal utility of each thing he buys (the utility of the last unit) will be equal. To illustrate his fact he used a table like Table 3.

The Roman numerals across the top of the table indicate needs of decreasing importance. The Arabic numbers in the columns show the decreasing satisfaction obtained as each additional unit of the good is consumed. Menger assumed that each unit of each good cost the same (in terms of money or some other good). He argued that the economizing individual would purchase different goods such that the additional satisfaction provided by the last unit of each good would be equal. If he had six units of purchasing power, he would purchase three units of I, two units of II, and one of III; the marginal utility of each purchase would then be eight. As his purchasing power increased, he would in-

Table 3

Menger's Table of Diminishing Satisfactions

I	II	III	IV	V	VI	VII	VIII	IX	X
10	9	8	7	6	5	4	3	2	1
9	8	7	6	5	4	3	2	1	0
8	7	6	5	4	3	2	1	0	
7	6	5	4	3	2	1	0		
6	5	4	3	2	1	0			
5	4	3	2	1	0				
4	3	2	1	0					
3	2	1	0						
2	1	0							
1	0								
0									

Source: Carl Menger, *Principles of Economics, First, General Part*, trans. and ed. by James Dingwall and Bert F. Hoselitz, with an introduction by Frank H. Knight (Glencoe, Ill., Free Press, 1950), p. 127.

crease his consumption of each of these goods and also extend his consumption to satisfy new wants. With 15 units of purchasing power, he would purchase enough of the first five goods to obtain a marginal utility from each purchase of six. (Actually, of course, degrees of satisfaction were subjective and not objectively verifiable.)

Menger's theory of value led to his theory of exchange. Individuals with combinations of goods that were not ideal for their needs according to the marginal-equalization principle would seek to exchange units of goods of less subjective value for goods of more subjective value. In a barter situation involving only two individuals the ratio of exchange between the goods would reflect the final outcome of their haggling over terms. The exchange, if it occurred, would benefit each party even though, as Menger went out of his way to point out, the goods had an unequal subjective value in the eyes of each individual. Where there were many sellers and buyers of the two commodities, an exchange ratio would emerge that would clear the market. Use value and exchange value were therefore "only two different forms of the same phenomenon of economic life." (*ibid.,* p. 228) Adam Smith's famous paradox of the difference in value between water and diamonds was now no longer a paradox. Exchange values reflected marginal utility, not aggregate utilities. A greater supply of water lowered its marginal utility and hence its exchange value in comparison with diamonds. This low exchange value was perfectly consistent with its greater aggregate-use value.

Converting values into prices required a theory of money. Menger's analysis here was in keeping with his belief in the rightness of the unintended results of the organic process of social development:

> As *each* economizing individual becomes increasingly more aware of his economic interest, he is led by this *interest, without any agreement, without legislative compulsion, and even without regard to the public interest,* to give his commodities in exchange for other, more saleable, commodities, even if he does not need them for any consumption purpose. (*ibid.*, p. 260, Menger's italics).

Emphasizing the importance of custom, Menger argued that certain commodities, such as gold, became generally recognized as more desirable for monetary purposes and that governments eventually came to sanction behavior that evolved naturally.

His theory of allocation, which he detailed for goods of the first order, was also applicable to goods of higher orders. In pointing out that the value of these goods derived from their contribution to the want-satisfying qualities of goods of a lower order, he stood on the verge of a marginal-productivity theory of the determination of factor prices. However, although he advanced the proposition that the contribution of a productive factor to the satisfaction of a final want governed its value, he did not develop the concept of variable proportions necessary for such a theory (although he hinted at it). Instead he based his analysis on the assumption that factors were employed in fixed ratios.

The extension of the theory of the consumer's allocation of income to an allocation of productive resources among different final uses was by itself neither new nor revolutionary. The idea of allocation had been discussed or assumed by all economists in one way or another. What distinguished the Austrian theory from, say, John Stuart Mill's, was that Mill had believed it essential to take into account the workers' effort and the capitalists' abstinence as disutilities (costs) for which they had to be compensated or production would not continue. (In the case of nonreproducible goods, however, costs in this sense were irrelevant.)

Menger's theory of costs as related to allocation, especially as elaborated by Wieser in *Natural Value,* bypassed the classical cost position by the simple device of assuming that all factor supplies were fixed. Labor, raw materials, and other production inputs were treated as constant quantities, like the classicist's supply of agricultural land. Under these circumstances, the demand for different consumer goods became the demand for higher-order goods, and the only "costs" involved in producing more of one good from the fixed supply of resources were the opportunity costs, or the reduced production of other final goods.

In Wieser's analysis, values were assigned to productive factors by a process of "imputation" (*Zurechtnung*). If an additional unit of a productive factor increased the supply of a final good, the marginal utility of that good fell but the value of the entire stock of it increased. The gain in total value was attributable (i.e., "imputed") to that specific, additional factor input and no other. The value of a marginal input was therefore determined by the marginal increment in the value of the total stock. Having thus determined the value of the marginal input, Wieser then argued that due to competition the values of all other units of that factor of production would have similar value. This value, he said, was an opportunity cost. He used the term "cognate goods" to describe products that had at least one productive factor in common. If more of a factor was used to produce one good, there would have to be a drop in the production of cognate goods. That drop was the true cost of the first good; it was a sacrifice of utility, and "between costs and utility," he said, "there is no fundamental opposition."

IV

Using Menger's theory of allocation and his suggestions concerning the role of time in production, Böhm-Bawerk developed a unique theory of capital and interest. Unlike the classical writers, he made capital investment an allocation problem and time an unhistorical economic category. Interest, he claimed, was a universal phenomenon based on psychology, not on the limited supply of fertile land; it would not disappear in a stationary state. Furthermore, interest on capital was not an exploitative return, as Marx and the socialists claimed. It would exist even in an economic system organized in accordance with the socialist principle of government ownership of the means of production.

By interest, Böhm-Bawerk meant a return on capital, whether contractual or not, and he was concerned with pure interest, not the money needed to cover the cost of administration, replacement capital, and risk. The fundamental question, as he saw it, was why owners of capital goods should obtain an economic surplus in the form of a permanent net income. Interest, he said, "presents the remarkable picture of a lifeless thing producing an everlasting and inexhaustible supply of goods. . . . Whence and why does the capitalist, without personally exerting himself, obtain this endless flow of wealth?" (*Capital and Interest,* vol. I, *A Critical History of Economic Theory,* pp. 1, 2).

Böhm-Bawerk felt that previous economists had given either fallacious or inadequate answers to this question. In his extensive review of interest theories in volume one of *Capital and Interest,* he examined in detail five major types. The first group contained productivity theories, such as those advanced by Say, Lauderdale, and von Thünen. These theories assumed that capital was an independent factor of production which caused output to be larger than it otherwise would be. This point of view was fallacious according to Böhm-Bawerk. That capital goods were of use in production was clear enough, but not why the value of the output should be so high that a return on capital accrued over and above the cost of the production of the capital goods themselves. The second group of theories were "use" theories; they were based on a conception of interest as a price paid for the use of a capital good rather than the good itself. This idea was found, he said, in the writings of Say and also Menger. But it too was erroneous. The use of a good was the same thing as the consumption of it; a distinction between a capital good and its use was wholly improper.

A third group of theories stressed interest as a payment for abstinence. Senior's theory was typical. To Böhm-Bawerk, it was not so much erroneous as incomplete. Senior was correct in thinking that interest payments induced the individual to give up the consumption of present goods in order to produce future goods, but his theory did not answer the basic questions of where the interest surplus came from. A fourth group of theories held that the capitalists should receive interest because of the labor or effort connected with saving or with their indirect management and supervision of the enterprise. Finding such arguments in the writings of James Mill and others, Böhm-Bawerk replied that as wages are paid for efforts, why should a second wage be paid for capital once produced?

Böhm-Bawerk reserved his most cutting words, however, for the socialist theory of profits, the exploitation theory of Rodbertus and Marx.

> However serious the fallacies we may meet among the representatives of some of the other theories, I scarcely think that anywhere else are to be found together so great a number of the worst fallacies —wanton, unproved assumption, self-contradiction, and blindness to facts. The socialists are able critics, but exceedingly weak theorists. (*Capital and Interest,* vol. I, pp. 390–391)

The fatal error of the exploitation theory, according to Böhm-Bawerk, was its reliance on the labor theory of value, a theory based on the work of Adam Smith and David Ricardo among others. In a sense, these men were the "involuntary godfathers of the Exploitation theory" (*ibid.,* p. 316), although Böhm-Bawerk absolved them of drawing socialist conclusions from the labor theory. Nonetheless, he considered it a "decisive blunder" (*ibid.,* p. 94) of Ricardo not to have recognized that profit was independently determined and not just a surplus remaining after wages and rent were paid. On the other hand, Ricardo at least recognized that the labor theory of value had many exceptions, whereas Marx was blind to them. It did not explain all prices, as Menger's subjective theory did. It contained no explanation of the prices of nonreproducible goods, reproducible goods requiring different degrees of skill, or goods produced with different combinations of constant and variable capital—a point Böhm-Bawerk developed more fully in his book on Marx. Nor did it explain market prices. If all prices could not be explained by the labor theory of value, how could it be assumed that labor was entitled to the entire product? And if labor was not entitled to the entire product, the assumption that profit was a deduction from what was due the worker was a non sequitur.

Böhm-Bawerk's own theory of capital and interest was, in a real sense, a "positive" argument against the socialist doctrine. He began with Menger's analysis of the relationship of goods of a higher order to consumer goods. Capital was defined as the intermediate goods in the productive process—goods other than the final product that came into being as a result of particular combinations of land (physical resources) and labor. Such goods required time to ripen into final consumer goods. They were not an original factor of production; only labor and land were original. But, Böhm-Bawerk said, again taking his ideas from Menger, including more capital goods increases the productivity of the original factors.

Böhm-Bawerk called the time required for a good to ripen from its highest stage into a final good the "period of production." In any economy with a number of goods with different production periods, he believed one could find the "average period of production" (in years) for the system as a whole. An increase in the average period of production would be more "roundabout" (since it required more time), more "capitalistic" (since it implied more intermediate goods), and more productive (since it yielded a greater output). The increase in output as the period of production lengthened would, however, be subject to the law of diminishing returns.

At any given moment in society, there are many capital goods in one stage or another of the production process, and of course they are owned by someone. What determines their value? Since consumers value only final goods, values must be imputed to capital goods. Böhm-Bawerk's concept of imputed value differed somewhat from Wieser's, however. Since capital goods become consumer goods in the future, the valuation process, he believed, was essentially a comparison of future consumer goods and present consumer goods. In such comparisons, said Böhm-Bawerk, individuals will tend to place a higher value on present goods, for three reasons. First, individuals frequently feel a lack of present goods but believe things will be better in the future. Hence they prefer to have more goods now. Second, individuals tend systematically to undervalue future wants, they lack the "power to imagine" their future situation, their willpower fails them when it comes to saving, and moreover they consider human life so uncertain that they prefer the present to the future.

These two grounds, both of which were consistent with Menger's subjective theories, would by themselves have been sufficient to explain the difference in value of present and future goods. Since that difference, which Böhm-Bawerk called "agio," would vary from one individual to another, the exchange of present and future goods was at least a possibility. Those who valued the present more highly would become borrowers if the current interest rate was less than their own subjective rate of discount, while lenders could gain if the market rate was above *their* subjective discount rate.

Yet Böhm-Bawerk added a third argument, based on the "technical superiority" of present goods. The borrower, he said, was an investor who, by putting new resources to productive use, would reap a greater future output; hence, present goods were "superior" to future ones. He was able to pay the lender interest because of the increase in productivity obtained by lengthening the period of production. Thus the source of interest payments was a production process that took time, and not the process of exchnage.

However, Böhm-Bawerk was ambiguous on this point. In *A Critical History of Interest Theories,* he had explicitly denied that capital was productive. Yet in *Positive Theory,* he admitted that the third ground for interest was a theory of the marginal productivity of capital. "The rate of interest—on the assumptions already made—is limited and determined by the productiveness of the last extension of process economically permissible, and of the further extension economically not permissible." (*Capital and Interest,* vol. II, p. 393) He went on to acknowledge that the principle that the rate of interest is determined by the surplus return on the last permissible extension of production "coincides almost to a word with Thünen's celebrated law which makes the rate of interest depend on the productiveness of the 'last applied dose of capital' " (*ibid.,* p. 394)[3]

Böhm-Bawerk's confusion over the productivity of capital was due to the very nature of the Austrian theoretical system. Its heart was the allocative mechanism that responded to the needs of the final consumer; capital consisted of consumer goods in process; interest rates were prices, and like any price they represented a judgment by the ultimate consumer. In such a world, the investment-savings function was extraneous. The Austrian model of the universe was quite unlike the dynamic version of a growing economy found in the writings of Smith, Ricardo, Mill, and Marx. In their systems, investment meant production, additional aggregate output, and additional value. Such a view contradicted the Austrian premise that value was created by the exchange of goods, their production.[4] Wieser's marginal-productivity theory was more consistent with Austrian propositions than Böhm-Bawerk's because the latter had introduced the upsetting element of new investment.

Ambiguity was even more apparent in Böhm-Bawerk's description of how the interest rate is determined. His argument rested on the interdependence of five major variables: the supply of capital (i.e., intermediate goods), the amount of labor, outputs functionally related to inputs over time (i.e., a schedule of the output of different hypothetical periods of production), the wage rate, and the interest rate (i.e., the ratio of net profits to total stock). At any given time there is a certain

---

[3] Johann Heinrich von Thünen (1785–1850), a German economist, was the first to develop the principle of the marginal productivity of labor and of capital, as well as the first to examine the economics of industrial location. His major work, *The Isolated State,* the first part of which was published in 1826, was largely ignored at the time. In his statement of the marginal theory of wages and interest, he said that the contributions of labor and capital to production could not be distinguished except by a consideration of the changes in output that followed an incremental change in one factor when the other remained constant.

[4] Böhm-Bawerk's theory was not wholly accepted by other Austrians.

amount of final, finished goods (i.e., "subsistence"), the result of previous production. (Böhm-Bawerk's market for the "uses" of land can be omitted in this discussion.)

Böhm-Bawerk began by assuming that workers as a class were inadequately provided with subsistence so that they were unable to wait out the more productive roundabout methods of production. They therefore depended on advances of subsistence goods from the capitalists, who owned the intermediate goods and the maturing final products. Although this theory was similar to the classical wage-fund theory, Böhm-Bawerk modified it by introducing variable periods of production. If the period were lengthened, a given wage-fund would not support the same number of workers at the same wage for the duration of the productive process; hence a longer period would mean a lower wage (assuming that there is full employment because of competition in the labor market), and eventually, of course, a greater output. Given a fixed number of workers, a specific amount of subsistence goods, and a production schedule showing output increasing but at a declining rate as time went on, it then followed that there were a number of possible full-employment wage rates, each associated with a different (in length) period of production. According to Böhm-Bawerk, however, there would be only one wage rate (corresponding to only one production period) at which the surplus over costs would be highest. As investors sought to maximize profits, the entire system would arrive at an equilibrium point at which all the independent variables would be mutually determined: the wage rate, the interest rate, and the length of the production period.

The underlying principle, said Böhm-Bawerk, is the fact that the capitalists who own the stock of goods are able to exchange their present holdings for the labor of workers who later turn out a greater quantity of future goods:

> [The capitalists] are the fortunate possessors of a stock of goods which they do not require for the personal needs of the moment. They exchange this stock, therefore, into future goods of some form or another, and allow these to ripen in their hands again into present goods possessing full value. . . .
>
> In the circumstances, then it is very easily explained why capital bears an "everlasting" interest. . . . It is because the stock of present goods is always too low that the conjuncture [i.e., competition] for their exchange against future goods is always favourable. And it is because time always stretches forward that the prudently purchased future commodity steadily becomes a present commodity,

grows accordingly into the full value of the present, and permits its owner again and again to utilize the always favourable conjuncture.

I do not see that there is anything objectionable in this. (*ibid.*, pp. 358–359)

Böhm-Bawerk claimed that this theory of the determination of interest explained the permanent return on capital without relying on either a productivity theory of capital or an exploitation theory. Yet investment did lead to an increase in output. If the increase could not be attributed to the productivity of capital, why should the capitalists profit from it? Strangely, Böhm-Bawerk's answer was similar to Marx's. The capitalists were the "fortunate possessors" of a stock of goods; it was the juridical structure of capitalist society that enabled them to appropriate the gains from the production process. Böhm-Bawerk's justification for interest and Marx's charge of exploitation rested in the last analysis on different conclusions as to the morality of the system of property.

What Böhm-Bawerk added to the controversy, however, was a demonstration of the universality of the phenomenon of interest, no matter what the political arrangements of society might be. In *Positive Theory* he concluded that even in a socialist system interest could not be abolished; it would only be distributed differently.

Böhm-Bawerk's willingness to consider other social systems such as socialism was a debating tactic, however, and not meant to be taken too seriously. In his last significant publication, "Control or Economic Law?" (1914), he expressed convictions on social reform that were basically those of Menger. Government intervention for the purpose of reform was destructive of society. Thus in the end, economic laws were not universal. In the conservative philosophy of Böhm-Bawerk and the Austrians, they were applicable satisfactorily only within a particular political system.

Notes to Chapter vii

I

The editions of Carl Menger's works referred to are *Principles of Economics (Grundsätze der Volkswirtschaftslehre), First, General Part,* trans. and ed. by James Dingwall and Bert F. Hoselitz, with an introduction by Frank H. Knight (Glencoe, Ill., Free Press, 1950), and *Problems of Economics and Sociology (Untersuchungen über die Methode der Socialwissenschaften und der Politischen Oekonomie ins-*

besondere), ed. and with an introduction by Louis Schneider, trans. by Francis J. Nock (Urbana, University of Illinois Press, 1963). Menger's other essays and articles are included (untranslated) in *The Collected Works of Carl Menger* (London, London School of Economics and Political Science, 1934–36).

Also available in English are Friedrich von Wieser's two major works: *Natural Value (Der naturliche Wert),* ed. with a preface and analysis by William Smart, trans. by Christian A. Malloch (London, Macmillan, 1893), reprinted in 1930 by Stechert, New York; and *Social Economics (Theorie der gesellschaftlichen Wirtschaft),* trans. by A. Ford Hinrichs, with a preface by Wesley Clair Mitchell (New York, Adelphi, 1927). The first was originally published in 1889; the second appeared in 1914 as volume one of Max Weber's *Grundriss der Sozialökonomie (Outline of Social Economy).* Although a member of the Schmoller school with whom Menger had had his argument over method, Weber was far less hostile to theory than Schmoller and included two major theoretical works in the *Grundriss.* One was Wieser's book; the other was a study by Joseph S. Schumpeter entitled *Epochen der Dogmen- und Methodengeschichte (Eras of the History of Doctrines and Methods).* It was this book that became the foundation for Schumpeter's later *History of Economic Analysis* (New York, Oxford University Press, 1954). (See the editor's note, p. 819.)

Wieser's other major works were *Ursprung und die Haupgesetze des wirthschaftlichen Wertes* (1884), an exposition of Menger's marginal-utility theory, and books relating to his interest in history and sociology, *Recht und Macht* (1910) and *Gesetz der Macht* (1926). Although Wieser seems to have developed ideas that were not taken up by other Austrians (for example, his theory of "natural value" and his rejection of Böhm-Bawerk's theory of capital), his work nonetheless was impressive, and he was effective in making the economics of the Austrian school known to the English-speaking world, especially during the 1920s.

The references in the text to Böhm-Bawerk's writings are to *Capital and Interest (Kapital und Kapitalzins),* a two-volume work. The first volume, *A Critical History of Economical Theory (Geschichte und Kritik der Kapitalzinstheorien),* translated with a preface and analysis by William Smart in 1890, was reprinted by Kelley (New York) in 1970; the second, *The Positive Theory of Capital (Positive Theorie des Kapitales),* translated with a preface and analysis by William Smart in 1891, was reprinted by Stechert (New York) in 1923. A more recent translation of his work, by George D. Huncke and Hans F. Sennholz, was published by Libertarian Press (South Holland, Ill.) in 1959. This edition added a third volume to the two already mentioned, *Further Essays on Capital and Interest,* containing Böhm-Bawerk's replies to the numerous critics of his theory of interest and capital. His work on Marx, *Karl Marx and the Close of His System (Zum Abschluss des Marxchen Systems)* was reprinted, together with Rudolf Hilferding's *Böhm-Bawerk's Criticism of Marx* and an article by Ladislaus von Bortkiewicz, in 1949. The book, edited and with an introduction by Paul M. Sweezy, is published by

Kelley (New York). Böhm-Bawerk's article "Control or Economic Law?" is found in *Shorter Classics of Eugen von Böhm-Bawerk* (South Holland, Ill., Libertarian Press, 1962), vol. I.

For biographical information concerning the first Austrian writers, see Friedrich von Hayek's discussion of Menger and Wieser in Henry William Spiegel, ed., *The Development of Economic Thought: Great Economists in Perspective* (New York, Wiley, 1952), pp. 527–567; and "Schumpeter on Böhm-Bawerk," *ibid.*, pp. 569–579. The Austrian triumvirate is also discussed in Joseph A. Schumpeter's *Ten Great Economists* (New York, Oxford University Press, 1951), pp. 80–90, 143–190, and 298–301.

As for the younger Austrians, Ludwig von Mises wrote at first on money and credit (1912), then turned to attacking the "irrationality" of socialism (1922), and continued to develop Austrian subjectivism in the philosophical direction of extreme individualism and libertarianism, as typified in his *Human Action* (1949). Government economic control was anathema to him. Friedrich von Hayek first analyzed business cycles in terms of Böhm-Bawerk's theory of the period of production and Mises' doctrine of forced savings (see *Prices and Production,* 1931, and *Monetary Theory and the Trade Cycle,* 1933), then he too turned to attacking socialism (its deficiencies were a favorite Austrian theme) in *Collectivist Economic Planning: Critical Studies on the Possibilities of Socialism* by N. G. Pierson, Ludwig von Mises, Georg Halm, and Enrico Barone, edited with an introduction and a concluding essay by von Hayek (London,

Routledge & Kegan Paul, 1935). Hayek, like Mises, became obsessed with the belief that government intervention, democratically motivated or not, led straight to collectivism and coercion of the individual. See his *The Road to Serfdom* (1944), *Individualism and Social Order* (Chicago, University of Chicago Press, 1948), *The Counter-Revolution of Science: Studies on the Abuse of Reason* (Glencoe, Ill., Free Press, 1952), and other works.

Although Joseph A. Schumpeter differed somewhat from standard Austrian doctrines on certain economic issues, he nonetheless expressed the same *fin de siècle* attitudes toward the destruction of capitalism by hostile forces from within. In part, Schumpeter's thesis rested on his unique view of the entrepreneur as a figure whose innovations in production created temporary profits that provided a motive for further investment and expansion but whose functions were increasingly being automatized in large-scale businesses by the spread of bureaucratic procedures. In addition, he believed that there were growing anticapitalist attitudes that found expression in legislative controls and limits on entrepreneurial initiative. He considered intellectuals the class most articulate in their hostility toward capitalism. (See his *Capitalism, Socialism, and Democracy,* 3rd ed., New York, Harper & Brothers, 1947, chs. XII, XIII, and XIV.) Schumpeter's business-cycle theory appeared originally in 1912 in German; it became available in English as *The Theory of Economic Development,* trans. by R. Opie (Cambridge, Mass., Harvard University Press, 1949).

II

1. The Burke-Savigny thesis is a conservative ideology; yet, like most ideologies, it can receive various interpretations under different circumstances. The historical school of jurisprudence in Germany at the turn of the nineteenth century became the basis of a school of German romantic economists, such as Adam Müller, who attacked economic liberalism on the grounds that the state alone could give meaning and purpose to economic activities. This amounted to a glorification of medievalism and received further inspiration from the writings of the German philosopher Fichte. The older German historical school of the middle of the nineteenth century also had its roots in the Burke-Savigny thesis. Although it expressed criticisms of individualistic liberalism, its opposition was less vitriolic and it looked forward to historical development, not backward to the Middle Ages. Roscher claimed allegiance to Savigny's methods of research, although he did not seek to justify or reform existing institutions. The social-reform element in German historical economics came later and was influenced both by Rodbertus and "socialists of the Chair" (academic socialists like Adolph Wagner) and by nationalist desires to bring together dissident groups and forge a new German state. Menger's attack on the German historical school was leveled against the nationalists and reformers, whose method, he believed, were a travesty of the true methods of historical research. His *Principles* in 1871 had been dedicated to Wilhelm Roscher.

2. The relationship of Burke's theories to German romantic economics and to Menger requires further explanation, especially since Hayek has now implicitly amended Menger's analysis to claim Adam Smith as an intellectual comrade of Burke and hence an early proponent of Menger's theory of the organic nature of society. Hayek's argument is that Smith's exposition of the "invisible hand" clearly defined the beneficial, unintended results of individual actions and that, moreover, Smith was reported to have said that Burke thought about economic subjects "exactly as I do." Therefore, Hayek asserts, Burke and Smith together represent what he (Hayek) calls "true individualism." (See, for example, his "Individualism: True and False," in *Individualism and Economic Order,* Chicago, University of Chicago Press, 1948, ch. I, especially pp. 7f; and *The Counter-Revolution of Science, op. cit.,* p. 65.)

Burke, of course, did express the British utilitarian tradition of the importance of the individual, doubts concerning the power of governments, and liberal views with respect to free trade and colonies. It was his *Thoughts and Details on Scarcity* (1795) that contained these Smithian theories. In his *Reflections on the French Revolution,* however, he mourned the outcome of French schemes for social reform, which, he said, had extinguished the glory of Europe. The aristocratic element in Burke's thought, his distaste for the actions of the lower classes, his opposition to reforms of all kinds, these indicated a different theme—a theme that was avidly taken up by the German romantics, as well as by Menger and Hayek, but not by Smith. Smith's theory of the "invisible hand" was justification enough for institution reforms quite in accord with the "pragmatic orientation" of which Menger accused him.

3. Although the historical school of economics is primarily identified with German writers, the historical movement spread to other countries as well. In part the influence was direct. In the latter part of the nineteenth century, German universities, then considered the model for graduate education, attracted students from many countries, including the United States. The historical approach in economics was appealing to Americans, to whom British classical theories seemed increasingly unrealistic in view of the growth of trusts and the greater gulf between rich and poor in America. The American Economic Association was formed in 1885 by historically minded American economists, who wanted a focal point like Schmoller's *Verein* to express a message of social reform. American institutionalism was an outgrowth of the same movement. American writers, however, tended to be more pragmatic and less sympathetic to socialist interpretations or to philosophies of history, such as Hegel's, that gave a different character to the German approach. For a view of historical economics in the United States, see Joseph Dorfman, *The Economic Mind in American Civilization, 1865–1918* (New York, Viking Press, 1949), vol. III.

In Great Britain, historical economics was popular at about the same time. At first critical of all theory, the movement later receded to a position subordinate to analytical models. In France, however, the field of historical economics became a recognized part of the curriculum of the *Facultes de Droit* in 1878. See Charles Gide and Charles Rist, *A History of Economic Doctrines, From the Time of the Physiocrats to the Present Day*, 2nd English ed. (Boston, Heath, n.d.), p. 391.

III

For a general review of the development and spread of marginal-utility doctrines, see R. S. Howey, *The Rise of the Marginal Utility School, 1870–1889* (Lawrence, University of Kansas Press, 1960); Emil Kauder, *A History of Marginal Utility Theory* (Princeton, N. J., Princeton University Press, 1965); and George J. Stigler, "The Development of Utility Theory," *Journal of Political Economy* (August–October 1950), vol. 58, reprinted in his *Essays in the History of Economics* (Chicago and London, University of Chicago Press, 1965), pp. 66–155.

In *Production and Distribution Theories, The Formative Period* (New York, Agathon Press, 1968 [first published, 1941]), chs. VI, VII, and VIII, George J. Stigler devotes separate chapters to an analysis of the economics of the three major Austrian writers. Ben B. Seligman, in *Main Currents in Modern Economics: Economic Thought Since 1870* (Glencoe, Ill., Free Press, 1962), ch. 4, reviews the Austrian school through Mises and Hayek. For a different assessment of the economics of the school, see Leo Rogin, *The Meaning and Validity of Economic Theory: A Historical Approach* (New York, Harper & Brothers, 1956), chs. 12 and 13.

IV

Böhm-Bawerk's theories of capital

and interest stirred up massive controversies, and the debate still goes on. For a recent appraisal, see Robert E. Kuenne, *Eugen von Böhm-Bawerk* (Irvington-on-Hudson, N. Y., Columbia University Press, 1970). The controversies were aggravated in part by Böhm-Bawerk's polemical tactics (attacking the theories of others first), in part by his shifts in position (for example, on whether capital is productive), and in part by the loose way in which he expressed his arguments.

Marxist replies to his criticisms, however, were relatively few. Rudolf Hilferding, a German, specifically answered charges against Marx in his *Böhm-Bawerk's Criticism of Marx* (1904), translated and reprinted in the Sweezy edition of Böhm-Bawerk's work noted earlier. Nikolai Bukharin, a Russian Marxist, criticized the economics of the entire Austrian school in *The Economic Theory of the Leisure Class* (1919, Eng. tr., 1927).

A more significant challenge came from another quarter. The American economist John Bates Clark (1847–1938), who emerged at the turn of the twentieth century as one of the leading theoreticians in the United States, had independently, though belatedly, discovered the principle of marginal utility and had been one of the first to define the marginal-productivity theory of wages and interest. He had developed a unique theory of capital and sought to show that the existing system of distribution of income was justifiable. He wrote, in *The Distribution of Wealth* (New York, Macmillan, 1899), p. 10: "We have undertaken to solve a test problem of distribution—to ascertain whether the division of the social income into wages, interest and profits is, in principle, honest." (See the article on Clark by his son, John Maurice Clark, in Spiegel's *The Development of Economic Thought*, pp. 592–612.)

Clark's claim of the legitimacy of returns to capital was not so much a defense against Marx as it was a reply to the land-nationalization (single-tax) proposals of Henry George, the journalist-economist whose *Progress and Poverty* (1881) had achieved great popularity. George had simply extended classical arguments that rent paid to landlords was unearned, and that private land ownership was an obstacle to economic progress. Clark's attempts to disprove this were original and, in retrospect, quite simple. He lumped all factors of production into two categories, labor and capital, eliminating land as a separate factor. Each category could be viewed in two ways: first, in terms of the specific units that composed it, and second, as a fund. The units of labor were individuals with different skills, of different ages, and so forth; pure labor was a fund. Similarly, capital consisted of specific goods (including land), each with its own life cycle; but it was also a fund—born of new savings and timeless. Each specific capital good would, in the short run, under competition, earn rent; but in the long run through mobility and replacement the composition of capital in terms of specific goods could change to meet consumer demands, and the fund of capital would then receive a return determined by its marginal productivity (assuming that the fund of labor is fixed). The pure fund of labor would receive a wage (assuming that the fund of capital is fixed) in accordance with its marginal productivity.

Clark was well aware that his theory had an air of unreality. Moreover, it was static, and though he hoped to supplement it with a study of dynamics, he did not do so. Nonetheless, it was significant not only because it laid down the principle of marginal productivity but because it marked the end of the classical theory of capital as advances. Clark's point was that consumption was synchronized with production.

Despite a lengthy controversy between Clark and Böhm-Bawerk over the nature of capital and the theory of interest, little was resolved. Clark denied the existence of a period of production for pure capital, as well as the importance of time in the determination of interest. Böhm-Ba-werk, on the other hand, considered the concept of a "fund" that continually renewed itself a myth. (See his article in *The Quarterly Journal of Economics,* February 1907, vol. XXI, p. 282.)

The argument over these contrasting theories was renewed in the 1930s by Friedrick von Hayek and the American economist Frank H. Knight. (See Hayek's article, based on a quotation from Böhm-Bawerk, "The Mythology of Capital," and Knight's "Capital and Interest," both reprinted in the American Economic Association's *Readings in the Theory of Income Determination,* Homewood, Ill., Irwin, 1951, pp. 355–383 and 384–417 respectively. A bibliography of their controversy is given in footnote 1, pp. 355–356.)

Chapter viii

ECONOMIC AND MORAL
WELL-BEING:

Marshall's Neoclassical Economics

Political Economy or Economics is a study of mankind in the
ordinary business of life; it examines that part of individual and
social action which is most closely connected with the attainment and with the use of the material requisites of wellbeing.
Thus it is on the one side a study of wealth; and on the other, and
more important side, a part of the study of man.

Alfred Marshall, *Principles of Economics*

. . . I have devoted myself for the last twenty-five years to the
problem of poverty, and . . . very little of my work has been
devoted to any inquiry which does not bear on that.

Testimony of Alfred Marshall before the Royal
Commission on the Aged Poor, June 5, 1893

The dominant influence on economic theory from the 1890s to the
depression of the 1930s, especially in English-speaking nations, was
undoubtedly Alfred Marshall, the Cambridge economist who reaffirmed
and extended the classical traditions of Smith, Ricardo, and Mill. His
major work, *Principles of Economics,* published in 1890 after years of
careful preparation, seemed to many a definitive answer to the attacks
against the classical writers that came from all sides—from the historical
economists, the socialists, and the new marginal-utility theorists such as
Jevons and the Austrians. The response to his *Principles* was favorable,
and the book went through eight editions. The last edition appeared in
1920, just four years before he died, and sales were never higher than
during the decade of the 1920s. Marshall became the center and source

of inspiration of the Cambridge school of economics, and his influence was extended by his many and able students.

Marshall's success was due first to the contributions he made to the techniques of economic analysis. Economic theory, he said, was not dogma or a body of "concrete truth," but "an engine for the discovery of concrete truth." His theoretical "machine" was essentially a demand-and-supply analysis of normal value, with marginal utility and wants on one side of the equation and costs and efforts on the other. His theory of value encompassed not only consumer goods, but the distributive return to productive factors; every element in his economic universe was inter-dependent, its equilibrium position mutually determined. Marshall applied the principle of the margin not only to demand but to the use of economic factors under equilibrium conditions. He conceived of the concept of substitution at the margin as a process of small adjustments by consumers and firms. He was the first to introduce the concept of short-run values, as opposed to market or long-run values; and he was responsible for much of the modern geometrical approach to economics, although he was not the first to suggest treating variables in this way. Many specific analytical tools, such as the concepts of externalities, quasi-rents, and consumers' surplus, owe much to Marshall. It was he who devised the coefficient of elasticity.

Marshall was also successful because he was interested in the every-day economic problems of the general reader. He was concerned with applications of economic theory. For this reason, although he was fully aware that the general equilibrium of the economy depended on the interrelationship of all variables, he emphasized what came to be called partial equilibrium analysis and investigation of the principles of economics as they affected the individual consumer, the individual firm, the specfic industry.

Finally, Marshall was popular because he sought to show the relationship between economic forces and the general well-being of society. Well-being, to him, was both an economic and a moral state. Economic welfare was defined as the satisfaction of wants, or utility; and he believed, although he carefully pointed out its limitations, that the competitive economy, or system of freedom of enterprise (as he preferred to call it), was the best way to reach this goal. But in addition to requiring economic welfare, well-being had a moral side. Economics studied the social nature of man, not only his material position. According to Marshall, economic activity, especially productive activities, influenced a man's character. To him, the great virtue of the free-enterprise system was that it rewarded and stimulated those who produced. For this reason, he felt a kinship with the classical writers who, he believed, included in their study of economics the higher ends of mankind. In describing them in his *Principles* he also revealed his own ideals:

> . . . nearly all the founders of modern economics were men of gentle and sympathetic temper, touched with the enthusiasm of humanity. They cared little for wealth for themselves; they cared much for its wide diffusion among the masses of the people. . . . They were without exception devoted to the doctrine that the wellbeing of the whole people should be the ultimate goal of all private effort and all public policy. (p. 47)

I

Alfred Marshall (1842–1924) was raised in a religious family dominated by a father who, himself a cashier for the Bank of England, had visions of his son being ordained a minister. Even when it became apparent that young Marshall was an exceptional mathematician, his father remained convinced that he should enter Oxford, study classics, and prepare for a religious career. However, Marshall went to Cambridge instead, with the financial help of a kind uncle; in 1865 he received his degree, with honors in mathematics.

His early religious upbringing did not cease to affect him with the award of the degree, however. When he entered Cambridge he had planned to work toward ordination at a later date; but his interests began to change, in part because of the shock waves set off by the publication in 1859 of Charles Darwin's *Origin of Species*. The concept of evolution without divine intervention challenged religious orthodoxy and led some of the intellectual community, if not to atheism, at least to agnosticism. In Marshall's case, although he became an agnostic, he retained a moralistic orientation. He turned first to metaphysics, then to ethics, and finally to economics, a study of which he hoped would help him resolve ethical questions. In his biographical sketch and interpretation of Marshall, John Maynard Keynes quotes Marshall looking back on his own mental development:

> "From Metaphysics I went to Ethics, and thought that the justification of the existing condition of society was not easy. A friend, who had read a great deal of what are now called the Moral Sciences, constantly said: 'Ah! if you understood Political Economy you would not say that.' So I read Mill's *Political Economy* and got much excited about it." (*Memorials,* p. 10)

Upon graduation, Marshall tutored mathematics to repay the loan from his uncle. He began to read Mill and other economists, translating their ideas into mathematical form. In 1868 he discovered the work of Augustin Cournot, the French mathematician and economist, who had already developed mathematical schedules of demand and cost. Marshall later stated, in a letter to John Bates Clark, that in those years (1867 to 1870) he "practically completed" his "main position as to the theory of value and distribution." (*Memorials,* p. 416) It is little wonder that he was annoyed when Jevons' work, with its claim of originality in the mathematics of marginal utility, appeared in 1871. By 1875, he had completed practically all of the mathematical appendix that was to permanently establish his reputation as a major theorist when it finally appeared, with his *Principles of Economics,* in 1890.

Meanwhile, Marshall was appointed a lecturer in logic and economics at Cambridge. He was forced to resign in 1877, however, when he married Mary Paley, a former student; the regulations of St. John's forbade those who married to hold fellowships. He then accepted a position as principal and professor of political economy at University College, Bristol. While there, he published his first book, *The Economics of Industry* (1879), written in collaboration with his wife. This book was an elementary text, which Marshall later came to believe was unsatisfactory. Others, however, praised it.

In the same year, Henry Sidgwick, a professor of moral philosophy at Cambridge, had printed for private circulation several chapters of Marshall's "The Pure Theory of Foreign Trade. The Pure Theory of Domestic Values," a work never completed. In these chapters, Marshall used the diagrammatic method of exposition, a method that became associated with his work. Although the few economists who saw these chapters recognized their importance, the world at large was still unaware of his theoretical abilities.

After a year of rest in Italy from a sickness that plagued him for many years, Marshall returned to England, this time to become a fellow at Balliol College, Oxford, and a lecturer in political economy to candidates for the Indian civil service. He remained at Oxford only a short time: in 1885 he was elected to the chair of political economy at Cambridge. His predecessor, and the first to hold the Cambridge chair, was Henry Fawcett, a follower of Mill.[1]

[1] The chair of political economy at Cambridge was not established until 1863, even though George Pryme had earlier agitated for the official establishment of such a position and was often considered a professor of political

The *Principles,* which was close to final form when he received the Cambridge appointment, was finally published in 1890, nearly two decades after he had worked out the basic theoretical structure. His reluctance to leap into print without the most careful consideration of all the implications of his ideas, his periods of ill-health, and above all his wish to make the theory applicable and understandable to laymen largely accounted for the delay, regretted by both his colleagues and students. Because of it, his theories, except to the knowledgeable few, appeared to be elaborations of the ideas of others.

Principles was originally planned as the first of two volumes. By 1895, Marshall had expanded his plans to include three additional volumes—on industry, on credit and employment, and on the economic functions of government—and by 1907 he projected yet another. But he completed only two more books: *Industry and Trade,* a descriptive, historical study published in 1919, and *Money, Credit, and Commerce,* published in 1923, when he was over eighty. By this time, his ideas were no longer new; he himself had presented his monetary views a number of times before governmental commissions, and his former students had also been expounding his views in their own ways.

The view of economics presented in Marshall's first edition of *Principles* remained relatively unchanged in subsequent editions. The revisions in the third edition (1895), which took into consideration the rapidly growing literature of the early 1890s, were the most important; there were a few minor revisions in the fifth edition, which appeared in 1907, a year before he retired from teaching. Thus the structure of his economics went through very little development from 1890 to the final, eighth edition in 1920. The book's continued success not only attested to the care that he had lavished on it before publication and his painstaking quest for the comprehensive and exacting statements; it also reflected the fact that he had caught the spirit of his age—its belief in the underlying stability of the competitive market economy and in the inevitability of social improvement through a slow but sure evolutionary process.

---

economy. Henry Fawcett was elected to the chair in 1863; Marshall's term ran from 1885 to 1908. At that time Professor Arthur Cecil Pigou, Marshall's student, was appointed to the chair; he held it until 1943 and was succeeded first (in 1944) by Sir Dennis Robertson and later (in 1957) by Professor James E. Meade. The examination for the B.A. degree in economics, known as the Tripos, was established in 1903.

II

It was Marshall's firm faith in the underlying benevolence of the development of the free-enterprise system that governed his approach. Obviously influenced by the Darwinian theory of evolution through small changes, he saw the socioeconomic system of free enterprise growing by similar small changes into one that provided higher levels of living and greater freedom for the individual. The idea of change by small increments applied not only to historical evolution but to the theoretical adjustments of consumers and firms to achievement of optimum conditions under static conditions. Thus the motto of his *Principles* was *natura non facit saltum,* nature makes no jump.

In his concern for the historical development of the market economy toward greater economic welfare, Marshall was following the great tradition of the classical economists. But he had neither the Malthusian fear that economic development would reduce the standard of life of masses to the subsistence level nor Mill's feeling that economic development would soon come to an end. According to Marshall, the reason for optimism was that technological progress had made food so cheap that the pressure of population on food supplies had abated significantly. Technological changes in agriculture had reduced costs directly, and improvements in transport had "enabled Englishmen of the present generation to obtain the products of the richest lands of the earth at comparatively small cost." (p. 180) Moreover, there seemed to be a tendency for those with higher incomes to have smaller families. While this was a hopeful sign, he sometimes implied that it might have a bad effect on the caliber of future generations (if those whose higher incomes were due to their superior energies and abilities failed to pass these virtues on). The possibility of restraining future population growth seemed to him to be greatly improved as the economy became more and more productive and as more income reached the working classes.

Marshall's historical descriptions of the course of economic development in Appendix A of his *Principles* centered on the growth of free enterprise, which he believed promoted both technological change and an upward trend in real incomes. To him, three conditions were responsible for England's emergence as the world's leading industrial nation: (1) the desire of the population for greater material comforts; (2) the submission of "every action to the judgment of the reason," rather than custom, in order to maximize income; and (3) "complete political freedom and security," which enabled an individual to act in his own interest and "fearlessly" commit his person and property to "new and distant undertakings." (p. 744) This third factor was especially important; the "same qualities which gave [England and her colonies] political freedom gave them also free enterprise in industry and commerce." (p. 744) These qualities were essentially the moral virtues of applying one's energies to the invention and production of goods, of individualism and self-reliance, and of forethought and the careful calculation of alternatives.

Although Marshall applied the doctrine of evolutionary change to society, he did not accept the dogma of the Social Darwinists that the social struggle for survival led to a process of natural selection by which only the fittest survived and the weak were properly weeded out. Such a doctrine, he said, prevented men from "seeing and removing the evil that was intertwined with the good in the changes that were going on around them." (p. 246) There were evils in the process of economic development, evils that it was important to identify. For example, the early "capitalist employer . . . was tempted to subordinate the well-being of his workpeople to his own desire for gain." (p. 750) Marshall disapproved of the way the rich often tended to create envy by ostentatious displays; he noted that many of the "largest" fortunes were made by "speculation rather than by truly constructive work," by "anti-social" strategies, and even by "evil manipulation." (p. 719)

The greatest evil, as Marshall saw it, was poverty. It was the stark contrast between the upper classes and the "lower ones" in England that led him to study economics in the first place, and he later declared that the study of poverty was his principal life's work. In 1883, he said:

> There are two great questions which we cannot think too much about. The first is, Is it necessary that, while there is so much wealth, there should be so much want? The second is, Is there not a great fund of conscientiousness and unselfishness latent in the breasts of men, both rich and poor, which could be called out if the problems of life were set before them in the right way, and which would cause misery and poverty rapidly to diminish? (Quoted by Pigou, *Memorials,* p. 83)

At the very beginning of his *Principles,* Marshall wrote that the "study of the causes of poverty is the study of the causes of the degradation of a large part of mankind," (p. 3) and that it was the possibility of ending poverty that gave ecoonmic studies "their chief and their highest interest." (p. 4)

But how could widespread poverty coexist with the beneficent system of free enterprise? And if the problem was so intractable, were drastic measures to reform the system needed? Marshall's answers placed him in a middle position. The Social Darwinists argued that economic failure reflected an inherent lack of ability and character and that nothing much could be done about it. Others, ranging from trade unionists to socialists of various degrees, urged varied programs of institutional reform. To the advocates of untrammeled *laissez-faire,* Marshall replied that character did not determine economic position; the "physical, mental, and moral ill-health" of the poor was largely due to their poverty—to their inadequate income, to the type of work they did, and to the squalid, overcrowded conditions in which the urban poor were forced to live. (p. 2) Turning the evolutionary argument around, he claimed that

> partly through the suggestion of biological study, the influence of circumstances in fashioning character is generally recognized as the dominant fact in social science. Economists . . . have learnt to trust that the human will, guided by careful thought, can so modify circumstances as largely to modify character; and thus to bring about new conditions of life still more favourable to character; and therefore to the economic, as well as the moral, wellbeing of the masses of the people." (p. 48)

Yet Marshall rejected socialistic proposals. Restraints on the free-enterprise system, he believed, would impair the rate of technological advance and investment essential to economic progress, as well as the free movement of resources necessary to achieve an optimum allocation. He voiced numerous objections to government ownership and operation of industry: Socialism was likely to be bureaucratic and provide no incentive for improvement; it offered no alternatives for those who disliked its restraints and controls and hence tended to be tyrannical. (See Marshall's "Social Possibilities of Economic Chivalry," *Memorials,* pp. 323 ff., in which he considers both the advantages and disadvantages of socialism.) His overriding objection to socialism was that it would choke off the inventiveness of the entrepreneur and hence impair economic growth: ". . . every great step in the direction of collectivism is a grave menace to the maintenance even of our present moderate rate of progress." (*ibid.,* p. 342) He decried arguments for "untried" schemes of social reform on the grounds that the "rights of private property . . . have been inseparable from solid progress; and that therefore it is the part of responsible men to proceed cautiously and tentatively in abrogating or modifying *even such rights as may seem to be inappropriate to the ideal conditions of social life."* (*Principles,* p. 48, italics added)

Marshall did not see much hope for the abolition of poverty in Mill's proposals for workers' cooperatives, on similar grounds. Although he was sympathetic to certain objectives of trade unions, he believed that they were harmful to the extent that they could impose wages different from the competitive market rate, place obstacles in the way of worker mobility, or limit technological innovation. In a letter dealing with the engineers' strike of 1897, he wrote:

> I have often said that T.U.'s [trade unions] are a greater glory to England than her wealth. But I thought then of T.U.'s in which the minority, who wanted to compete with others to put as little work as possible into the hour, were overruled. Latterly they have, I fear, completely dominated the Engineers' Union. I want these people to be beaten at all costs: the complete destruction of Unionism would be as heavy a price as it is possible to conceive: but I think not too high a price. (*Memorials,* p. 400)

Marshall approved of certain types of protective legislation for women and children on the grounds that since the nation seemed strong and wealthy enough to impose new restraints on free enterprise it could absorb "some temporary material loss . . . for the sake of a higher and ultimate [sic] greater gain." (*ibid.,* Appendix A, p. 751) He did not carry this argument very far, however; he opposed all minimum-wage legislation. (*Principles,* pp. 715–716, note 1).

Marshall's answer to the problem of poverty was education, supplemented by the molding of character and the encouragement of a chivalrous attitude on the part of the rich. His argument—basic to modern theories of human capital investment—was that since an individual's discounted lifetime earnings equaled the cost of his training, poverty perpetuated itself through the failure of the poor to invest in the education of their children. Pointing out that there was no market for such investments—and believing that it was best that none existed, as it would mean slavery—Marshall said that poor parents without resources, without the power to forecast the future, and unwilling to sacrifice themselves for the future do not give their children any more advantages than they had themselves. "The worse fed are the children of one generation, the less will they earn when they grow up, and the less will be their power of providing adequately for the material wants of their children; and so on to following generations." (*ibid.*, p. 562) Thus poverty is cumulative unless the chain of circumstances is broken by public outlays to educate the children of the poor. Education would not only increase their skills; it should improve their tastes and change their attitudes toward work.

Marshall's reluctance to abandon individual initiative even in the case of education is revealed by his emphasis on the importance of education in changing attitudes. In a letter in 1902, he wrote that character-development of the young was most important: "I have always held that poverty and pain, disease and death are evils much less important than they appear, except in so far as they lead to weaknesses of life and character. . . ." (*Memorials*, pp. 443–444) In his *Principles*, he wrote that "the schoolmaster must learn that his main duty is not to impart knowledge. . . . It is to educate character, faculties and activities; so that the children even of those parents who are not thoughtful themselves, may have a better chance of being trained up to become thoughtful parents of the next generation." And he added: "To this end money must flow freely." (p. 178) Going beyond the economics of human capital investment in monetary terms, Marshall stressed the importance of the mother. Unlike Mill, who believed in the emancipation of women, he felt strongly that a woman's place was in the home, raising her children: "The most valuable of all capital is that invested in human beings; and of that capital the most precious part is the result of the care and influence of the mother, so long as she . . . has not been hardened by the strain and stress of unfeminine work." (p. 564)

Improvement of the moral climate was important. Marshall urged that businesses adopt fairer and more benevolent attitudes toward their employees and others. This philanthropic approach, which emphasized the personal relationships between employers and their workers and businessmen and the public, he called "economic chivalry." He defined it as a "delight in doing noble and difficult things . . . a delight in succouring those who need a helping hand," a pride in achievements "only in the second degree for the value at which they are appraised in the money of the market." (*Memorials*, pp. 330–331) Unless such a spirit is developed, Marshall said, the "world under free enterprise will fall far short of the finest ideals. . . ." (*ibid.*, p. 342)

In short, there was nothing fundamentally wrong with the institutions of the capitalist and the free-market system. One should "guard against the temptation to overstate the economic evils of our own age," he wrote. (*Principles,* p. 722) Free enterprise, through an upward, evolutionary process, was substantially improving the material and moral well-being of the masses. Poverty and other social ills could be gradually eradicated by education and appeals to the chivalrous spirit of the rich, but the process required time and, above all, Marshall warned, no interference with the basic institutions of the system by the impatient with their collectivist schemes.

III

Marshall's economic analysis took for granted the stability and permanence of capitalist institutions. He did not question the belief that the free play of prices, mobility, and competition within the system would promote human welfare—perhaps not perfectly, but better than any rival form of organization. Nor did he doubt that business fluctuations were self-correcting because of the inherent ability of the system to maintain full employment in accordance with the traditional doctrines of Say's Law.

Within the limits created by these assumptions, he extended and modified the classical theories of value and distribution into a comprehensive, complex theory of equilibrium of demand and supply in the determination of prices. His special objective was to show how the seeming confusion of the marketplace could be analyzed in terms of the interaction of demand, supply, and price, and how changes worked slowly but consistently toward long-run equilibrium prices for goods and services. Those long-run prices Marshall called normal, not because they existed or would eventually exist, but because they indicated the direction in which the changes were leading. The tendencies in this direction were continuously interrupted by "outside" forces, by changes in consumer tastes and in production methods that disturbed the mutually determined equipoise of long-run prices. But the inherent counterbalancing tendencies of the system worked always toward a state of normalcy.

According to Marshall, problems of adjustment arose because of the "time that must be allowed for causes to produce their effects"; but analyzing the time dimension of adjustment was "a source of great difficulty in economics." (p. 36) In the preface to the first edition of his *Principles* he noted that the "element of time . . . is itself absolutely continuous: Nature knows no absolute partitions of time into long periods and short; but the two shade into one another by imperceptible gradations. . . ." (p. vii) Darwin's theory of biological evolution had been acclaimed as a great scientific achievement; Marshall sought, in a similar fashion, to capture the essence of economic change with his new theoretical technique.

The special characteristic of Marshall's economics was his careful elucidation of the adjustments by which the system moved toward a long-run equilibrium. It was because this process was so widely misunderstood by the general public, he believed, that people were tempted, when difficult problems arose, to support intemperate demands for institutional reforms that could only thwart the attainment of welfare in the long run. He recognized a need, in short, for a system of economic analysis that would be relevant to the problems that the ordinary person faced, not one that, however formally correct, failed to investigate the great social questions of the day. Economics was both a pure and an applied science, he said, but its "dominant aim . . . is to contribute to a solution of social problems." (Marginal note, p. 32) His emphasis in the text of *Principles* was on applied economics. Pure science laid down general relationships or laws concerning men's actions, but its necessary assumption that everything else remains equal did not hold in real life. Pure laws, therefore, represented only "tendencies, more or less certain, more or less definite." (pp. 32, 33)

Certain aspects of Marshall's approach flow directly from his stated purpose of relating the complexities of demand and supply to the real world. For example, he believed that as essential as pure theory, and especially mathematical theory, was to economists, it needed to be carefully interpreted. In the mathematical appendix to *Principles,* he wrote:

> But while a mathematical illustration of the mode of action of a definite set of causes may be complete in itself, and strictly accurate within its clearly defined limits, it is otherwise with any attempt to grasp the whole of a complex problem of real life, or even any considerable part of it, in a series of equations. For many important considerations . . . do not lend themselves easily to mathematical expression: they must either be omitted altogether, or clipped and pruned till they resemble the conventional birds and animals of decorative art. And hence arises a tendency towards assigning wrong proportions to economic forces; those elements being most emphasized which lend themselves most easily to analytical methods. (Note XIV, p. 850)

Marshall accordingly placed his own mathematical and geometrical explanations in footnotes and appendices and devoted the body of his work to verbal explanations.[2]

Second, Marshall believed in the value of historical information about specific problems. It was the acquisition of such information, rather than the formulation of pure theory, that required lengthy research and long periods of study. Early in his career he himself had hoped to prepare a series of comprehensive monographs on special areas of economic life before attempting to write his *Principles,* but the task proved too great. Nonetheless, in his writings and in his testimony before governmental investigatory groups, he revealed a thorough grasp of detail and an understanding of historical factors other than purely economic ones. In a perceptive passage in "The Old Generation of Economists and the New," an address given in 1897, he pointed to the coming era of quantitative economics:

> Speaking generally, the nineteenth century has in great measure achieved *qualitative* analysis in economics; but it has not gone farther. It has felt the necessity for *quantitative* analysis, and has made some rough preliminary surveys of the way in which it is to be achieved: but the achievement itself stands over for you. (*Memorials,* p. 301)

Unlike the economists of the historical school, however, he saw no opposition between theory and fact. The better the theory the greater stimulus it would be to the study of reality.

Third, Marshall, like Mill, agreed that the closer an economist came to a study of reality the more willing he must be to accept the importance of noneconomic motives. It was the variety of human motives, the "ever changing and subtle forces of human nature" (p. 14) that made not only economic theories but all social theories inexact. Pure economic theory had an advantage over other social sciences because it assumed the strength of motives could be measured with money: Economics laws "relate to branches of conduct in which the strength of

[2] He was also critical of those economists who seemed to find greater fascination in mathematical formulas than in analyses of problems. Of F. Y. Edgeworth, the Oxford economist, Marshall said, "It will be interesting . . . to see how far he succeeds in preventing his mathematics from running away from him, and carrying him out of sight of the actual facts of economics." (Quoted by Keynes in *Memorials,* p. 26. He thought Jevons' book, *The Theory of Political Economy,* would have been better if the mathematics of utility and exchange—which Jevons had believed to be his greatest achievement—had been omitted.

the motives chiefly concerned can be measured by a money price." (p. 33) This was not entirely true in applied economics. Money did not measure the motives of individuals with different tastes or different incomes. As Marshall often pointed out, a shilling was worth more to a poor man than to a rich one. Moreover, in studying any particular social problem he said one must recognize the complexity of human motives. Some are undesirable and evil and should be softened and modified in the interests of society as a whole.

It was the latter point that led Marshall to modify the economist's usual warning with respect to value judgments. As early as his inaugural address at Cambridge (given in 1885) he stated, on the one hand, that "an economist, like any other citizen, may give his own judgment as to the best solution of various practical problems. . . . But in such case the counsel bears only the authority of the individual who gives it: he does not speak with the voice of the science." (*Memorials,* p. 165) But he also left open a door: "Sometimes indeed the economist may give a practical decision as it were with the authority of his science," although usually such decisions were negative ones that a particular proposal would not work. In his *Principles,* he went further, taking a position similar to that of Adam Smith. Although economics shuns many political issues, he said, it does aim at helping the statesman determine what the ends of policies might be, and which ways are best for reaching them. (p. 43) Although he did not clarify the distinction between "political issues" and other ends, his work contained many normative judgments. For example, he defended a policy of "generous expenditure" by governments for education of the masses of the people by claiming that "living economists with one consent maintain that such expenditure is a true economy, and that to refuse it is both *wrong* and bad business from a national point of view." (*Principles,* p. 47, italics added)

Finally, concern with the way things worked in the real world led Marshall to begin his analysis by focusing on the particular rather than the general. His method, known as the partial equilibrium approach, was to examine a given market, firm, or industry, show how individuals and firms in it reacted to changes, and only then indicate the indirect, or ripple, effects on other markets. "Thus we begin," he said, "by isolating the primary relations of supply, demand and price in regard to a particular commodity." Later the other forces, which had been held constant, "are released from the hypothetical slumber that had been imposed on them: changes in the conditions of demand for and supply of particular groups of commodities come into play; and their complex

mutual interactions begin to be observed." ("Preface to the Eighth Edition," pp. xiv-xv)

Marshall's approach was unlike the general equilibrium theory of Walras and Pareto.[3] The latter were interested in the final equilibrium after each economic unit had adjusted to all the direct and indirect effects of the changes that upset the initial equilibrium. Marshall, on the other hand, concentrated more on the adjustment process. He understood quite well that all markets were interdependent; but his analytical tools were devised primarily to dissect not the final equilibrium, which would never be attained, but the process of change.

IV

Although it is neither necessary nor possible here to review in detail Marshall's comprehensive and intricate demand-and-supply theory of the determination of prices in product and factor markets, there are three significant areas of his analysis in which he developed concepts and theories, highly useful to later economists, that bore the marks of his particular orientation to the study of the economic world. These concepts and theories we shall discuss, in brief.

In his analysis of demand, Marshall used the partial equilibrium approach. He examined the demand for a given commodity in a market at a particular time; to simplify the analysis he assumed that consumer expenditures for that good were only a very small part of their total outlay. Demand, he said, could be described as a schedule of quantities that would be purchased at different prices; represented geometrically, that schedule was a downward-sloping function.[4] The "one general *law of demand*" was that the "greater the amount to be sold, the smaller must be the price at which it is offered in order that it may find pur-

[3] These writers, who were Marshall's contemporaries, are discussed in Chapter x.

[4] The modern geometrical presentation of a demand schedule owes much to Marshall. Although he was not the first to diagram the relationship between the quantity of a good demanded at a series of prices, it was he who established the present convention of putting prices on the vertical axis and quantities on the horizontal axis. He also originated the coefficient of elasticity to describe the shape of the curve.

Earlier writers, like Cournot, had recognized different-shaped demand schedules, noting that higher prices meant larger revenues for sellers in some cases (an inelastic demand) but lower revenues in others (an elastic demand.) Marshall gave precision to the concept.

chasers." (I, p. 99) The market demand schedule was the sum of the demand schedules of individual consumers. Each individual schedule was downward-sloping because of the marginal-utility principle. The additional utility derived from another unit of a good diminished as more of it was acquired. Consequently, reasoned Marshall, an individual would not purchase more of it except at a lower price.

Because of this partial equilibrium approach, Marshall's demand analysis had certain unique features. In defining the demand schedule for a particular good, he explicitly assumed that "everything else was equal." This assumption admitted no changes in a person's tastes, in his income, or in the prices of other goods. If any one of these restrictions was lifted, the schedule would be different; it would shift. However, Marshall's logic was faulty. Price changes for one commodity were not consistent with his assumption that everything else was equal. For example, a change in price could affect an individual's income, although the effect might be very small. If the demand for a good was inelastic, an increase in its price would mean a greater financial outlay and the purchaser would have less money to buy other things. Marshall himself said that income changes affected the marginal utility of money; if an individual had less money left over its marginal utility would rise, contradicting the assumption in his analysis of demand that the marginal utility of money remains constant. If a decline in income caused an individual to purchase more of a certain kind of good—today termed an "inferior" good—an anomalous situation might develop. A rise in price (of one good), through its effect on income, might cause more of the good to be purchased, contradicting Marshall's law of demand.[5] Marshall, however, called this not an inconsistency, but an exception, and did not revise his analytical technique. (p. 132) A similar problem arose in the case of commodities that were substitutes. A change in the price of one had to affect the demand schedule for the other, again contradicting the *ceteris paribus* assumption. For example, a rise in the price of coffee would cause some consumers to switch to tea, shifting the demand schedule for tea and raising its price. Marshall did not resolve this problem of interdependence among demand schedules except to make the rather lame suggestion that substitute commodities (such as coffee and tea) could be treated as one good. (p. 100, note 1)

[5] A contemporary of Marshall's, Sir Robert Giffen, associated with the British Board of Trade, had noted this exceptional behavior in the case of the consumption of bread by the British working class. The phenomenon later became known as the Giffen paradox.

Marshall attempted to derive from the demand schedule a measure of welfare in the form of consumers' surplus—a concept previously used by the Frenchman DuPuit. The "excess of the price which he [the consumer] would be willing to pay rather than go without a thing, over that which he actually does pay, is the economic measure of this surplus satisfaction." (p. 124) On the marginal unit purchased, there would be no surplus; but there would be excess utility on the other units purchased (assuming the demand curve was not infinitely elastic), and the consumer's surplus would be the sum of the excess on each of those units. Marshall thought the exact measurement of consumers' surplus might "become of high practical importance." It might make possible a measure of the change in relative welfare resulting from a change in the price of one commodity in comparison with another. It would therefore measure the benefits an individual obtained from his "environment," as Marshall called the social system within which he lived.

But the concept of consumers' surplus also presented theoretical obstacles. It required that utility be measurable (i.e., cardinal) and interpersonally comparable, for welfare to be evaluated. Marshall admitted that utility was a subjective phenomenon: "we cannot speak of measuring marginal utility in general, because the wants and circumstances of different people are different." (p. 100) But he was willing to put aside this objection in the case of individuals with similar tastes—for example, when considering English consumers of tea—and similar incomes, or a similar range of incomes. Although, he was not wholly clear on this point, Marshall seemed to accept the implication that where tastes were not the same, and where levels of income were not similar, the concept could lead to misunderstandings. One other conceptual difficulty with consumers' surplus was the inability of anyone to add the surpluses arising from the consumption of different commodities if those commodities were substitutes. Marshall considered this an unimportant exception. (See p. 131, note 1, and his mathematical appendix, p. 842.)

Marshall's analysis of the economics of the firm was unique and innovative and opened new fields of investigation for subsequent economists. In his own system, it furnished the key to the establishment of equilibrium prices, other than the market price, through demand and supply. In calculating the market price at any given moment, supplies of a good in the hands of distributors in the markets could be considered as fixed in quantity; the equilibrium market price resulted from the interaction of demand and the supply curve that represented those existing quantities. Given more time, however, firms would react to the current market price by changing their output, and this would alter the level of supplies. Marshall introduced two categories for classifying output adjustments. In what he called the short-run normal period, existing firms could vary their output within the limitations set by their fixed capital. In the long-run normal period, this restriction was lifted: Existing firms could increase or decrease the size of their plant, and new firms could enter the industry or old ones leave. Short-run adjustments would affect the equilibrium price of the commodity quite differently than long-run changes. In the case of an increase in market demand, the output response to a higher market price in the short run would be less elastic as firms sought to increase production from fixed facilities. But with a longer period of time, said Marshall, if the higher price seemed likely to prevail, firms would be tempted to enlarge their capital facilities, and new firms would be attracted to the industry. These changes would increase supplies, that is, make the supply curve of the industry more elastic. Under these circumstances the long-run normal price would be lower than the price in the short run.[6]

The assumption that supported Marshall's short-run analysis of the firm's behavior was that its costs of production could be divided into two parts, prime costs and supplementary costs. The first type—now termed "variable costs"—included special, or direct, costs such as the wages of production workers and outlays for raw materials; the second type included fixed capital charges, "salaries of the upper employees," and similar costs that did not change quickly in response to changes in output. No firm would operate in the short run, said Marshall, unless its prices enabled it to cover its prime costs; no firm would operate in the long run unless it could cover all its costs, both prime and supplementary.

Marshall's partial equilibrium approach led him to an analysis of the types of adjustments that the firm might make in its cost structure to increase efficiency. For example, it might seek more efficient combinations of factors of production by substituting a little more of a cheaper factor for a more expensive one. (This principle will be discussed below.) It might also make changes in its plant. With a larger

[6] Marshall also presented a fourth period of adjustment in which there occurred secular changes. These were normal price movements "caused by the gradual growth of knowledge, of population and of capital, and the changing conditions of demand and supply from one generation to another." (p. 379) The concept has been largely forgotten.

plant the firm might be able to introduce more expensive equipment and achieve large-scale purchasing economies that would reduce production costs. Marshall called these changes *internal economies*. There were also *external economies,* the gains resulting from cheaper, or more productive, services made possible by economic progress elsewhere. The firm might benefit from a more educated labor force within a particular locality, the development of specialized auxiliary industries, or improved means of transportation and communication. Although later economists found it more convenient to assume in analyses of price determination that firms adjusted by the principle of substitution to the lowest cost position to realize all economies of scale, Marshall did not do so. Instead, he concentrated on the "representative firm" as the reality he was attempting to illuminate. Beginning with the assumption that in the real world firms are born, grow in size, and then die, he wanted neither a struggling new firm, nor a powerful one, to illustrate his principles. The "representative firm" was "one which has had a fairly long life, and fair success, and which is managed with normal ability, and which has normal access to the economies, external and internal, which belong to that aggregate volume of production. . . ." (p. 317)

In generalizing about the long-run supply curves of particular industries, Marshall assumed that they could have different shapes. If the industry was an agricultural one where land was limited as the classical economists had assumed, expansion would probably mean a rising supply curve because of the principle of diminishing returns. In manufacturing, he believed there were greater opportunities for economies of scale. Hence he argued that the long-run supply curve could indicate constant or even decreasing costs as the industry increased its output. These possibilities would arise if economies of scale more than compensated for rising prices due to increases in the cost of raw materials or other productive agents. Marshall did not feel he could exclude technological change and still produce realistic appraisal of long-run industry supply curves. This conclusion was later challenged by the supporters of formal, general equilibrium theory, who believed that his failure to isolate the effects of changes in scale impaired his analysis. But Marshall's logic, which was classical in spirit, was concerned primarily with price changes in specific industries over time. His conclusions, he believed, offered realistic explanations of reality.

One of Marshall's major conclusions from this line of analysis was the importance of costs in determining normal prices, especially in the long run. In fact, where the long-run cost curve showed constant returns, it was costs and not demand that determined the equilibrium normal price. This was the exact opposite of the conclusion arrived at by Jevons and the Austrians. Of course Marshall argued that both utility and costs determined price: "we might as reasonably dispute whether it is the upper or the under blade of a pair of scissors that cuts a piece of paper, as whether value is governed by utility or cost of production." (p. 348) But he went on to add that although demand is more important at first, production costs have a greater influence during longer periods.

The third general area of analysis affected by Marshall's methods of analysis was distribution, or the division of the national income into wages, rent, interest, and profit. He was primarily interested in factor pricing, not aggregate payments. The importance he placed on the firm led him to add to the classical three factors of production, land labor, and capital, a new fourth factor—the entrepreneur, or as he called it, the organization. Marshall's approach was again a partial equilibrium, supply-and-demand analysis with a heavy emphasis on the time required for adjustments. In addition, he continued the British tradition of including real costs, or disutilities.

There was one difference between Marshall's approach to the market demand for factors of production and his analysis of consumer demand. The demand for agents of production, he said, was a joint demand; the agents cooperated (and competed) with one another in production. Firms, in their search for greater profits, constantly took into consideration the effects of different combinations of those agents on output and profit. The demands for different agents of production were therefore interrelated, and price changes in a product market would affect the demand in a number of factor markets. Thus Marshall perceived the interconnections within the competitive system as a whole.

The firms' demands for agents of production were called, by Marshall, derived demands, and he laid down rules that governed the elasticity of such curves. Elasticity is increased, he said, if substitute factors are readily available, if the product-demand schedule is elastic, if the proportion of the cost of the factor to total production costs is large, and if a rise in the price of one factor price will not be followed by an increase in the prices of competing factors.

In its attempts to find a more efficient combination of productive factors, the firm would eventually discover that using more of any one factor would yield diminishing returns. This gave Marshall a clue that the demand for a factor was governed by the principle of marginal productivity. The firm seeks to use just enough of each agent so that "in its marginal application, its cost is proportionate to the additional new product resulting from its use." (p. 518)

> [The businessman] estimates as best he can how much *net product* (i.e., net addition to the value of his total produce) will be caused by a certain extra use of any one agent, *net* that is after deducting for any extra expenses that may be indirectly caused by the changes, and adding for any incidental savings. He endeavors to employ each agent up to that margin at which its net produce would no longer exceed the price he would have to pay for it. (p. 406) [7]

Although Marshall can be credited with having presented a form of the modern theory of marginal productivity (even in his first edition), his interpretation was somewhat different. He made a special point of denying that the doctrine of marginal productivity governed value. "It is not so; the doctrine says we must *go to the margin to study the action of those forces which govern* the value of the whole: and that is a very different affair." (p. 410) In his discussion of wages, he again denied that the theory of marginal productivity underlying the demand curve of labor was a theory of wages. By itself, he said, such a statement has no "real meaning." One has also to consider other expenses and the supply curve of the factor.

Marshall sought to make his analysis of the supply side of factor markets realistic by emphasizing the diversity of the productive agents within the larger categories of land, labor, capital, and organization. Not only were there different grades of land, there were different grades of managerial ability, different types of workers, and highly differentiated arrays of different types of capital goods. It took time for the supply of each of these specific agents of production to adjust to continually shifting demands; sometimes an adjustment was not possible at all. In the case of labor, Marshall extended the Mill-Cairnes theory of non-competing groups, pointing out many obstacles to the mobility of workers, especially manual workers—their lack of resources, the "perishability" of their labor, and the difficulty of obtaining funds for training and investment in human capital. He argued that there was "no such thing in modern civilization as a general rate of wages." (p. 533). He also concluded that it was "certain that manual labourers as a class are

[7] Technically, the present-day concept of marginal productivity assumes that only one factor is increased, by a small amount, and all others remain the same. Marshall's concept of "net" reflects his concern with realism, not logical rigor.

at a disadvantage in bargaining; and that the disadvantage wherever it exists is likely to be cumulative in its effects." (p. 569) It took far longer, he noted, for the supply of labor to adjust to changes in demand than it took commodity supplies to adjust. Under these circumstances, Marshall had great reservations about the very concept of a national wage rate.

In the performance of its functions labor incurs disutility, which is a subjective real cost. Marshall assumed that the supply curve of labor consisted of those prices that would just compensate workers for additional expenditures of effort. It would be a forward-rising curve, since higher wages would be necessary to induce greater effort.

Capital goods, like labor, tended to be relatively immobile and specialized. If a good were absolutely immobile, the return on it would be like a rent; Marshall called it a *quasi-rent*. Over time, when the supply of the good increased or decreased to meet changes in demand, the return would be less rentlike. Money paid to workers with special skills and abilities, such as some professional men and artists, was also, at least in part, a quasi-rent in the sense that the supply was fixed.

Marshall distinguished between existing stocks of capital and what he termed "free" or "floating" capital. This was new savings, which could be freely invested. The return on these invested savings was interest, and the rate was determined by supply and demand. Marshall argued that such funds had a disutility cost because saving required the sacrifice of present for future goods. He termed this type of disutility "waiting" in order to avoid the moral implications of Senior's "abstinence." The free-capital supply curve was forward-rising since it, like the supply curve of labor, reflected increasing marginal disutility.

Returns to business management, according to Marshall, were not a return on capital, although gross profits often included interest on capital invested by the management. Profits were essentially wages of management, not contractually fixed and subject to variation due to risks and uncertainties. Marshall treated them as quasi-rents, that is, as payment for managerial abilities not easily duplicated, and for effort.

In discussing rent, Marshall accepted the fact that to an individual firm land rents were an alternative cost that had to be paid to prevent the land's being put to other uses. In considering land as a whole, however, he returned to the Ricardian position that true rent was a payment for resources whose quantity could not be altered. It was not price-determining, and it was not a real cost.

V

At no point in his analysis of the adjustments in product and factor markets caused by the interaction of demand, supply, and price did Marshall lose sight of the welfare connotations of the free-enterprise system. With the wants and demands of consumers, on the one hand, and disutilities and costs of production on the other, competition within the system tended to produce the best allocation of resources to meet those demands, relative to costs; to promote, in short, "maximum satisfaction." Marshall's *simpliste* example was the boy in the blackberry patch. The boy enjoyed eating the blackberries he picked, but the more he picked and ate the less marginal satisfaction he drew from eating and the greater the marginal disutility of picking became. At the point where the marginal utility of his consumption equaled the marginal disutility of production, the boy would stop, his satisfaction would be "at its *maximum*." (p. 331) The economy of England was much more complicated than a blackberry patch, but the forces of demand and supply tended toward the same goal—maximum satisfaction.

Although there were many exceptions and hazards in the drift of society toward greater satisfaction through market adjustments, as Marshall always carefully pointed out, nonetheless the direction of the movement was unmistakable even if sometimes exasperatingly slow. One fundamental limitation of the system, however, was the inequality in the distribution of wealth and income. The balance between wants and disutilities would be different if incomes were equally distributed, and since the rich gained less utility from a unit of income than the poor the aggregate satsfaction of society would increase. Marshall resisted the implication that there should be any redistribution of property on the grounds—similar to those first expressed by Bentham—that any disturbance of property arrangements would precipitate a drop in innovation and in the supply of entrepreneurs and curtail economic progress. Education of the poor, he believed, was a much better solution, although a slower one.

According to Marshall, another limitation of the system, a more technical one unrelated to the distribution of property, was the fact that in some industries there was a tendency for the supply-price to rise in the long run (because of increasing costs). On the other hand, there were also industries in which supply prices tended to fall in the long run (because of production economies). If people purchased more goods whose costs tended to decline, they would receive more goods for less resources than if they purchased goods from rising-cost industries. Although it would contradict the doctrine of consumer sovereignty to persuade consumers to switch from one type of good to another, it would be possible to induce them to do so by taxes and subsidies. Consumers would realize a net gain if decreasing-cost industries were stimulated by subsidies to produce more and increasing-cost industries were taxed to make them produce less.

Marshall did not pursue this suggestion, however. His overall conclusions with respect to government policy were consistent with his favorable orientation to the free-enterprise system. It was better to accept the system, with all its limitations, than to invite government interference.

Notes to Chapter viii

The following works of Marshall are referred to in the text.

1. Alfred Marshall, *Principles of Economics,* 9th (Variorum) ed., with annotations by C. W. Guillebaud (London and New York, Macmillan, 1961), two vols. The first volume contains the text (and pagination) of the eighth edition. Unless otherwise stated, references are to the first volume.

2. A. C. Pigou, ed., *Memorials of Alfred Marshall* (London, Macmillan, 19295). This is a collection of articles, reviews, addresses and a number of letters of Marshall, in addition to biographical essays and reminiscences by John Maynard Keynes, Pigou, F. Y. Edgeworth, and others.

3. *Official Papers of Alfred Marshall,* published for the Royal Economic Society (London, Macmillan, 1929). This volume also contains papers of Marshall, relating to his

testimony before various government agencies.

As noted in the text, Marshall wrote two books in addition to *Principles: Industry and Trade* (London, Macmillan, 1919) and *Money, Credit, and Commerce* (London, Macmillan, 1923).

I

The biographical sketch of Marshall is based primarily on the essays of Keynes and Pigou in *Memorials;* on the "Editorial Introduction" by Guillebaud in *Principles,* vol. II; on Guillebaud's "The Evolution of Marshall's *Principles of Economics,*" *Economic Journal,* vol. LII (December 1942), pp. 330–349; and on Jacob Viner's "Marshall's Economics, in Relation to the Man and his Times," *American Economic Review,* vol. XXXI (June 1941), pp. 223–235. Information on the sales of the *Principles* and the statement that little of the book's content was changed, especially after the third edition, are found in the Guillebaud's references.

The ambivalent attitude of Marshall toward Jevons deserves special comment. William Stanley Jevons (1835–82) used the principle of marginal utility to explain exchange and price in his *Theory of Political Economy*. The book appeared shortly before Menger's in 1871. Until then, Jevons had had exceptional difficulty in getting anyone to give serious consideration to his theory, and even after its publication the reaction was unfavorable. Cairnes condemned the book, and Marshall in his published review gave it only partial approval. Jevons later ran into more trouble: As marginal utility ideas became accepted, he was accused of lack of originality. It was true, he found, much to his disappointment, that others had preceded him—especially Herman H. Gossen (1810–58), whose exposition of the laws of exchange based on marginal utility and expressed mathematically had appeared in 1854—but he had not known of them when he developed his theory. Marshall, who had been drawing on the little-understood works of Antoine Augustin Cournot (1801–77) and von Thünen for his own mathematical approach to economics was caught unawares by the publication of Jevons' work in 1871.

It was not only the reaction bordering on dismay that distressed Marshall about Jevons' publication of ideas on which he had already been working. Jevons' approach was, he believed, too mathematical for students of economics in general, and certainly for the public. Moreover he believed that Jevons did not

understand the importance of classical economics and its continued relevance. Jevons, in fact, had gone out of his way to attack Ricardo and Mill. In the preface to his *Theory*, he wrote:

> When at length a true system of Economics comes to be established, it will be seen that that able but wrong-headed man, David Ricardo, shunted the car of Economic Science on to a wrong line, a line, however, on which it was further urged towards confusion by his equally able and wrong-headed admirer John Stuart Mill. (*The Theory of Political Economy*, 4th ed. (London, Macmillan, 1924), p. li. The quotation is from the preface to the second edition.)

No statement could have been better calculated to irritate Marshall. Yet Marshall tempered statements about Jevons. In his *Principles*, he would note that Jevons was given to overstating his case with remarks that were inaccurate and sometimes mischievous (e.g., see note 1, p. 90), and then praise his excellent work (note 1, p. 91).

Marshall's major criticism of Jevons, however, concerned the latter's denial of the classical doctrine on the influence of costs on price. Jevons' short summary of the role of marginal utility—he called it the final degree of utility—was as follows:

> Cost of production determines supply.
> Supply determines final degree of utility.
> Final degree of utility determines value.

Marshall's rebuttal was effective and to the point:

> Now if this series of causations

really existed, there could be no greater harm in omitting the intermediate states and saying that cost of production determines value. For if *A* is the cause of *B*, which is the cause of *C*, which is the cause of *D;* then *A* is the cause of *D*. But in fact there is no such series. (*Principles*, Appendix I, p. 818)

Ricardo's doctrine of the importance of costs, said Marshall, "though unsystematic and open to many objections, seems to be more philosophic in principle and closer to the actual facts of life." (p. 819) His point, of course, was that there were interactions between utility, costs, and price.

Marshall's emphasis on the classical writers, on costs, and on applying economics to problems of the day rather than perfecting mathematical theories largely won over British economists in the period before World War I. (See, for example, the analysis of journal articles in Marmadeshwar Jha, *The Age of Marshall: Aspects of British Economic Thought, 1890–1915* (Ashoka Rajpath, Novelty, 1963), foreword by Sir Dennis H. Robertson.)

II

The social and moral attitudes of Marshall toward society have been the subject of much discussion. Paul T. Homan, in his *Contemporary Economic Thought* (New York and London, Harper & Brothers, 1928), pp. 195 ff., builds his analysis of Marshall's economics around the man's moral and social perspectives, which he claims made him both great and an inspiration to others: ". . . by rescuing economics from barren controversy and formal logic, and by inspiring much of the best work in economics during the past generation, he established himself as the greatest of modern economists." (*ibid.*, p. 280) Marshall's preoccupation with the problems of his day, his traditional philosophical outlook, and his Victorian values undoubtedly account for the datedness of many of his attitudes. But, as Homan points out, Marshall was well aware of the transient qualities of his economics.

Jacob Viner (*op. cit.*) also examined the relationship of Marshall's concern for the betterment of society and his economic analysis. As a social philosopher, Marshall, said Viner in 1941, was "not yet merely a period piece. If he should become so in the near future, it would properly be a matter for concern, but not for surprise." Clark Kerr, in *Marshall, Marx and Modern Times: The Multi-Dimensional Society, The Marshall Lectures, 1967–68* (Cambridge, University Press, 1969) contrasts the ethical views and insights of Marx and Marshall.

As G. F. Shove points out in "The Place of Marshall's *Principles* in the Development of Economic Theory," *Economic Journal*, vol. LII (December 1942), reprinted in Spengler and Allen, *Essays in Economic Thought* (*op. cit.*), p. 734, and note 124, p. 739, Marshall himself was well aware of the probable obsolescence of his ideas. He accepted the relativity of economic doctrines to a particular age and country. In a letter in 1915 (*Memorials*, pp. 489–490), he wrote: "A thousand years hence 1920–1970 will, I expect, be *the* time for economic historians. It drives me wild to think of it. I believe it will make my poor *Principles*, with a lot of poor comrades, into waste paper."

III

For a description of Marshall's methods and assumptions, see Talcott Parsons, "Wants and Activities in Marshall," *Quarterly Journal of Economics,* vol. XLVI (November 1931), pp. 101–140, and his *The Structure of Social Action* (New York, McGraw-Hill, 1937), ch. 4. See also T. W. Hutchison, *A Review of Economic Doctrines, 1870–1929* (London, Oxford University Press, 1953), ch. 4. For evaluations from other viewpoints see Herbert J. Davenport, *The Economics of Alfred Marshall* (Ithaca, N. Y., Cornell University Press, 1935), and Leo Rogin, *The Meaning and Validity of Economic Theory: A Historical Approach* (New York, Harper & Brothers, 1956).

IV

Because Marshall's theories have been so dominant in modern economics, the literature concerning his specific concepts and theories is naturally very large. For an appraisal of his demand theory in relationship to the work of other marginal-utility theorists, see George J. Stigler, "The Development of Utility Theory," *Journal of Political Economy,* vol. LVIII (August-October 1950), pp. 307–327, 373–396. This article, along with Stigler's "Notes on the History of the Giffen Paradox," is reprinted in his *Essays in the History of Economics* (Chicago and London, University of Chicago Press, 1965). Milton Friedman interprets Marshall's demand analysis in his "The Marshallian Demand Curve," *Journal of Political Economy,* vol. LVII (December 1949), pp. 463–495. See also Kenneth E. Boulding,

"The Concept of Economic Surplus," *American Economic Review,* vol. 35 (December 1945), pp. 851–869, reprinted in the American Economic Association's *Readings in the Theory of Income Distribution* (Homewood, Ill., Irwin, Blakiston Books, 1946), pp. 638–659).

For a view of Marshall's theory of production in relation to the work of other theorists of the period, see George J. Stigler, *Production and Distribution Theories: The Formative Period* (New York, Agathon Press, 1968, reprinted from the 1941 edition), ch. IV. Frank H. Knight discusses Marshall in his *Risk, Uncertainty, and Profit* (1921), reissued in New York by Harper & Row, 1965), and in his *The Ethics of Competition and Other Essays* (New York, Harper & Row, 1935), chs. 7 and 8.

Marshall's ideas about long-run industry supply curves and the significance of internal and external economies of production ran into considerable opposition from economic formalists, especially Frank H. Knight (*op. cit.*). Were not external economies to an industry the internal economies of some other industry or industries? If so, then the appearance of increasing returns in the one case (assuming the absence of technological change) simply resulted from the chance situation that the other industries had not as yet reached their long-run normal-price equilibrium positions. A key article that restated Marshall's cost analysis of the firm and industry was Jacob Viner's "Cost Curves and Supply Curves," *Zeitschrift für Nationalökonomie* (1931), reprinted in the American Economic Association's *Readings in Price Theory* (Homewood, Ill., Irwin, 1953), pp. 198–232.

Daniel H. Buchanan gives a good review of Marshall's rent theory in his "The Historical Approach to Rent and Price Theory," in the AEA's *Readings in the Theory of Income Distribution* (*op. cit.*), ch. 31. For a review of his work on wages, see Kerr, *op. cit.*, passim.

For a discussion of Marshall's contributions to monetary theory, see Eprime Eshag, *From Marshall to Keynes: An Essay on the Monetary Theory of the Cambridge School* (Oxford, Basil Blackwell & Mott, 1963).

V

Marshall's concern with realism rather than formalism in economics became the hallmark of the Cambridge, or neoclassical, school and led his intellectual followers to develop from his works new criticisms of the doctrine of maximum satisfaction in a competitive market system. Two criticisms became of key importance in subsequent economic thought. One was the theory of imperfect competition; the other was an analysis of the divergence of social costs from private costs.

Among those who wrote on the structure of markets that fell between the two extremes of perfect competition, on the one hand, and monopoly (including duopoly) on the other, were Piero Sraffa, "The Laws of Returns under Competitive Conditions," *Economic Journal,* vol.

XXXVI (December 1926); Joan Robinson, *The Economics of Imperfect Competition* (London, Macmillan, 1933); and Edward Chamberlin, *The Theory of Monopolistic Competition* (Cambridge, Mass., Harvard University Press, 1933). The first two economists were at Cambridge University. Like many other intellectual discoveries, new ideas about imperfect competition burst forth from many writers at about the same time. Other economists who contributed to the new theory were Jacob Viner, Roy Harrod (who first used the term "marginal revenue" in 1930), T. O. Yntema, Harold Hotelling, F. Zeuthen, and Heinrich von Stackelberg. Mrs. Robinson later criticized her original presentation in "Imperfect Competition Revisited," *Economic Journal,* vol. LXIII (September 1953), pp. 579–593.

The social-cost vs. private-cost controversy also grew out of Marshall's criticisms of the doctrine of maximum satisfaction. A. C. Pigou, who assumed the Cambridge Chair of Political Economy following Marshall's retirement, developed the implications of Marshall's welfare theory in *Wealth and Welfare,* first published in 1912, but revised and expanded under the title *The Economics of Welfare* in 1920 in light of criticisms by Knight, Allyn Young, and D. H. Robertson. In brief, Pigou argued that the competitive system often generated certain costs that were not borne by private firms, but forced upon an unwilling public.

Chapter ix

THE NECESSITY OF GOVERNMENT INTERVENTION:

The Keynesian Heresy

> . . . the characteristics of the special case assumed by the classical theory happen not to be those of the economic society in which we actually live, with the result that its teaching is misleading and disastrous . . . .
>
> . . . the enlargement of the functions of government . . . I defend . . . both as the only practicable means of avoiding the destruction of existing economic forms in their entirety and as the condition of the successful functioning of individual initiative.
>
> John Maynard Keynes, *The General Theory of Employment, Interest and Money*

John Maynard Keynes's *General Theory of Employment, Interest, and Money,* published in 1936, had a profound impact on the world of professional economics and on the economic policies of nations. Keynes was a leading British economist, a brilliant essayist and university lecturer, editor of the *Economic Journal* (the official organ of the British Economic Society), and a successful financier and businessman. The book became an instant sensation, especially in Great Britain and the United States, for it challenged some of the most widely held and cherished beliefs in economics.

Keynes claimed that the competitive market mechanism did not automatically provide full employment of labor; he attacked the teachings of classical economists, including those of his former teacher, Alfred Marshall, as pernicious; and he advocated an increased role for

229

the state in controlling the level of investment, a policy that seemed contrary to the quintessence of capitalism itself. To economists who sought a rationale for government full-employment policies to end the nightmare of the Great Depression, the *General Theory* became a bible that needed only to be popularized, understood, and applied. But to economists who held that classical theories of competition were faultless, and to old-style liberals for whom *laissez faire* was a religion, Keynes's economics was heresy.

The controversies that swirled around Keynes's *General Theory* were intense, often bitter. Arguments arose over his evaluation of the role of government in economic affairs, over his attacks on classical propositions, and over the technical adequacy and scope of his theories. At first, these separate issues were confused. But as the controversies continued, they produced what has been called the Keynesian revolution, the speed and magnitude of which were phenomenal. The revolution successfully penetrated nearly all the subrealms of economic thinking, including theory, econometrics (which it greatly stimulated), monetary theory, business cycles, public finance, international economics, and labor. Within a decade or two the new economics of income determination had become a standard topic in economics textbooks—the pinnacle of success for any new theory. In addition to their impact on economics, some have attributed to Keynes and his followers a significant role in the emergence of national full-employment policies in the early-World-War-II period. One writer has called the twenty-five years after the *General Theory* "The Age of Keynes."

I

The effect of changes in social value judgments on the development of theory is vividly illustrated in the case of Keynes. His outlook on the world began to change from that of his Cambridge colleagues long before the depression of the 1930s. It was not that he perceived problems in the traditional analysis no one else had seen. But as a participant in world affairs he had become sensitive to the fact that political opinion was moving in directions orthodox economists did not consider relevant or perhaps even notice. Early in this career he began to be aware that the economy of Great Britain was running into difficulties, that it had lost the dynamic qualities that made the country a world leader in the nineteenth century, and that its inability to perform satisfactorily was creating a restlessness and disaffection particularly among workers, who saw little in the arguments of economists to calm their fears of unemployment and economic insecurity.

The first hint Keynes gave which indicated that he perceived a gap between the worlds of theory and reality came as early as 1919, and he became increasingly critical of the failure of fellow economists to face the growing social and economic problems of Great Britain during the 1920s. By 1930 he was attacking orthodox theories of savings and investment. The *General Theory* of 1936 was not a bolt from the blue, nor a response to a single depression; it was the culmination of a series of attempts to explain the inability of an economic system to perform the way it was supposed to according to theory. Keynes viewed the intellectual process he went through as "a long struggle of escape" from the orthodox views in which he had been raised.

In John Maynard Keynes (1883–1946), born and raised in Cambridge, England, the traditions of classical and neoclassical economics ran deep. His father, John Neville Keynes, who had come to Cambridge as a young student, remained as a young don, lectured and wrote on logic and political economy, and became registrary of the university. His mother had studied under Henry Sidgwick, the professor of moral philosophy who sympathetically interpreted John Stuart Mill. Although John Maynard, after Eton, studied mathematics at King's College, Cambridge, he began reading intensively in economics during his last year, when he also attended Alfred Marshall's lectures. Marshall wrote the father that fall "your son is doing excellent work in Economics" and hoped he would decide on a career as a professional economist.

After holding, briefly, a position with the British India Office, Keynes finally wrote his dissertation (on probability) and was elected a fellow of King's College in 1909, a position that meant a lifetime appointment if he wished to keep it. He began lecturing in economics and writing a few articles, and his star began to rise. With Marshall's support, he was picked as editor of the *Economic Journal* in 1912, when he was twenty-eight, succeeding Francis Y. Edgeworth. He remained its editor for thirty-three years. He was appointed to the Royal Commission on Indian Currency and Finance in 1913, and the following year published his first major book, *Indian Currency and Finance*. This book, which became a standard work on the monetary problems of India, recommended adoption of the gold exchange standard. In it, Keynes revealed his ability to express himself verbally with ease; but he gave no hint of future apostasy. He worked for the British Treasury from 1915 to 1919, serving as its principal representative at the Paris Peace Conference. Dismayed by the punitive system of reparations proposed by the allies, he resigned his position and wrote an indictment of the settlement, *The Economic Consequences of the Peace,* published · in December 1919.

The impact of the book, which was polemical in tone, was immediate; it was a best seller. Although it was written very quickly, the style was polished and sparkling, the analysis clear and incisive, and the argument authoritative. Keynes's principal point was that Germany simply would not be able to pay the amounts demanded because of balance-of-payments difficulties exacerbated by the loss of productive resources, such as coal deposits in the Saar and Upper Silesia, demanded by the allies. His analysis proved prophetic. The reparations were in fact unpayable; first the American Dawes Plan of 1924 and then the Young Plan of 1929 sought to scale down the financial obligations. The crowning irony was the fact that German payments to the allies and allied payments on war debts to the United States were eventually made possible only by United States loans to Germany. The whole irrational system of reparations, its problems doubly compounded by the American Smoot-Hawley protective tariff, collapsed with the Great Depression.

Although *Economic Consequences* was an analysis in the classical tradition, in it Keynes revealed for the first time an awareness that perhaps the economic foundation of the pre-World-War-I era had not been quite as firm as economists had assumed. The new rich of the nineteenth century, he said, had acquired "vast accumulations" of wealth. Fortunately, they did not spend their wealth only on luxuries, for the world would have found the inequalities of such a regime "intolerable"; rather, they invested it, and the whole community gained. The book also showed that Keynes had a mind of his own and that when he made it up he was not afraid to speak it even if it meant challenging the establishment. (He was *persona non grata* at the Treasury because of the book, and he did not enter government service again until World War II.)

It was in the post-World-War-I period of the twenties that Keynes first began, seriously, to question orthodox economic policy. The chief issue at that time was whether Great Britain, which had gone off the gold standard during the war, should when it returned to it purchase gold at the prewar price. Keynes believed that since the price level of Great Britain and most other nations had risen substantially since 1914, a return to prewar parity was likely to bring deflation, unemployment, and hard times.

As early as 1923, when the Bank of England raised its lending rate, Keynes sensed a developing political and economic conflict over policy. In *The Nation,* the Liberal Party weekly, of which he was board chairman, he wrote that the rate increase was "misguided," that the Bank was "acting under the influence of a narrow and obsolete doctrine . . . ." Its only purpose could be to deflate the price level to prepare the way for resumption of the prewar gold standard. But why aggravate unemployment further for the sake of paying an arbitrary number of shillings for an ounce of gold?

Before the year was out Keynes had completed a new book, *A Tract on Monetary Reform,* in which he argued for stabilizing the domestic price level. His case was that price-level changes have different effects on the three major classes of the population, which he identified as the investors, who furnished savings; the businessmen, who were the active entrepreneurs; and the wage-earners. In general, inflation harmed the first class, and deflation harmed the other two by restricting production and employment. If one had to compare the evils of inflation and deflation, said Keynes, deflation is the worse, "because it is worse, in an impoverished world, to provoke unemployment than to disappoint the *rentier.*" But Keynes did not think that a choice was necessary. Stabilizing the price level would prevent both evils, but that could not be done if the nation insisted on adhering to the prewar type of international gold standard. That standard, which required a nation to expand or contract its money supply as gold flowed in or out of the country, caused the domestic price level to fluctuate. But it was not necessary to sacrifice domestic tranquility to preserve the external value of the monetary unit in terms of gold. In fact, said Keynes, some nations, like the United States, did not raise domestic prices when gold flowed in; thus the rules of the international-gold-standard game were already being broken. Currencies were being managed, "whilst the economist dozed." In truth, he said, "the gold standard is already a barbarous relic."

England returned to the old gold standard, however, and the painful process of rising unemployment and deflation began. Labour Party officials called for public-works expenditures, and even the Liberal Lloyd George urged government action. Writing in *The Nation* in 1924, Keynes supported the need for government outlays and went on to suggest state encouragement of domestic investment in housing, transport, and electric-power transmission. He rceognized that he was guilty of a heresy—"if it is a heresy. I bring in the State; I abandon *laissez faire*—not enthusiastically, not from contempt of that good old doctrine, but because, whether we like it or not, the conditions for its success have disappeared."

The idea of government control of the level of investment he elaborated further in a series of lectures at Oxford, published in 1926 under the title *The End of Laissez-Faire.* Here he stated:

> I believe that some coordinated act of intelligent judgment is required as to the scale on which it is desirable that the community as a whole should save, the scale on which these savings should go abroad in the form of foreign investments, and whether the present organization of the investment market distributes savings along the most nationally productive channels. I do not think that these matters should be left entirely to the chances of private judgment and private profits, as they are at present.

Capitalism, he felt, was in many ways extremely objectionable. But if it was "wisely managed" it could be made "more efficient for attaining economic ends than any alternative system yet in sight."

Keynes was certain that government intervention was needed to prevent depression and economic stagnation. Yet he had not been able to put his finger on the exact nature of the problem. It was more than simply a question of the gold standard or government outlays during a depression. The bothersome fact to Keynes was that the *rentier* class, as he called it, produced the savings that were used by the active entrepreneurial class for investment. At certain times investment seemed to be stifled; did the savings of the *rentiers* help or hinder the investment process?

His first attempt to answer this question was a theory of savings and investment presented in his major work in monetary theory, *A Treatise on Money,* published in 1930 in two volumes. The writing of it took five years.[1] While the book was a treatise in the sense that it covered many topics, such as banking, the gold standard, international-exchange mechanisms, and central-banking policy, it sought above all to explain

---

[1] Keynes was in no ivory tower during these five years. On the contrary, he was immersed in many enterprises. He played an important role in the organization of several investment and insurance companies; he continued to edit *The Nation* (later he was a member of the board of *The New Statesman and Nation*). He guided the investment policy of King's College with spectacular results. His interests in the arts also took a personal turn when he married ballerina Lydia Lopokova.

the causes of economic instability. In writing it, Keynes was influenced by such writers as Swedish economist Knut Wicksell and especially by Cambridge economist Dennis H. Robertson, whose book *Banking Policy and the Price Level* had appeared in 1926. Wicksell had stated in 1898 that there were two rates of interest, the natural rate and the market rate. If the monetary authorities kept the latter below the former businessmen would find investment more profitable and would borrow funds, causing a capital-investment boom. Prices would rise, said Wicksell, and rise without limit. If the market rate were higher than the natural rate, businessmen would not borrow, and prices would fall. Robertson's approach to savings and investment was somewhat different. He claimed that savings and investment were not necessarily the same, that one could be larger than the other, and that no automatic mechanism made them equal.

Keynes now embraced Robertson's view. Not only was investment important in determining national income, but there was a possibility of too much saving in comparison with investment. Keynes argued that the interest rate would not necessarily make the two equal. Thus although thrift could be beneficial when an economy was pressed for new funds with which to pursue attractive investments, when investment opportunities were lacking it was no virtue.

> It is Enterprise which builds and improves the world's possessions. . . . [A]s soon as Thrift gets ahead of Enterprise, it positively discourages the recovery of Enterprise and sets up a vicious circle by its adverse effects on profits. . . . For Enterprise is connected with Thrift not directly but at one remove; and the link which should join them is frequently missing. For the engine which drives Enterprise is not Thrift, but Profit.

To the Keynes of the *Treatise,* the most important job of the central-banking authorities was to promote a stable price level by pursuing a proper policy with respect to interest rates.

However, the *Treatise* turned out to be only a step in the development of his economics. His ideas were shifting even as he was writing it, and he said in its preface, ". . . [T]here is a good deal in this book which represents the process of getting rid of the ideas which I used to have. . . . It follows that I could do it much better and much shorter if I were to start over again."

Keynes did start over again. With a world depression gathering momentum, he approached the problem of economic instability from the point of view not of a theory of money but of a theory of aggregate output. In making the transition he was influenced by Richard F. Kahn's article "Home Investment and Unemployment," published in the *Economic Journal* in June 1931. One of Keynes's students, Kahn formulated the theory of the employment multiplier, which showed how new investment could generate a greater amount of output and employment under conditions of unemployment.

Named to the Macmillan Committee on Finance and Industry, Keynes advanced the view that government pump-priming would break the "vicious circle" of depression and declines in investment. But his ideas were not accepted. In 1933, he published a pamphlet, *The Means to Prosperity,* based on four articles he had written for *The Times,* in which he advocated a government public-works policy and used Kahn's multiplier to show how government deficit spending would raise income and employment. In 1934, on a visit to the United States, he talked with President Franklin Delano Roosevelt, but found the same resistance to his proposals that he had met in England. He could not convince Roosevelt of the desirability of greater government expenditures.

Keynes completed the draft of the *General Theory* in 1934 and obtained private reactions from fellow economists. As expected, they were highly critical of his new theory of employment. Keynes felt that even his objectives were misunderstood. When the *General Theory* was published in 1936, economists trained in the older theories found its terminology unfamiliar, different even from that of the *Treatise;* its attacks on classical and neoclassical theory unnecessarily derogatory; and its concepts difficult to grasp. To the younger generation, however, the new theory made sense. As Keynes himself said, the new ideas were not difficult; but it was hard for those who had been indoctrinated in the old way of looking at things to accept a new viewpoint.

The outbreak of World War II turned Keynes to an analysis of war finance. In 1940, in a new book, *How To Pay for the War,* he showed that his theories applied to problems of inflation as well as depression. The last years of his life were years of recognition and attempts to find a way to end international economic instability. He returned to government service during World War II, for the first time since 1919. He was appointed a member of the Court of the Bank of England and became Lord Keynes of Tilton in 1942; coming back to the Treasury, he gave more and more attention to the international economic problems sure to emerge in the postwar world. He believed it was imperative for the nations of the world to avoid any future gold standard that would lead to new conflicts or instability. Instead he proposed an International Clearing Union as an orderly way of determining exchange rates and preventing competitive, unilateral currency devaluations. He sought to make full employment the primary international goal, not the defense of money in terms of gold. To this end he proposed a new international-bank money, christened *bancor,* whose value was to be fixed, but not unalterably, in terms of gold. Actually, it was not unlike the paper-gold arrangement devised by the western nations a quarter of a century later. Although Keynes led the British delegation to the International Monetary Conference at Bretton Woods in 1944, he was unable to win American support for his plan. In the end, he accepted the American proposal for an International Monetary Fund, although he considered it a less satisfactory compromise.

In 1945, after the end of the war against Japan, Keynes made another trip to the United States, this time to discuss financial assistance for Great Britain. Although he had hoped for better terms, he agreed to the offer of a loan of $3.75 billion. He came to the United States only once more, for the inaugural meetings of the International Monetary Fund; shortly after returning to England in 1946, he died of a heart attack.

II

The controversies that erupted over the *General Theory* were fundamentally over the necessity of government intervention in a market economy to offset fluctuations in aggregate income and employment. The classical writers had no theory of aggregate income, other than that it would always, or almost always, be at a full-employment level; any deviation from full employment would be due to forces not connected with the market mechanism. Keynes had come up with a new theory of national income, which showed that an equilibrium could occur at many positions of less-than-full employment. The assumption in classical theory that full employment was automatically attained was only a special case of a more general theory; hence, he used the word "general" in his title.

But before Keynes could advance his own theory of employment, he first had to show why classical theorists had erroneously concluded that less-than-full-employment equilibria could not occur under competition. According to Keynes, the errors were not in classical writers' reasoning but in their postulates. He leveled his attack at two classical constructs: the classical theory of wages and the classical theory of money and interest.

The Classical Theory of Employment

The classical postulates concerning competition in the labor market were, said Keynes:

1. "The wage is equal to the marginal product of labour," and
2. "The utility of the wage when a given amount of labour is employed is equal to the marginal disutility of that amount of employment." (p. 5)

These Marshallian assumptions meant a falling demand curve and a rising supply curve respectively: the competitive wage was determined by their point of intersection. Only two types of unemployment were compatible with such markets: frictional and voluntary. The first type occurred as workers moved from one job to another in search of better positions and as firms adjusted their labor force to meet the changing needs of society. The second occurred when a worker withheld his labor because the utility of the wage (equal to the marginal product) was less than the disutility attached to the work. The classical writers would admit of no involuntary unemployment, unless the wage was above the point of intersection of demand and supply (i.e., not at its proper equilibrium position). Their remedy for that type of involuntary unemployment was a reduction in wages. As wages fell to the point of intersection, employers would hire more workers, and some of the unemployed, unwilling to incur the disutility of labor at the lowered wage, would withdraw from the labor market (i. e., become voluntarily unemployed).

Keynes offered two criticisms of this theory. The first was that, although it was expressed in real-wage terms, it did not distinguish between a cut in money wages and a fall in the value of money wages due to cost of living (i. e., in the prices of wage-goods). In the former case, unemployed workers may refuse to work at a money wage lower than the one they had become accustomed to. But in the latter case, where the reduction in the real wage occurs as the result of a rise in the price of wage goods, while the money wage remains the same, there would be no diminution in the number of workers seeking work. Said Keynes, this can only mean that the real wage does not measure disutility, and that the second postulate is not controlling.

Keynes's second and more fundamental criticism was that the real wage is *not* determined by employers and workers. If money wages are reduced, costs of production will fall; and under competition, product prices will fall as well. There may be *no* way, said Keynes, for labor and management to negotiate a fall in real wages. Thus involuntary unemployment could persist: "Men are involuntarily unemployed if, in the event of a small rise in the price of wage-goods relatively to the money-wage, both the aggregate supply of labour willing to work for the current money-wage and the aggregate demand for it at that wage would be greater than the existing volume of employment." (p. 15)

Later in his book, Keynes elaborated his opposition to money-wage cuts by stating that they might not stimulate investment if entrepreneurs believed that further wage declines were coming. They could give rise to unfavorable expectations on the part of entrepreneurs. The orthodox position was that if the quantity of money was unchanged, and money wages fell, expectations would improve. The quantity of money would be larger relative to incomes as less cash was required for business purposes at the lower price level; and as the demand for liquidity fell interest rates would fall, providing a favorable stimulus to investment. But, said Keynes, such a result would not necessarily follow; if a wage reduction gave rise to unfavorable expectations among investors (as indeed it might), and if the reduction in wages disturbed "political confidence by causing popular discontent," there would be a greater demand for liquidity than before and interest rates would not fall. Would it not be easier to increase the amount of money in circulation, leave money wages alone, and let rising prices reduce the real wage?

Keynes did not dispute the first postulate, linking wages and marginal productivity; on the contrary, he accepted the theory that greater employment would mean a lower real wage. But he did not believe that a direct reduction of money wages would achieve that objective. In short, he disagreed with the classicists on how to lower wages, not whether they should be lowered.

The Classical Theory of Money and Interest

Keynes's criticism of wage policy was only a preliminary, and to some extent diversionary, move. He knew he had to mount his major attack against the classical and neoclassical doctrine of savings and investment. According to Say's Law, there could be no general glut because production created its own demand. Prices of specific commodities

would always equilibrate supply and demand: If too much of a particular good was produced, its price would fall, leading to a shift of resources to the production of other goods for which demand was higher.
If too many investment goods were produced (through miscalculation,
for example), the demand for funds would drop, the interest rate would
fall, and resources would be switched from the production of investment goods to the production of consumer goods. The demand for the
latter would be higher because the low rate of interest would make
savings less attractive. The classicists assumed that the demand curve
for new capital and the supply curve of savings determined the rate of
interest and that if either or both of the curves shifted the new rate of
interest would be found at the point of intersection.

Keynes called this "a nonsense theory," and attempted to show
what was erroneous about it. The basic fallacy, he said, was the assumption that income would remain constant if either the investment
or the savings schedule changed. Such an assumption might be plausible
in the long run; it was unacceptable in the short run.

In Keynes's own analysis, as we shall see, an increase in investment
outlays, for example, would raise the level of aggregate income; an
increase in savings, for example, would reduce consumption and hence
lower income. The impact of such shifts on the level of aggregate income
was what was missing in the classical analysis of savings and investment, precisely because of the unwarranted postulate that national income was always at a full-employment maximum. As soon as that
postulate is dropped, said Keynes, it becomes clear that the interest rate
is *not* the price that equilibrates the supply of and demand for funds;
it is not a reward for waiting in the Marshallian sense; it is rather a
reward for "not hoarding."

Keynes explicitly rejected the idea, used in the *Treatise,* that the
natural interest rate equated savings and investment with a stable price
level in the Wicksellian sense. The concept of a natural rate was no
longer useful, because Keynes now claimed there was a different natural
rate for each hypothetical level of employment. Only in the case of full
employment would the concept be appropriate. But then, he said, we
all would be "safely ensconced in a Ricardian world." (p. 244)

The main difficulty with the classical theory of interest, according
to Keynes, was its failure to recognize the relationship of the interest
rate to money. The classical writers, he said, understood the monetary
aspect of interest when they showed that an increase in the supply of
money could cause interest rates to fall, at least temporarily; but they

did not use this insight in constructing a theory of value. Interest rates, however, are monetary phenomena and arise because money serves as a store of value and not simply as a means of exchange. Developing the Marshallian cash-balance approach to money, Keynes specified three motives for holding money: for transactions and for outlays in advance of receipts, as a precaution against contingencies; and for speculation. The amounts of cash that individuals and firms would hold as a result of the first two motives were related more or less directly to the size of the national income. The higher the national income, the more money would be required for transactions and as a hedge against the unforeseen. But the speculative motive was not so related. While Marshall only hinted at the last point, Keynes fashioned it into his major weapon against the classical system. Considering money as an asset, individuals would express a preference for liquidity that would in general vary inversely with the interest rate. At higher rates of interest, individuals would be less inclined to hold cash and would put their money into interest-bearing assets (such as bonds) instead; at lower rates of interest they would be more willing to hold cash. In fact, said Keynes, at extremely low rates of interest, the public's willingness to hold cash might be infinite. Given the liquidity-preference function, the amount of money in the system then determines the interest rate that prevails in the market. An injection of new money, for example, will increase cash holdings beyond the level that individuals feel is necessary; the additional funds will be invested (in fixed-interest-bearing securities), their price will rise, and hence their yields will fall. Interest rates on other types of assets will also fall. If the injections of money continue beyond a certain point however, interest rates may become so low that those with cash will not consider it worth their while to part with it: They will be willing to hold as much cash as the monetary authorities can pour into the system, and interest rates will then decline no more. It was this tail-end of the liquidity-preference function that later became known as "the liquidity trap." When this portion of the curve was reached, said Keynes, the monetary authorities "would have lost effective control over the rate of interest." (p. 207)

But this was not the end of the story of money and the interest rate. The liquidity-preference function could shift as attitudes toward holding money—the propensity to hoard—shifted, and thereby hinder full employment. In one context, Keynes stated that the rate of interest was "a highly psychological phenomenon"; in another, he called it "highly conventional," a matter of group psychology. He even expressed the view that the rate might become "conventionalized" at a level that was chronically too high for full employment.

Keynes's criticisms of classical theories drew blood, yet the attack on the classical postulates was actually less substantial than it appeared at first sight. For example, both he and the traditionalists agreed that wage rigidities accompanied unemployment. Keynes, however, said that wages were sticky downwards, that it was not desirable to try to force them down during a depression, and that it was easier and socially more expedient to raise prices in order to lower real wages. The primary criticism of this argument was that workers were not so irrational that they could not distinguish between a cut in money wages and one caused by a rise in the price of wage goods. But this criticism was beside the point if workers did in fact resist a reduction in money wages.

In the case of interest rates, the problem was more complex. The importance of liquidity preferences was a new development in monetary theory, although the idea itself was an old one. Yet in terms of orthodox economic analysis, it could be argued that Keynes's point was only an addition to traditional theory and not a substitute for it. The importance of the desire for liquidity, in the last analysis, was due to uncertainty about the future. Money was sought as a store of value when prices fell or were expected to fall and avoided for that purpose when prices rose. In the logic of the classical system uncertainty was not a factor and the *theoretical* problem by definition could not arise. But if uncertainty was a factor, and an important one at that, liquidity preferences could be significant. Questions arose about the effect of liquidity preferences on the structure of interest rates (as related to yields on assets of different risks and maturities) and particularly about the liquidity trap. Critics quickly and correctly showed that there were in fact many types of financial instruments which could be used speculatively and that a precise definition of money in comparison with many types of "other" assets was missing in Keynes's analysis. The liquidity trap in particular was attacked as a highly unlikely phenomenon. Two arguments were used against it. One was Keynes's own point that a decline in prices would increase the ratio of money to income so that interest rates would tend to fall; this was labeled (patronizingly) "the Keynes effect." The other, advanced by Pigou, was that with a decline in prices the ratio of money to *assets* would increase so that money's price in terms of assets—the interest rate—would fall. Called "the Pigou effect," this doctrine preserved the classical function of interest as a *theoretically* satisfactory device for bringing about the equality of savings and investment at full employment. Ironically, Pigou prefaced his counterattack on Keynes by admitting that a deflationary solution to the problem of unemployment was undesirable from a political standpoint.

The controversy over classical postulates was essentially qualitative. Keynes offered no empirical data to support his position; nor did his immediate critics. The controversy later stimulated many empirical investigations, but the outcome was a somewhat uneasy compromise: The defenders of the classical system believed that they had upheld its integrity; on the other hand, the Keynesians believed they had won the battle and established a rationale for government intervention in times of depression. No one, even the supporters of the classical view, had much stomach for a *laissez-faire* policy of price and wage deflation as a remedy for unemployment.

III

If traditional wage policies could not cure unemployment, if interest rates did not serve to bring savings and investment into balance at the level of full employment, what then determined the aggregate level of output, income, and employment within a market economy? Keynes answered this question with a theory of aggregate demand, his most important theoretical innovation.

He postulated an aggregate demand function relating entrepreneurs' expected receipts with employment of different quantities of labor and an aggregate supply function based on the relationship between the cost of producing output and the number of workers employed. Both functions had a positive slope, but the former began above the latter and rose more slowly. The point of intersection was the equilibrium level of employment; at that point entrepreneurial expectations of proceeds from sales of output from that employment equaled the cost of that output. The point of equilibrium did not have to be at full employment. Since the supply function (in the short run) was likely to remain the same, the crucial influence on the level of employment was the aggregate demand function.

The two major components of aggregate demand were consumption and investment.

The Propensity to Consume

Keynes defined the propensity to consume as the functional relationship between consumption and income. He pointed out that other factors influence consumption, but that the effect of income was the most significant and the relationship between the two was "fairly stable." The fundamental psychological law that governs the function, said Keynes, is that "men are disposed, as a rule and on the average, to increase their consumption as their income increases, but not by as much as the increase in their income." Thus if C is the amount of consumption and Y is income (both measured in wage-units), $\dfrac{dC}{dY}$ is "positive and less than unity." (p. 96)

The propensity to consume function was without doubt Keynes's most significant theoretical innovation, even though the basic idea was old, going back to Lauderdale, Hobson, and others. Keynes's statement of it was simple but its implications were revolutionary. It meant that as income increased, aggregate consumption would increase but by a lesser amount; thus what was "not spent" (i. e., "savings") increased also. But savings are not outlays; new investment is an outlay. If "employment and hence aggregate income increase, *not all* the additional employment will be required to satisfy the needs of additional consumption. . . . [T]he increased employment will prove unprofitable unless there is an increase in investment to fill the gap." (pp. 97–98) Keynes was discussing, of course, an economy operating at less than full employment.

Keynes's propensity to consume had other implications too. First, it implied that the consumer was not the rational calculator in command of his own destiny, as had traditionally been assumed. The concept of the individual consumer balancing his consumption of present goods against the purchase of future goods and taking into consideration the going interest rates might be adequate in isolated cases; but one could not add up the actions of individual households to find the aggregate effects of these actions on the economy as a whole. That was the logical fallacy of composition. The decisions to save were not made, usually, by those who made investment decisions. If those making investment decisions continue a given level of outlays, while households attempt to increase their savings (i.e., shift the consumption function downward), then total outlays (consumption and investment) will decline, the level of output will decrease, and at the lower output (and income) households will save *less,* not more as intended. What seemed rational turns out to be irrational.

Second, Keynes pointed to the importance of the distinction between the average propensity to consume, $\dfrac{C}{Y}$, and the marginal propensity to consume, $\frac{dC}{dY}$, the slope of the function. The latter had a special significance since it determined the value of the "multiplier." The multiplier, a concept adapted from Kahn, expressed the change in income that resulted from a change in investment. Income could increase by more than an increase in investment in a less-than-full-employment economy. At full employment, new investment would be possible only if consumption decreased: In Keynes's wage-unit terminology, real national income could not change at all. If some resources were unemployed, however, new investment would generate new income, because some of the investment funds would be spent and respent. (The exact amount would depend on the marginal propensity to consume.) Each round of spending adds to national income. The aggregate effect on the national income, per dollar of the original additional investment depends on the size of the multiplier, k, which is equal to $\frac{1}{1-C'}$, where C' is the marginal propensity to consume.[2]

Keynes was able to calculate the effects of investment on income because he assumed a period long enough for the effects to be worked out, although he did not specify its length. He was comparing the changes in investment and income between two points in time, each of which represented an equilibrium position. He was not concerned with the disequilibria that the movement from one period to another required. Since in an equilibrium state, income equaled investment plus consumption, investment also had to equal savings. For this reason, he abandoned the theory that savings could be larger or smaller than investment, the theory that Robertson, the Swedish economists, and even he in the *Treatise* had used. During disequilibria, the two could differ; in an equilibrium state they would always be the same.

This analytical framework allowed Keynes to estimate the exact size of the multiplier in a different way. With new investment, aggregate income must increase sufficiently to generate additional savings equal to the amount of the new investment. If the latter is 1 billion, then the national income must increase by an amount that will yield $1 billion in savings. If the marginal propensity to consume is 0.9, national income will rise by $10 billion; if it is 0.5, Y will rise only $2 billion. The dollar

---

[2] If $Y = C + I$, where I represents investment, differentiation in terms of Y gives $1 = C' + \frac{dI}{dY}$. With a slight alteration, the equation becomes $\frac{dY}{dI} = \frac{1}{1-C'}$, or k.

effect of new investment on the economic stability of the economy will be relatively greater where marginal propensities to consume are high than where they are low. Keynes pointed out, however, that the absolute effect on the economy will also depend on the size of the *average* propensity to consume. If that is high, then investment is by definition small relative to total income, and the impact of its variations (even when the k's are high) is small.

The Inducement to Invest

The other component of aggregate demand was new investment. To Keynes, this component was a source of greater "disturbance" to employment than consumption because it was more volatile.

The determinants of investment were the marginal efficiency of capital and the rate of interest. If the expected gains from a new investment were greater than the interest rate, or the cost of borrowing funds, then an investment would be made. If the expected gains were less, no investment would be made. We have already reviewed Keynes's theory of the interest rate; we come now to examine his concept of the marginal efficiency of capital. By this, he meant the relationship between the prospective yield of one more unit of a capital asset and its supply price. More precisely, it was that rate of discount that would make the present value of the anticipated returns from an asset equal to the cost of the asset. There are many assets, each with its own rate of discount; the greatest of these is society's marginal efficiency of capital.

The algebra of the concept presented no problem. If Q_1, Q_2, Q_3 . . . Q_n was the anticipated return from an asset at the end of 1, 2, 3 . . . n years respectively, the rate of discount r, that would make its present value equal to the cost of purchasing it, C, was

$$C = \frac{Q_1}{1 + r} + \frac{Q_2}{(1 + r)^2} + \frac{Q_3}{(1 + r)^3} + \ldots + \frac{Q_n}{(1 + r)^n}$$

The higher the expected Q's, the higher the marginal efficiency of capital, r. On the other hand, the higher the supply price of the asset, C, the lower the marginal efficiency of capital.

Keynes's concept of the marginal efficiency of capital differed from the concept of the marginal productivity of capital in terms of physical increments in two ways. The latter created, he believed, insoluble and unnecessary problems in converting physical input-output ratios into money values. These problems he said, arose from a failure to perceive the importance of expectations in investment decisions. It is not current output, but expected future yields, that governs. Such expectations are influenced by many factors, including anticipated changes in labor costs, new technology as it affects future sales, and changes in the value of money.

The prospective yields of investment, said Keynes, are based on knowledge that is usually "very slight and often negligible." In Chapter 12, "The State of Long-Term Expectation," he described the volatility of expectations, accentuated by waves of speculative activity. In stock markets, the major occupation is forecasting the psychology of the market, for it is the investor's state of mind that often affects the prospective yields of new capital. Keynes was critical of the system saying, "When the capital development of a country becomes a by-product of the activities of a casino, the job is likely to be ill-done." (p. 159) Nevertheless, although he recognized that "we should not conclude from this that everything depends on waves of irrational psychology," he saw that the marginal efficiency of capital could shift because of changes in investors' outlooks unexplained by "strict mathematical calculations." (pp. 162–163)

In sum, the "general theory" of the level of output and employment in the economy was that aggregate demand was determined by the propensity to consume, the expected rate of return of capital (its marginal efficiency), liquidity preference, and the quantity of money. The last two determined the rate of interest; the last three determined the amount of investment; and the first governed the size of the multiplier effect. These four independent variables determined the equilibrium position of the economy, which might or might not be a full-employment position. There was no inherent reason for the economy to shift from a less-than-full-employment level toward full employment. Market forces did not operate that way. Unemployment would not lead automatically to low enough wages to restore full employment, and the rate of interest would not automatically fall far enough to stimulate investment if the latter were insufficient. Thus the traditional "Law" of J. B. Say did not hold. Nor was there any assurance that the monetary authorities, by increasing the amount of money, could restore full employment, since liquidity preferences could prevent the necessary fall in interest rates.

Keynes rooted the first three of his determining variables in psychological propensities. The consumption function was based on the psychological propensity to consume, the marginal efficiency of capital on expectations, liquidity preferences on psychological attitudes toward holding cash and the future. If all men behaved rationally all the time, had perfect knowledge and perfect foresight, the Keynesian theory of underemployment equilibria would be untenable. But Keynes was concerned with the real world, not an ideal one. Above all, he emphasized the effect of uncertainty. Expectations about the future affected the marginal efficiency of capital and liquidity preferences, and hence output. Although Keynes analyzed equilibrium positions that were necessarily *ex post* in Swedish terminology, his stress on expectations revealed an awareness of uncertainty similar to the Swedish concept of *ex ante* as applied to savings and investment plans.

Critics recognized that Keynes's theory of income determination broke with tradition, at least in its treatment of short-run forces. With regard to the consumption and savings functions particularly, Keynes had radically changed the scope of the analysis. His consumption function was a behaviorial function that could be investigated empirically; it reflected the actual decisions made by individual spending units; whether individuals rationally calculated the marginal utility of their choices in the last analysis was irrelevant. In fact, one could not assume that rational decisions by individuals, about saving, for example, would have a desired effect. Everyone trying to save more might result in less savings for all.

The virtue of a concept that could be tested empirically and hence scientifically, however, was not developed by Keynes at all. He used statistics only sparingly in his *General Theory*. As his controversy with Tinbergen revealed, he was dubious about the use of multiple correlation techniques even in getting at the heart of business-cycle problems. One could hardly deny that Keynes was knowledgeable about the statistics of the world of finance and business; yet he thought more in terms of the shifting psychological propensities to invest and to hold liquid assets. Critics found Keynes's formulation of the consumption function useful but ignored many of its implications. Was consumption a function of today's income, or of yesterday's? Empirical testing of actual relationships could help answer such questions, and it was in this direction that the Keynesians quickly moved.

IV

Keynes's new theory of income and employment led him to reexamine the trade cycle, problems of economic growth, and the role of the state. He did not claim to have a complete theory of business fluctuations, but he argued that his theory of employment, if correct, should be able to explain the business cycle. The key, he believed, was the fluctuations in the marginal efficiency of capital, although every element in the employment theory had a role. Booms were the result of the multiplier effects of a "favorable marginal efficiency of capital [and] a lowering of liquidity, both resulting from optimistic expectations." But as the boom continued, eventually there would be a shift in expectations because of changes in both the expected returns from capital and the interest rate. The marginal efficiency of capital would fall as the stock of capital goods grew (undermining expectations of future profit) and as the supply price of new capital goods rose. At the same time, the interest rate would tend to rise because of increasing demands for money for transactions. The rise in interest rates, however, was less important than the downward pressure on the marginal efficiency of capital. These forces gradually undermined investment prospects, and at some point there was a "collapse" in the marginal efficiency of capital—a psychological shift in expectations—that set off a business crisis and brought on a depression. The bubble of overoptimism burst as investors realized that the future was not so rosy after all.

A slump, when it comes, tends to be "intractable" because of (a) a new wave of pessimism about future profits and (b) a shift in liquidity preferences. It is the latter that prevents the interest rate from falling far enough to stimulate the investment necessary to restore a full-employment equilibrium. Moreover, the propensity to consume may also shift downward during the slump, further aggravating the problem of recovery.

The only offsetting factor that Keynes recognized was what has been already discussed as "the Keynes effect," namely that as the amount of money used for transactions (and precautionary purposes) was reduced, more money was available for speculative holdings and could satisfy, in part at least, the public's desire for liquidity. But this was "the only element of self-righting in the system" and it arose at a much later stage and in an "uncertain degree."

These ideas gave Keynes an opportunity to reflect on the nature of economic growth. In his section on mercantilism, he said the "early pioneers of economic thinking" of the sixteenth and seventeenth centuries advanced such practical precepts as "keeping down the rate of interest, . . . maintaining the domestic stock of money and . . . discouraging rises in the wage-unit; and in their readiness in the last resort to restore the stock of money by devaluation." (p. 340) Their interest in protectionism and the balance of trade was legitimate in view of the problems of a nation in the early stages of growth and development, although Keynes pointed out that such avowedly nationalistic policies would not be likely to benefit the rest of the world. A large supply of money kept down the rate of interest, control of the labor supply prevented rises in the wage-unit that harmed trade balances, and protectionism stimulated both investments and money inflows, saturating demands for liquidity. (India, Keynes noted, was an example of a country so obsessed with a preference for liquidity that even an enormous influx of specie could not bring down the rate of interest enough to stimulate economic growth.)

In the nineteenth century, Great Britain entered into "the exuberance of the greatest age of the inducement to investment," and in a century built up its capital from primitive tools into a vast stock of capital equipment. This was possible, in part, because liquidity preferences (and hence the interest rate) were low due to the great discoveries of gold. But with economic growth came another problem. Britain and the other advanced nations found that the wealthier they became the lower their propensity to consume became, the more savings were generated by full employment, and the more difficult it was to invest productively. It was not that excessive savings led to excessive investment, as Hobson had said; rather a "relatively weak propensity to consume help[ed] to cause unemployment by requiring and *not* receiving the accompaniment of a compensating volume of new investment . . . ." (p. 370) The abstinence of the rich, he said, was more likely to impede than promote the growth of wealth; the inequalities of wealth and income, to the extent that they promoted higher rates of savings, aggravated the problem.

Stagnation was likely as the supply of capital assets was gradually built up. Ricardo had said that economic development would lead to the stationary state and full employment. Keynes admitted that with the growth of capital goods the marginal efficiency of capital would approach zero. But if the monetary system prevented the interest rate from falling low enough, he anticipated not full employment, but a rise in unemployment as income dropped to that "miserable" level at which savings were zero. And if the economy does not automatically move toward a full-employment equilibrium, it becomes imperative for the government to intervene to bring about full utilization of the nation's resources. The grounds for a policy of *laissez-faire* no longer exist.

Keynes did not develop systematically the economics of state inter-

vention through public investment. When there was involuntary unemployment in the short run, government "loan expenditures" would
"enrich the community on balance." (p. 128–129) By such expenditures, Keynes meant both public investment financed by borrowing from
individuals and "any other current public expenditure which is so financed." He believed it would be sensible "to build houses and the
like" but had little faith that the cultivated myths of the past which
claimed that government spending was downright immoral would permit
it. He reserved his greatest sarcasm for that view. "If the education of
our statesmen on the principles of the classical economics stands in the
way of anything better," then let them engage in wasteful activities, as
these will have a multiplier effect upon the national level of income and
employment in any case. (p. 129) As examples of such activities he offered pyramid-building, wars, "digging holes in the ground," gold mining
(a respected form of hole-digging), etc. However, he believed that once
the theory of effective demand was understood, a "sensible community"
would no longer be content to depend on wasteful and fortuitious outlays. In any case, he believed that "the duty of ordering the current
volume of investment [could not] safely be left in private hands." (p.
320)

In the long run, Keynes believed that as the problems of Great
Britain and the United States were those of mature economies in which
too much saving tended to be endemic they could be resolved only by
public investment. But Keynes also expressed the hope that the problems of maturity could be permanently eliminated if the economy were
so saturated with capital goods that its marginal efficiency approached
zero. Like Mill, he considered the stationary state and zero profits not
too far distant. With the end of the scarcity of capital would come the
disappearance of the economic basis of the *rentier,* whose existence
should be considered "transitional," a phase in the development of
capitalism. The "euthanasia of the rentier, of the functionless investor,
will be nothing sudden . . . and will need no revolution." (p. 376)
The entrepreneur would remain (although Keynes believed that his remuneration could safely be reduced); his skills would still be vital to
economic progress.

Keynes was not specific about how governments should go about
assuring the necessary high level of investment in the long run. As a
general rule, he hoped that they would interfere as little as possible with
private actions. Given full employment, then there can be no objection,
he said, to "the classical analysis of the manner in which private self-

interest will determine what in particular is produced, in what proportions the factors of production will be combined to produce it, and how the value of the final product will be distributed between them." (pp. 378–379)

Keynes's incomplete views on the trade cycle, growth, and government intervention were not testable hypotheses, but they were provocative. The spectacular development of models of business-cycle behavior and of economic growth owes much to the stimulus of his ideas. But the later models quickly achieved a far greater sophistication. Following Keynes, economists began to analyze in detail the effects of government outlays and taxes. The analysis turned technical, and the philosophical issues, although debated in political arenas, tended to fade into the background of the more empirical investigations. The reason, of course, was not that the role of the government was unimportant; rather the government intervention that Keynes had sought had become a fact.

Notes to Chapter ix

The Collected Writings of John Maynard Keynes (New York, St. Martin's Press) is currently being published. Three of the twenty-four volumes now planned appeared in 1971; vol. I, *Indian Currency and Finance* (1913); vol. XV, *Activities and Associated Writings: India and Cambridge* (1906–14); and vol. XVI, *Activities and Associated Writings: The Treasury and Versailles* (1914–19).

In addition to *Indian Currency and Finance,* Keynes's major works include *Economic Consequences of the Peace* (1920), *A Treatise on Probability* (1921), *A Revision of the Treaty* (1922), *A Tract on Monetary Reform* (1923), *A Treatise on Money,* 2 vols. (1930), and *The General Theory of Employment, Interest, and Money* (1936). All were first published by Macmillan, London.

His shorter works include *The Economic Consequences of Mr. Churchill* (1925), *The End of Laissez-Faire* (1925), *The Means to Prosperity* (1933), and *How To Pay for the War* (1940). There are two collections of his essays: *Essays in Persuasion* (1931) and *Essays in Biography* (1933). Two autobiographical papers dealing with his early career appeared posthumously as *Two Memoirs* (New York, Kelley, 1949).

The page references in the text are to John Maynard Keynes, *The General Theory of Employment, Interest, and Money* (New York, Harcourt, Brace, 1936).

I

The best full-length biography of Keynes is R. F. Harrod's *The Life of John Maynard Keynes* (London, Macmillan, 1951). Also see E. A. G. Robinson's lengthy obituary, "John Maynard Keynes, 1883–1946," in the *Economic Journal* (1947), reprinted in Robert Lekachman, *Keynes' General Theory: Reports of Three Decades* (New York, St. Martin's, 1964), pp. 13–86. For a more recent study of Keynes's life see Robert Lekachman, *The Age of Keynes* (New York, Random House, 1966), chs. 1–7. G. L. S. Shackle in his *The Years of High Theory: Invention and Tradition in Economic Thought, 1926–1939* (Cambridge, University Press, 1967) gives an excellent account of the development of Keynes's *General Theory*.

The quotations in the text from Keynes's writing in *The Nation* are from Harrod, *op. cit.,* pp. 338 and 348. The quotations from *A Tract on Monetary Reform* (London, Macmillan, 1924) are from pp. 40 and 172. For Keynes's statement on *laissez-faire*, see his *The End of Laissez-Faire* (London, Leonard & Virginia Woolf, 1926), pp. 48–49. The quotation from his *A Treatise on Money* (London, Macmillan, 1960) is from vol. II, pp. 148–149.

II

For a cross-section of pro and con reactions to Keynes's criticisms of orthodox economics from prominent economists, see Seymour E. Harris, ed., *The New Economics* (New York, Knopf, 1947); Henry Hazlitt, ed., *The Critics of Keynesian Economics* (Toronto, Van Nostrand, 1960); Robert Lekachman, ed., *Keynes' General Theory* (op. cit.); Robert Lekachman, ed., *Keynes and the Classics* (Boston, Heath, 1964); and Kenneth Kurihari, *Post-Keynesian Economics* (New Brunswick, N. J., Rutgers University Press, 1954).

The fact is that Keynes did not stray far from neoclassicism. He accepted the neoclassical assumption that the demand curve for labor reflected diminishing marginal productivity—even in periods of unused plant capacity—so that more labor could be hired only if real wages fell. He also assumed the prevalence of competition.

Keynes had no sympathy for (nor understanding of) Marx and socialism. He thought Marx both obsolete and a bore. In a 1935 letter to George Bernard Shaw, who was a prominent Fabian socialist as well as a dramatist, Keynes wrote about about Marx and Engels: "But if you tell me that they discovered a clue to the economic riddle, still I am beaten —I can discover nothing but out-of-date controversialising." (Quoted in Harrod, *op. cit.,* p. 462.) He went on to claim that in his forthcoming book (*The General Theory*), "the Ricardian foundations of Marxism will be knocked away." (*ibid.*)

III

The best straightforward expositions of Keynes's ideas are Dudley Dillard's *The Economics of John Maynard Keynes: The Theory of a Monetary Economy* (New York, Prentice-Hall, 1948) and Alvin H. Hansen's *A Guide to Keynes* (New York, McGraw-Hill, 1953). For three analyses of his economics, each from a different viewpoint, see Lawrence R. Klein's *The Keynesian Revolution* (New York, Macmillan, 1947); David McCord Wright, *The Keynesian System* (New York, Fordham University Press, 1961); and Axel Leijonhufrud, *On Keynesian Economics and the Economics of Keynes: A Study in Monetary The-*

ory (New York, Oxford University Press, 1968).

Keynes considered his greatest achievement to be the formulation of the theory of effective demand. To him, this theory had its roots in the Malthus-Ricardo controversy, but Malthus lost the contest. The "great puzzle of Effective Demand . . . vanished from economic literature. . . . It could only live furtively, below the surface, in the underworlds of Karl Marx, Silvio Gesell or Major Douglas." (*General Theory,* p. 32) (Gesell was a little-known advocate of free land and cheap money; Major Douglas was a monetary reformer whose schemes for monetary expansion rested on a diagnosis of depressions Keynes himself admitted was a "mystification.") Keynes also added Bernard de Mandeville and John A. Hobson (1858–1940), a British "economic heretic," to his list of writers whose hearts had been in the right place with respect to understanding the truth about underconsumptionism, even though their analyses were deficient.

Keynes's puckish attitude toward his predecessors reflected a strange ignorance of the history of non-British economic thought. He did not seem to be aware of many writers who had seriously investigated fluctuations in aggregate demand, including many business-cycle theorists. He made no mention of Thorstein Veblen, the American economist whose *The Theory of Business Enterprise* (1904) emphasized the role of investment in short-run fluctuations of income, the importance of expectations, and even the possibility of economic stagnation.

An even more fundamental gap in Keynes's knowledge concerned the pioneering work of contemporaries such as Gunnar Myrdal, Ragnar Frisch, and Michal Kalecki. Myrdal's *Monetary Equilibrium,* which laid the basis for modern Swedish theories of national-income determination, however, appeared in Swedish in 1931, in German in 1933, but not in English until 1939. Frisch, a Norwegian economist who later shared the first Nobel Prize in economics with Jan Tinbergen, distinguished between static and dynamic analysis and was the first to employ the terms "micro" and "macro." "Macro-dynamic" analysis, as he termed it, "tries to give an account of the fluctuations of the whole economic system taken in its entirety." See his seminal article, "Propagation Problems and Impulse Problems in Dynamic Economics" (1933), reprinted in the American Economic Association's *Readings in Business Cycles* (Homewood, Ill., Irwin, 1965), pp. 155–156. Frisch employed quantititative methods and was the first editor of *Econometrica,* which began its existence in January 1933.

Independently of both Myrdal and Keynes, Kalecki, a young Polish economist who had been influenced by Frisch, constructed an econometric model of aggregate income determination in 1933. The English version, "A Macro Dynamic Theory of Business Cycles," was published in *Econometrica* in 1935. Kalecki developed functional relationships for national income, investment, and capital stock.

Although Keynesian economics later became identified with quantitative, econometric models, Keynes himself had little relish for empirical investigations, as his criticisms of Jan Tinbergen's work revealed. Tinbergen, who along with Frisch received the first Nobel Prize in economics, is a Dutch economist who also pioneered in developing various econometric models. He was one of the first to develop the dynamic-cobweb theory of price. In 1937, he constructed an econometric model of the Netherlands' economy, and in 1939 he published two volumes under the auspices of the League of Nations, *Statistical Testing of Business Cycle Theories* and *Business Cycles in the United States of America, 1919–1932.* In a lengthy review in *The Economic Journal,* vol. XLIX (September 1939), pp. 558–568, of the first of these two volumes, Keynes catalogued his complaints against statistical models. After beginning by admitting that instead of preferring the "mazes of arithmetic to the mazes of logic" his tastes were "the other way round," Keynes argued that statistical analysis rests on assumptions open to serious dispute. How, he asked, can the statistician know for certain that he has included all the relevant variables, that such variables are necessarily quantifiable, that they are truly independent of each other, that correlations are linear, and that the beginning and ending dates of time series are not arbitrary? More important, Keynes went on, the assumption that analyses of lengthy periods of time can yield statistically significant relationships requires that the "environment in all relevant respects, other than the fluctuations in those factors of which we take particular account, . . . be uniform and homogeneous . . . ." (p. 566) To Keynes, "uniformity in the environment" over time was not obvious.

The fact that the Keynesian rev-

olution that was to follow flourished on econometric models à la Tinbergen, despite Keynes's aversion to them, is understandable. The subsequent development of national-income accounting and statistics and the introduction of high-speed computers, and the sheer necessity of finding ways to handle and interpret the flow of statistical information so vital to the formulation and administration of governmental policies for full employment made such models essential. But Keynes's historical role was not to provide those details; rather his *General Theory* helped to create the intellectual climate in which such tools would be not only developed but used.

IV

The extent of Keynes's influence on government policies to secure full employment will undoubtedly be debated endlessly. There is no question that Keynes revolutionized economics and that his name was associated with many of the full-employment policies governments initiated during and after World War II. He himself was thoroughly convinced of the power of ideas, including his own. In an often-quoted passage in *The General Theory* (p. 383), he wrote:

the ideas of economists and political philosophers, both when they are right and when they are wrong, are more powerful than is commonly understood. Indeed the world is ruled by little else. Practical men, who believe themselves to be quite exempt from any intellectual influences, are usually the slaves of some defunct economist.

On the other hand, the depression

of the 1930s was brought to an end not by Keynes or his followers, but by World War II. When government policies are devised that promote employment the question always remains whether economic advisers controlled the formulation and implementation of those policies or whether other political influences happened to have similar effects. An economist a century earlier took a view contrary to Keynes's. Augustin Cournot, in *The Mathematical Principles of the Theory of Wealth* (1838) (Homewood, Ill., Irwin, re-printed 1963), pp. 144–145 said:

it must be recognized that such questions as that of commercial liberty are not settled either by the arguments of scientific men or even by the wisdom of statesmen. . . . Up to a certain point it is possible to compare the influence of economic theories on society to that of grammarians on language. Languages are formed without the consent of grammarians, and are corrupted in spite of them; but their works throw light on the laws of the formation and decadence of languages . . . .

Chapter x

THE POLITICAL NATURE
OF ECONOMIC WELFARE:

From Walras to Pareto

> From the viewpoint of pure science, all that we needed to do, and all that we actually have done . . . was to treat free competition as a datum, or rather as an hypothesis. . . . It was in this light that we studied the nature, causes and consequences of free competition. We now know that these consequences may be summed up as the attainment, within certain limits, of maximum utility.
>
> Léon Walras, *Elements of Pure Economics*

> How can one compare agreeable sensations, or painful ones, and add them?
>
> Vilfredo Pareto, *Manuel d'économie politique*

> In summation, pure economics gives us no truly decisive criterion to choose between a society based upon private property and a socialist form of organization.
>
> *ibid.*

Although Keynesian economics overshadowed all else in the period from just before to immediately after World War II, another revolution in economics was unobtrusively occurring with many implications for the relevance of economics to the modern world. This was the introduction of theories that stemmed from the works of Léon Walras and Vilfredo Pareto, economists who had written before World War I at the University of Lausanne in Switzerland. In terms of the general-equilibrium-theory analysis of price determination, Pareto was a follower of

Walras, his predecessor at Lausanne, who had also been one of the first to develop theories of marginal utility. But Pareto did not accept Walras's theories of utility and economic welfare. And in these areas, it was Pareto's views that became influential.

General equilibrium theory expressed the interdependence of economic variables in formal equations, eliminating many of the troublesome features of Marshall's partial-equilibrium analysis. Unlike Marshall, both Walras and Pareto were unconcerned with the process by which changes occurred in the chain of connected markets over time. They were concerned with the final equilibrium effects and considered the adjustment process of less interest. On the one hand, this made their analysis less realistic than Marshall's; but on the other hand, it concentrated attention on the final results.

Although Walras had been one of the first to express the marginal-utility theory, Pareto minimized its importance and argued in favor of a concept of choice based on the indifference-curve technique of F. Y. Edgeworth, the British economist. However he disagreed with Edgeworth's cardinal utility theory that the value of goods to individuals, in terms of utility, could be measured, added, or compared. He called the standards of valuation laid down by Bentham and his utilitarians, Marshall, and even Walras, metaphysical.

Pareto's logic led him to deny that a market economy based on private property led to maximum utility. This was Walras's favorite theme, but to Pareto such a proposition could not be proved. All that economists as economists could support was a criterion of efficiency, and according to Pareto there was no reason why a socialist economy could not achieve as efficient an allocation of resources as a capitalist one. Although this conclusion was unexpected, since Pareto himself denounced socialist arguments, his point was simply that welfare could no longer be used as grounds for judging the desirability of a particular social system, of a given distribution of income, or of a precise form of political organization. To do so was unscientific. Pareto became an exponent of the doctrine that economics as a science should be, and could be, free of all welfare judgments (except efficiency).

The views of Walras and Pareto did not make much headway in the English-speaking world at first, in part because of the prestige and relevance of Marshallian economics and in part because their mathematics was unappealing to "the literary economists" as Pareto called them. But in the post-World-War-I period, as it became apparent that new types of economies were coming into being—communist, fascist, and welfare-statist—all characterized by an increasing economic role for government, older models of a competitive economy began to seem out of date. In the underdeveloped and the developed areas of the world, the economic effect of governmental actions went beyond the stabilization of business fluctuations in the Keynesian sense. Questions arose about the direct and indirect impact of governmental actions on resource allocation. How could governmental efficiency be tested without the profit-and-loss statements of a market economy? What were the indirect effects of government decisions on the private sector? And as always, what was their effect on social welfare? How, in the final analysis, were government actions to be judged?

In the theories of Walras and Pareto some economists began to find a basis for examining these questions in a new way. They found in them a more comprehensive view of the economy as a whole. In Pareto they discovered a way of appraising resource allocations without an actual price system, through traditional markets.

I

Marie-Esprit Léon Walras (1834–1910) independently discovered the concept of marginal utility—he called it *rareté*—and founded the general equilibrium approach to economics. His major work, *Elements of Pure Economics,* appeared in two parts, in 1874 and 1877. It presented his ideas in the mathematical form he deemed essential to scientific economics. Although the book had no immediate impact because of its concern with the formal aspects of pure theory and because of its mathematics (which most of his contemporaries found forbidding), its influence gradually began to be felt, first among a few leading theorists of the day. As the significance of his views of the inherent unity of the economy as a whole gradually became understood, the book became recognized as a major event in the history of economic theory. The first English translation appeared in 1954.

Walras's early record as a student was inauspicious: He failed his entrance examinations to the École Polytechnique twice, did not complete his studies at the École des Mines, and tried his hand at a variety of business ventures and at writing novels. He eventually settled down to prepare a paper on tax reform for a competition sponsored by the International Tax Congress at Lausanne in 1860. Although Proudhon, the French socialist, won first prize, Walras's paper was adjudged fourth best and used as evidence to support his appointment in 1870 to the chair of political economy at the Faculty of Law of the Academy of Lausanne. Although Walras was born in France and always considered himself a French citizen, he spent most of his adult life in Lausanne.

Walras's training in economics came from his father, Antoine Auguste Walras, a professor of philosophy and an economist. Walras claimed that he owed the fundamental principles on which his own economic doctrines were based to his father. The importance of scarcity and utility in the determination of price had been basic to his father's major economic work, *On the Nature of Wealth and the Origin of Value,* published in 1831. *Rareté* was his father's term, although it was Walras who used it to describe marginal utility, or the extra satisfaction attributable to an additional unit of a stock of goods. Although Walras was not aware of the works of Gossen, Jevons, or Menger when he completed his manuscript in 1874, he did know the works of Cournot. Cournot's mathematical demand and supply functions, in fact, helped open the way for Walras's development of mathematical economics.

Walras was a believer in the competitive economy. Competition, he argued, would maximize utility, although state intervention was necessary to control monopoly, to stop abuses of the competitive mechanism for private advantage, and to enforce standards of performance in certain areas of private industry. Developing these ideas in two other books, *Studies in Social Economics* (1896) and *Studies in Applied Economics* (1898), Walras advocated such proposals as nationalization of land, regulation of public utilities, control of advertising, and labor legislation. Land nationalization was the most important plank in his reform platform. If lands were purchased by the state, Walras believed, rents could be used to finance governmental expenditures and taxation could be abolished. Rising land values would enable the state eventually to pay off the cost of the original purchases. Walras's reform program was in the tradition not of socialism, as some of his critics complained, but of English reformers such as John Stuart Mill and Gossen. He wanted to strengthen the competitive system by preventing private control of a resource that he believed belonged to all the people and by eliminating private windfalls from rising land values caused by population growth.

These issues were related to what Walras called the art of economics (the application of economic principles to real-world problems) and to ethics (what ought to be in terms of justice). Pure economic theory, on the other hand (the study of which should precede both art and ethics), was concerned with the universal relationships that governed "social wealth"—all things, material or immaterial, that were both scarce and useful. It was, he said, "a science that resembles the physico-mathematical sciences in every respect." (p. 71) It used the mathematical method but in a rational, not an empirical, sense. That is, it dealt with abstract, ideal concepts, and not with real life, although the ideals were drawn from reality. Once the theories of pure economics were perfected, and only then, said Walras, could they be applied to reality.

Walras's method for the study of economics nonetheless reflected his ideas as to what aspects of economic behavior were significant. To him, what was important about the competitive system, viewed as a whole, was first, that it maximized satisfaction through a system of exchange and production; second, that it was, in theory, a logical, internally consistent system; and third, that despite the abstractness of the proof of its internal consistency that proof was relevant to the real world. In his pure theory Walras did not attempt to explain real-world problems:

> what we have in mind throughout this volume is not to pose and solve the problem in question as if it were a real problem in a given concrete situation, but solely to formulate scientifically the nature of the problem which actually arises in the market where it is solved empirically. (p. 157)

In demonstrating that competition promoted maximum satisfaction, Walras relied on marginal utility, which he called *rareté,* namely, the "intensity of the last want satisfied by any given quantity consumed of a commodity." (p. 119) Mathematically, he defined the marginal-utility curve as a downward-sloping function of the quantity of the good consumed or possessed. Given initial stocks of goods in the hands of various owners, exchanges would take place as individuals traded some of their supplies for other goods whose marginal utilities (to them) were higher. Satisfaction would be maximized for each trader, said Walras, when the ratios of the *raretés* were equal to price ratios, that is, when the marginal utilities of the stocks of goods held by each consumer (after the exchanges) were proportionate to their prices. At that point an individual would no longer be able to improve his position through trading.

Walras was not wholly clear about this interpretation of utility. He recognized that the concept was "elusive," but said: "I shall . . . assume the existence of a standard measure of intensity of wants or intensive utility, which is applicable not only to similar units of the same kind of wealth but also to different units of various kinds of wealth."

(p. 117) In a market where full competition reigned and equilibrium prices were arrived at, "all holders of one, several or all of the commodities exchanged can obtain the greatest possible satisfaction. . . ." (p. 173) Although Walras did not explicitly say in the *Elements* that the utilities of different individuals could be added to form a social maximum, he assumed as much in most instances. He explicitly indicated (for example, in Lesson 22) that he had given a priori proof of the desirability of *laissez-faire* principles, but only within certain limits. Because he had proven the desirability of free competition to satisfy private wants, he said, it should be clear that he had *not* proven the desirability of competition in "the production of things where public interest is involved," in the case of monopolies, and where matters of justice are involved. In the latter case:

> Though our description of free competition emphasizes the problem of utility, it leaves the question of justice entirely to one side, since our sole object has been to show how a certain distribution of services gives rise to a certain distribution of products. The question of the [original] distribution of services remains open, however. And yet, are there not economists who, not content with exaggerating the applicability of *laisser-faire, laisser-passer* to industry, even extend it to the completely extraneous question of property? p. 257)

His theory of the interdependence of economic phenomena in the competitive economy is considered Walras's greatest achievement. His system of equations defined the theoretical conditions for the equilibrium of the economy as a whole. This was not an equilibrium of aggregates, but rather of each element in the system: Each individual buyer of goods and supplier of resources, and each individual firm, when in equilibrium, would have no incentive to change his pattern of buying and selling because he would be making the best possible use of the resources he had in accordance with his particular tastes.

Walras's model included the demands of individual for goods in product markets and the supplies of productive agents available in factor (services) markets. In addition, he assumed that entrepreneurs knew the technical coefficients of production—namely, the specific combinations of factors required to produce final goods. At the beginning of the period he assumed the existence of a supply of consumption goods. What he sought to explain was the prices and quantities of goods produced during the productive process and the prices and quantities of factor services used in production.

In demonstrating the second point that the competitive system was a logical one, Walras made a number of simplifying assumptions. First, he designated one commodity as a common unit of account in which prices could be stated. This was the *numéraire*. Second, he assumed competition throughout the economy. This implied perfect knowledge of (and hence no uncertainty about) the market on the part of buyers and sellers and perfectly mobile factors of production. It also required that entrepreneurs (i.e., those who brought factors of production together in order to produce final goods) be sufficiently numerous so that no one of them could influence price; final prices would then equal costs, and profits in the sense of a recompense to the entrepreneur as such would be zero. (As an individual, however, he could sell or rent whatever productive services he had.) Third, Walras assumed a static, no-growth economy. Not only were the supplies of land and labor fixed, but capital goods as well. This required, of course, that savings be zero. Hence when the economy was in equilibrium, each individual would spend exactly as much on consumption goods as he received in the factor markets for his productive services.

Having set these conditions, Walras sought to develop a mathematical representation of the competitive system—a system of equations whose simultaneous solution would yield a set of prices that would clear the markets for both products and services. In it he included demand functions, cost functions that related inputs of factor services to output, and factor-supply functions, as well as the functions that equated the quantities of each good and each factor demanded with the amounts supplied. Walras's system met the formal requirements of equilibrium because the number of equations equaled the number of unknowns; hence it was logical and internally consistent.

But the third problem remained: Was his system of equations relevant to the real world? Could the market process of competition, theoretically at least, yield a set of prices that met the requirements of general equilibrium? These requirements were twofold: The price in any particular market had to be consistent with the equilibrium prices existing in all other markets at the same time; and no transactions could take place at any price other than the final equilibrium one. In short, all equilibrium prices had to be established, and all transactions had to occur, at one and the same time. If equilibrium prices were not established simultaneously, and if actual transactions were made prior to the final adjustment, then the prices arrived at would not be those mathematically predicted.

Walras's answer was yes, competition could yield such prices, by a process of groping ("par tâtonnement"). In the case of the exchange of goods, he said (forgetting about production for the moment), assume each individual has given stocks of different commodities which he is willing to trade to others to increase his own satisfaction. The process by which a general equilibrium of prices is achieved is similar to an auction in which a price is "cried out" at random to start the bidding, but in which no final exchanges take place until supply and demand forces have produced an equilibrium within that market *and in all other markets.* As the bidding proceeded in one market, each new price would lead both buyers and sellers to alter their purchases and sales in other markets. No transactions would be final until this process of "groping" had produced equilibrium values in all commodity markets.

Extending his example to include the production of goods and the factor-service markets, Walras introduced the idea of tickets (*"bons"*), which were tentative purchase agreements made through the auctioning process in each market. Since production transformed factors services into final goods, it could not take place until the final matching, through trial and error, of the demand and supply (at zero profits per entrepreneur) of every good and factor service. When the tickets in the hands of entrepreneurs indicated that all markets would be cleared, production would take place. Furthermore, the whole auctioning process had to take place "within a given time period during which no change in the data is allowed"; that is, no changes in tastes, production functions, and so on could occur. (p. 242)

The mechanics of "groping," no matter how cumbersome, Walras believed, demonstrated that general equilibrium could be achieved through competition, at least in the *pro forma* sense. He was under no illusions that the real world operated in this manner.

There were several important criticisms of Walras's general equilibrium theory. One was that, in the case of exchanges of goods only, the final prices and level of maximum satisfaction depended on the stocks of goods initially held; in the system as a whole (including production), they depended on the distribution of factors. If the initial distribution of stocks was different, or changes occurred in the ownership of nonlabor factors, would not the system of equations yield other answers? Walras was not only aware of this, but turned the argument around. Ownership of property, he said, raises the issue of justice. "The question of the [original] distribution of services remains open." (p. 257)

And he went on to argue that it was one of the failures of the *laissez-faire,* literary economists not to see that a sytem of competition offered no proof at all that the existing property structure was the best in terms of maximum satisfaction.

A second criticism was that there could be several solutions to the system of equations, rather than just one. Walras appears to have admitted this possibility. If this were true then it would be logical to conclude, along with Wicksell, who first raised the issue, that *all* the multiple-equilibria solutions could not represent positions of maximum satisfaction.

A third criticism of Walrasian theory disputed the conclusion that the process of groping would have no influence on the final equilibrium. As various prices were "cried out," would it not follow that stocks of goods and factor resources would be valued and revalued as market prices changed? In short, the values of the initial stocks of goods and resources were not "fixed," but were themselves unknown, changing as prices changed during the adjustment process.

The net effect of these criticisms was to strengthen doubts concerning the validity of the doctrine of maximum satisfaction under competition. It was Pareto who brought the issue to a head, from quite another direction.

II

Vilfredo Pareto (1848–1923) became a professor of political economy at Lausanne in 1893, taking the place of Walras, who retired to devote all his time to research. Pareto's political views were in sharp contrast to Walras's, and as time went on it became apparent that Pareto's economics was so substantially different from Walras's as to make any designation of a Lausanne school of economics that included both misleading. Both, however, accepted the general equilibrium theory, and Pareto always honored Walras for his contributions to it. When the latter died in 1910, Pareto wrote: "Walras' name will endure in science, and his reputation will continuously grow." Walras had originally recommended Pareto's appointment at Lausanne precisely because he found Pareto to have exceptional mathematical ability and a firm understanding of general equilibrium theory. But soon thereafter the relationship between the two men became strained, and there is no record of any communication between them in the last eight or so years of Walras's life. On many matters Pareto had come to dislike the position of Walras. For example, he disputed Walras's utility theory of demand and of value. Pareto's social philosophy was the opposite of Walras's. Whereas Walras was a social reformer, concerned with justice, Pareto was an aristocrat who saw humanitarianism and social idealism as a sign of decadence destructive of the will of the elite to rule. Moreover, whereas Walras had had difficulty in getting his ideas accepted, Pareto had a school of supporters, mostly in Italy, who emphasized his, not Walras's, position.

Pareto was born in Paris, where his father, an Italian *marchese*, was in exile, having been a supporter of the Mazzini movement for Italian national unity. After a general amnesty in 1858, the family returned to Italy. Pareto was educated as an engineer at the Polytechnical School of the University of Turin, where he received a thorough grounding in mathematics and physics. He next entered business (railroads and iron and steel) and acquired a thorough knowledge of industrial-management problems before retiring in 1882 at the age of 34. (Later, an inheritance contributed to his relative affluence.) Although he began to pursue studies in philosophy and history, he soon turned to economics and politics. After a chance meeting with Maffeo Pantaleoni, a leading economist of the time, he recognized the power of Walras's analysis and later corresponded with him. Following his appointment at Lausanne, Pareto lectured at first on pure and applied economics and to some extent in the field of sociology. Later he turned exclusively to sociology. He resigned his professorship in 1909 after a number of years of poor health and spent the remainder of his life at his villa near Céligny on Lake Geneva.

The first of Pareto's major works was the *Cours d'économie politique,* published at Lausanne in two volumes, in 1896 and 1897. In it he presented the general equilibrium theory, modifying Walras only in minor details. He substituted the concept of *ophélimité* (or desiredness) for Walras's *rareté,* thereby weakening somewhat the "utility" aspect of the Walrasian system. In 1906, he published *Manuale d'economia politica* (translated into French in 1909), in which he discarded the Walrasian theory of value and shifted to the indifference-curve technique of Edgeworth and Fisher, but without the cardinal-utility connotations. He developed further his own views of the pricing of factors of production. Although still a general equilibrium theory, Pareto's *Manuale* was essentially a new system of economic analysis. Devoid of a value theory, it claimed ethical neutrality in the interest of scientific validity.

Although Pareto's economics was in the realm of pure theory, he nonetheless had a consuming interest in economic and political policy. It was these interests that led him to turn to sociology for a unifying theory of society. His *Trattato di sociologica generale,* published in 1916 (translated into English in 1935 as *The Mind and Society*), attracted worldwide attention, even before his economics. In it he included not only the logic of economic behavior but also an analysis of nonlogical human actions, which he considered in some ways even more significant for understanding society than the slice of reality studied by economics. He also elaborated his theory of the elite. In his sociological works, Pareto strove for the same ethically neutral type of analysis that characterized his economics.

Pareto's attitude toward social and economic policy was at first ultraliberal, in the European sense. He believed in total economic freedom, free trade, and *laissez-faire.* He found Italian politics disillusioning, however, and came to believe that corruption and incompetence were an integral part of the democratic process. His antipathy toward the Italian political scene, in fact, had led him to want to leave the country even before he received the appointment at Lausanne in 1893. His opposition to government actions, unlike that of British *laissez-faire* advocates, stemmed not from a dislike of strong governments, but from a belief that the ruling classes of Italy had lost their vitality and ability to rule effectively. Pareto, in short, believed in the importance of a strong government, an elite, that insisted on discipline and took a firm hand in providing the social and political stability essential for economic activity.

The concept of the elite is the key to understanding Pareto's theory of society, as well as the key to the philosophical underpinning of his economics. His initial approach to the idea of an elite came in his first major work in economics, the *Cours,* with his theory of the unequal distribution of income. This was an empirical generalization, based on statistical evidence from a number of countries, to the effect that an unequal distribution of income existed in all societies, irrespective of their particular form of political or economic organization, and irrespective even of attempts to impose egalitarian policies. Although Pareto admitted that his theory could be invalidated by contrary evidence, his position (and that of his followers) was essentially that no such evidence had been found, nor was it likely to be forthcoming. Inequality, as he defined it, was an empirical law of nature, often called Pareto's Law.

The second step in the development of Pareto's analysis of social structure was his identification of political slogans such as "justice" and "democracy" as rationalizations that veiled the true state of affairs and thereby misled and confused those who sought to analyze society. In his historical writings, in his *Les systèmes socalistes* (1902, 2 vols.), and later in his *Trattato,* Pareto argued that these were nonlogical terms that served only to cloak drives and bids by elites to obtain or keep power. They appealed to sentiment, not logic. At one stage, he criticized his own earlier beliefs by admitting that he had been unaware his reasoning attempted to give logical clothing to beliefs that were fundamentally emotional.

Once the verbal screen was penetrated, Pareto arrived at his theory of the circulation of elites. This theory, like that of Mosca, his contemporary, claimed that the history of society was a history of successive elites. One elite rises to power and assumes control, it then becomes decadent, loses its will to govern, and descends into oblivion as a new, highly motivated and disciplined group takes its place. In his essay on *The Rise and Fall of the Elites* (1901), in the *Manuel* (French ed., ch. II), and in the *Trattato,* Pareto developed and elaborated this theme. In essence, he claimed that there were various types of elites. Some emphasized innovation and achieved solutions through combinations, threats, and manipulation; others stressed consolidation and security, through force if necessary, and appealed to men's consciences, to religion and faith. The failure of an elite to include both groups, the innovators and the consolidators, led to its decline, quite possibly through revolution. Pareto's earlier empirical law of economic inequality was simply a description of the class relationships he now analyzed.

Pareto's social theory, formed before the advent of fascism in Italy, was later claimed as an ideological justification of that regime. The fascist government itself acclaimed his work and made him an honorary senator, a title he accepted. Yet he did not consider himself an advocate of fascist goals. He considered his sociological theory ethically neutral. There is little doubt, however, that he had strong motives for denying the desirability of reformism as a social philosophy and that he believed the establishment of a new government that would preserve order in Italian society after World War I was desirable.

Pareto's theory of the elite provided the framework for his pure economics. Although one of his followers described him as, in a sense, "two people," the lucid scientist and the polemicist, his perspective of the nature of economic analysis was nonetheless guided by the assumption that since noneconomic forces governed political power, the rational motivations underlying economic behavior could be examined without considering the political implications. It is not necessary here to review in detail his sociological theories of nonrational action. Briefly, he believed that political and other noneconomic motivations were what he called "residues," nonlogical motivations akin to instincts and variously distributed among individuals from birth, along with native abilities. They were unrelated, analytically, to man's rational, logical actions to satisfy his wants. Men attempted to justify their nonrational behavior by "theories," rationalizations he called "derivations." Since these were designed to explain the unexplainable, they were essentially myths, or ideologies like Marxism and utilitarianism.

Pareto argued that there was no unique relationship between the state and the economic forces within it. This made it possible for him to assume that economic analysis could be nonpolitical. We shall review four aspects of his analysis here: his theory of scientific method in economics, his analysis of demand, his general equilibrium theory, and certain characteristics of his approach to welfare theory.

The scientific objective of studies of economic relationships should be, said Pareto, solely the examination of the uniformities of economic phenomena, "that is, their laws, with no view of their direct practicality, without preoccupation in any manner with giving prescriptions or precepts, without even seeking the happiness, utility, or well-being of humanity or any one of its parts. The objective . . . is exclusively scientific; one wishes to understand, to know; and nothing else." (*Manuel,* p. 3) Pareto used the term "logico-experimental" to describe his method. By this he meant that theory was like a hypothesis, one that is worked out logically and tested by experience. (He recognized of course that in the social and economic world theories could not be tested by scientific experimentation.) In his article on "Mathematical Economics" (p. 58), he wrote, "From the purely theoretical point of view, these laws [of pure economics] could be any laws whatsoever; but it is evident that we must deal in particular with those which, in abstract form, can more or less readily correspond to concrete cases." And in his treatise on sociology, he wrote: "Theories, their principles, their implications, are altogether subordinate to facts and possess no other criterion of truth than their capacity for picturing them." (*The Mind and Society,* p. 30)

Pareto's method meant that all theories should be hypothetical in the sense that their verification was dependent wholly on experience and factual testing. Any assumption that there is an "essential property" of behavior—as in concepts of utility, for example—which cannot be tested empirically is metaphysical. Hypotheses would, of course, have to be revised as facts and observation revealed limitations and certain ones might be abandoned entirely. This procedure he called the process of "successive approximations."

Despite its hypothetical nature, however, it was essential to develop pure theory as such. There was no other way to analyze the complex interdependence of variables as individuals sought to satisfy their wants. In a response to criticism of his method from Benedetto Croce, a well-known Italian philosopher, Pareto wrote that he believed the economist's central problem to be this: "given certain individuals who have certain tastes revealed by their choice, and who encounter obstacles in satisfying their tastes, predict the phenomena which will occur in that society." On the basis of the fact of choice, and with the aid of mathematical logic, he said, one can establish the equations of interdependence needed to make those predictions.

Pareto argued that there was no difference in the methods of the natural sciences and economics. Pure economics was like pure mechanics or geometry. One began with an equilibrium and investigated the forces that produced it. Just as the area of an actual, more-or-less imperfect rectangle differed from the area defined by a geometrical theorem, so too the real economic world differed from the true, theoretical world. He also believed that economics must be mathematical. From the time economics "began to discuss quantities and to establish quantities and to establish the variations of those quantities it found itself within the realm of mathematics." ("Reply to Croce," p. 182) With mathematics, pure economics could describe exactly the interdependence among variables; "literary economists" who thought in terms of causal relationships, rather than interdependence were wrong when they sought to prove that costs of production *determined* value or that marginal utility was the *cause* of value. At the same time, however, Pareto believed in the desirability of attempting to translate pure mathematics into words; and like Marshall, he put the mathematics of his *Manuel* in an appendix.

Pareto assumed, finally, that his method made economics a science that was relatively free of ethical judgments which might impair its objectivity. This was true, however, only in ideal cases. Thus he stated in *Mind and Society:*

> Experimental science has no dogmas. . . . [T]he history of human knowledge clearly shows that all attempts to explain natural phenomena by means of propositions derived from religious or metaphysi-

cal principles have failed. Such attempts have finally been abandoned in astronomy . . . and all other similar sciences. If traces of them are still to be found in sociology and its sub-branches, law, political economy, ethics, and so on, that is simply because in those fields a strictly scientific status has not yet been achieved." (p. 26)

A value-free economics was a goal that probably could not be fully reached, and he admitted in another passage in *Mind and Society:*

The man entirely unaffected by sentiments and free from all bias, all faith, does not exist; and to regard that freedom as an essential prerequisite to profitable study of the social sciences would amount to saying that such study is impossible. (p. 72)

However he added immediately, "But experience shows that a person can as it were divide himself in two and, to an extent at least, lay aside his sentiments, preconceptions, and beliefs when engaged in a scientific pursuit, resuming them afterwards." Perhaps Pareto was examining his own behavior; after all, he himself had given the impression of being "two people," the pure scientist and the social critic.

Pareto's analysis of demand reflected his belief that theory should be testable with experience. This belief led to what is known as the generalized utility function, the abandonment of cardinal for ordinal utility, and indifference-curve analysis. In developing the first and last of these concepts, he was preceded by F. Y. Edgeworth, the British economist who authored *Mathematical Psychics* in 1881; [1] in the abandonment of cardinal utility he was preceded by Gustav Cassel, the Swedish economist, in 1899. Pareto seems, however, to have reached his position independently; moreover he was the only major World-War-I economist who tied the three concepts together.

The generalized utility function as defined by Pareto stated that the utility derived from the consumption of one good was dependent also on the supplies of other goods. Marshall and Jevons did not use this concept; rather, they assumed that the utility of a good was derived

---

[1] Francis Ysidra Edgeworth (1845–1926) was Drummond Professor of Political Economy at Oxford from 1891 to 1922, occupying the chair first held by Nassau Senior. His original work on contract curves, indifference curves, and statistics was done in London, before his appointment at Oxford. In 1881, he became the first editor of the *Economic Journal* of the Royal Economic Society, a position he held until his death in 1926. Edgeworth did not develop his ideas in economics into a larger, more systematic statement. A confirmed bachelor, he once told John Maynard Keynes, who was later joint editor of the *Journal* with him, that "large-scale enterprise, such as Treatises and marriage, had never appealed to him."

solely from that particular good and that the sum of the marginal utilities of all goods to the individual was obtainable through addition. Walras also accepted this position. In Marshall's analysis this approach led to an inconsistency, pointed out earlier in the discussion of his concept of consumers' surplus, because utilities of substitute goods could not be added. A further problem arose in connection with complementary goods. Pareto recognized the limitations of the additive utility function and saw that Marshall's assumption of the constant utility of money could not be maintained in a more general analysis of the demand function. One striking aspect of the generalized demand function was that when the possible interrelationships of demands for more than one commodity were considered it did not follow that the demand curve for a particular good necessarily sloped downward and to the right. The exception of the Giffen paradox, which Marshall had noted (see p. 216) was explainable within the context of the new approach. A price change of one commodity could affect the marginal "utility of money"; in later terminology, a price change could generate income effects which in turn affected the quantities of goods consumers purchased.

Pareto's development of ordinal utility came slowly. In the *Cours,* he dealt essentially with measurable utility, although even then he called utility *ophélimité* (desiredness) in an attempt to escape the implication that utility was cardinal and observable. Dissatisfaction with his original statement led him, in the *Manuel,* to a nearly complete avoidance of utility. All one needed to know, he said then, was whether a given collection of goods, in comparison with another, was more, less, or equally desirable, not the different amounts of "utility" involved. Economics, he said, was concerned with the concrete facts of experience, not with metaphysical states of mind. The "fact" here was the individual's actual choice:

> In the fact of the choice between ordinary wine and Rhine wine, it is not necessary for me to go beyond the bare fact of choice. Whether I have chosen it because I prefer Rhine wine, or because the doctor ordered it and I dislike ordinary wine, or because I want to drink a bottle with a friend who likes Rhine wine, or for any other reason; all this does not matter. I stop at the fact.

Ophélimité was only a word used to show that a choice (among alternatives) had been made.

Pareto easily incorporated indifference-curve analysis into an ordinal view of utility. In 1881, Edgeworth had used indifference curves to express equal amounts of measurable utility from combinations of two goods. In the *Manuel* Pareto found this unnecessary:

[Edgeworth] assumed the existence of utility (ophélimité) and deduced indifference curves; I assume, on the contrary, indifference curves as a given fact and deduce from them all that is necessary for equilibrium theory, without recourse to ophélimité. (p. 169, note 1)

An indifference curve, to Pareto, only represented various combinations of two commodities to which the buyer was indifferent; it separated those combinations he preferred from those that were less desirable. Higher indifference curves meant "more utility," but Pareto did not believe one could say how much more; nor did he believe it necessary to be able to do so. An index of *ophélimité* could be constructed, but it would indicate only higher preferences and have no quantitative significance.

One aspect of Pareto's theory of general equilibrium that also reflected his willingness to avoid a theoretical generalization when in doubt about the possibility of its empirical verification was the marginal-productivity theory of factor returns. At the turn of the century various economists in a number of countries were approaching the problem in different ways. Walras had not introduced the possibility of variable factor proportions until the third edition of his *Elements* in 1896, having based his original theory on the proposition that factors were used together in production in fixed proportions. When Pareto took up the problem at about the same time he came to the conclusion that the "exhaustion" of total receipts assumed in some statements of the marginal-productivity theory was unnecessary and made it "erroneous." (One common version of the theory stated that if each factor in a productive combination received a price that was equal, because of competition, to its marginal contribution to the final product, the sum total of factor payments would exhaust (i. e., equal) the total receipts. It was further implied that if all factors were increased proportionately the output of the firm would increase in the same proportion.)

Pareto argued against this doctrine, saying that in certain instances one factor could not be increased without increasing others (i.e., technical coefficients were often fixed), that in other cases the supplies of certain factors might be so limited that expansion could not occur, and that in yet others a factor might not be divisible into small units. He did not deny that the achievement of general equilibrium conditions in a free, competitive market required the payment of factors in accordance with their marginal productivity; what he denied was the assumption that if each factor received its marginal product there would be nothing left. In other words, he denied that the sum of the marginal productivity times the quantity of each factor equaled the total product: There could be something left, something unexplained by marginal productivity. Pareto's own conclusion was that the excess was related to the phenomenon of rent. (See his "Mathematical Economics" p. 99f.)

Using his concept of ordinal utility and general equilibrium theory, as a basis, he constructed a theory of social welfare that became known as the *Pareto optimum*. This theory stated simply that the optimum welfare of a society is achieved when each of its members has found, through the process of production and exchange, an equilibrium position impossible to improve, assuming that the prices obtaining in the market are established through competition. This position of "maximum of ophélimité" occurred where

> it was impossible to find a way of moving a very small distance from that position so that the ophélimité enjoyed by each individual increases or decreases. That is to say, that any small departure from that position necessarily causes an increase in the ophélimité which some individuals enjoy and diminish that which others enjoy: It will be agreeable to some and disagreeable to others. (p. 354)

The theory also said that with different initial stocks of goods in the hands of individuals, a new general equilibrium would be reached, through competition, and that this new equilibrium could not be considered better or worse in terms of welfare than the former one. Pareto, in short, considered any equilibrium reached through competition an optimum-welfare situation. If for any reason a general equilibrium was not reached, then further exchanges (assuming competition) could improve the position of the trading parties without injury to any party. But in any unilateral transfer of property from one individual to another, one would benefit while the other would lose. Pareto's argument via the ordinal chain of reasoning was that as there was no way of comparing the subjective worth of such gains and losses, one could not conclude that aggregate welfare was raised or lowered by the transfers.

Pareto's theory of welfare had significant political implications. What was essential to his theory of the optimum was competition, not the distribution of income. On the one hand, he was criticizing writers like the British classical and neoclassical economists who had used cardnal utility to justify reducing inequalities in income. But on the other hand, he was subtly undermining the long-cherished belief that the market economy as it had evolved historically inevitably maximized welfare. To Pareto, competition was not a necessary result of the market system. He castigated the society of his day as one ruled not by competition, but by monopoly, greed, intrigue, and deceit: "Our ruling class is insatiable; as its power wanes, its fraudulent practices increase." (*The Rise and Fall of the Elites*, p. 69) In the *Manuel*, he denounced this type of monopolistic society as one in which prices diverged from costs (pp. 166f) and it was impossible to maximize *ophélimité* by private trading.

In addition to private market systems governed by competition and private market systems run by monopolists, Pareto defined a third type of social system which he called a collectivist system, an economy where monopoly power was exercised by the government in the interest of the economy as a whole. In this system, prices did not equal costs, but were set in accordance with whatever criteria the central authority considered relevant. On the basis of its ethical principles or other guidelines, such a government could establish whatever distribution policy it deemed best. But how should production be organized in order to achieve the maximum welfare of all citizens? Pareto believed that production in such a society should be organized in a way that approximated the allocation of resources that would have occurred if, given the new distribution, the economy were run competitively. If the collectivist society wanted to abolish private property and hence the payment of interest on capital, it could do so; but it would still have to estimate returns on capital in its planning. Moreover, even though prices are set to achieve social goals rather than to cover costs, the central planners must know the true prices of things (their value) if "the minister of production" is not to "proceed blindly," not knowing "how to organize production." (*Manuel*, p. 362). Pareto saw no reason why welfare could not be maximized in a collectivist economy if the planners applied the principles of general equilibrium theory to allocation problems.

Pure economics alone, said Pareto, could give "no truly decisive criterion" for choosing between a society founded on private property and one based on socialist principles. (*Manuel*, p. 364) He was no socialist himself, but he believed that no welfare optimum could be obtained under the conditions prevailing in his day. His pure economics did, however, provide a foundation for his hopes that a new political elite could reorganize the economy, ending the arbitrary exercise of private monopolistic power and making possible a "maximum of *ophélimité*."

Criticism of Pareto's theories, especially his approach to welfare economics continues, and in one basic respect he was his own critic. He made clear the importance of distinguishing between problems of income distribution and problems of resource allocation. But whether the actual divorce of one from the other can be so easily arranged is less obvious. Pareto's own theory of the elite argues against it. If elites dominate social systems, how can the distribution of wealth and income be manipulated except within the limits imposed by the elite itself? Pareto's attack on measures of social welfare in terms of the common good, aggregate utility, or whatever broad gauges of social benefit other economists might employ turn out in the end to be one of his own "derivations"—a justification of elite decision-making.

Notes to Chapter x

Arthur L. Bowley was one of the first to present mathematical versions of the theories of the Lausanne school. His book *Mathematical Groundwork of Economics* appeared in Great Britain in 1924. Gustav Cassel, the Swedish economist who followed Walras but weeded out utility connotations from demand theory, introduced Walrasian analysis without mathematics in his *Theory of Social Economy* (1918; English trans., 1924). In the 1930s, Pareto's ordinal theory began to take hold. R. G. D. Allen and John R. Hicks brought out the power of indifference curves, and Hicks' Pareto-based *Value and Capital* (1939) soon became standard fare for aspiring economists. In the United States, the first exposition of general equilibrium was by Henry Schultz in 1929. The influence of the ordinal theory was especially clear in the works of Paul A. Samuelson on revealed preference in the 1930s and in his *Foundations of Economic Analysis* (1947).

Pareto's views on welfare theory, which had to compete with the dominant Marshall-Pigou point of view based on cardinal utility, began to win converts and gradually became

the acknowledged fountainhead of modern welfare economics. The line of development ran from Pareto to Enrico Barone, one of his followers, whose 1908 article on the possibility of a rational allocation of economic resources in a socialist state was translated and published in 1935 by F. A. Hayek in *Collectivist Economic Planning*. With the writings of Abram Bergson, A. P. Lerner, Oscar Lange, Samuelson, and others that appeared at about the same time or shortly thereafter, the new field of welfare economics grew, guided by Pareto's belief that utility could neither be measured nor made interpersonally comparable. The Pareto-Barone position also stimulated a new interest in the economics of socialism and planned economies. Pareto's views on the scientific necessity of avoiding value judgments meanwhile found support in a highly influential work by British economist Lionel Robbins, *An Essay on the Nature and Significance of Economic Science* (1932).

Input-output analysis, which seeks to establish the empirically relevant economic relationships among industries so that the effects of a change in one can be estimated, quantitatively, for every other industry, was built on Walrasian foundations (with Quesnay's *Tableau Économique* and Marx's theory of interindustry relationships more distant influences). The founder of the technique, which has many uses, was Wassily W. Leontief (b. 1906), who examined first the Soviet balance of trade and then the American economy in "Quantitative Input-Output Relations in the Economic System of the United States," published in *The Review of Economics and Statistics* (August 1936) and in *The Structure of the American Economy* (1941).

The Lausanne school stimulated the use of mathematics in economics, statistical data-gathering, and econometric methods. R. G. D. Allen, for example, published his *Mathematical Analysis for Economists* in 1938. (Allen had earlier introduced Paretian value theory in an article co-authored by John R. Hicks, "Reconsideration of the Theory of Value," *Economica*, in February–May 1934). The historical roots of empirical economic research, of mathematics in economic analysis, and of statistical and econometric testing of hypotheses, however, are found in many different places and schools of thought. The founding of the Econometric Society in 1930, for example, resulted from an initial meeting of Ragnar Frisch of Oslo and Charles F. Roos of Cornell with Irving Fisher of Yale. Fisher, who had long been engaged in mathematical and statistical research, was the organization's first president. (See John Perry Miller, "Irving Fisher of Yale," in William Fellner *et al., Ten Economic Studies in the Tradition of Irving Fisher,* New York, Wiley, 1967, pp. 12–13.) Another American economist who pioneered in this area before World War I was Henry Ludwell Moore, a professor at Columbia. (See George J. Stigler, "Henry L. Moore and Statistical Economics" in his *Essays in the History of Economics,* Chicago and London, University of Chicago Press, 1965, pp. 343–373.) Both Fisher and Moore had met Walras and Pareto on trips to Europe.

Pareto's influence also was apparent in the shift of economic opinion away from Keynes's criticisms of the inequality in the distribution of income as a source of the difficulty in maintaining an adequate level of investment. In contrast to Keynes the new Keynesians, like Hicks and Samuelson, believed that, properly applied, the rules of government finance ("functional finance," to use Abba P. Lerner's phrase) for achieving and maintaining full employment could work, regardless of the distribution of income. They attempted to convert his economics into a set of value-free, instrumentalist techniques that could be subsumed within the larger framework of Paretian analysis.

I

References in the text to Walras are to Léon Walras, *Elements of Pure Economics, or The Theory of Social Wealth,* trans. by William Jaffé, published for the American Economic Association and The Royal Economic Society (Homewood, Ill., Irwin, 1954). The work, under the title of *Elements d'économie politique pure,* appeared originally in two parts, the first (on exchange) in 1874 and the second (on production) in 1877. They were published together in subsequent editions, the second in 1889, a third in 1896, and a fourth in 1900. Walras introduced variable proportions into his production theory in the third edition. Jaffé's translation is of the fourth definitive edition, published posthumously in 1926, which incorporates corrections made after 1900 but unpublished by Walras. Jaffé is also the editor of *Correspondence of Léon Walras and Related Papers* (Amsterdam, North Holland Publishing, 1965), 3 vols.

Walras's two other major publications, *Etudes d'économie social* (1896) and *Etudes d'économie politique appliquée* (1898), have not been translated. They are actually collections of studies on separate topics. For biographical material on Walras, see Jaffé's introduction to the two works cited and Joseph A. Schumpeter's *Ten Great Economists: From Marx to Keynes* (New York, Oxford University Press, 1951), pp. 74–79.

Walras's attitudes toward land reform were based on the premise that individual faculties and abilities were naturally the property of the individual, whereas land was naturally the property of the state. (See, for example, his letter of April 2, 1902, to Paul Jules Pic, in *Correspondence* (*op. cit.*), vol. III, pp. 200 ff.) Walras distinguished his attitude from that of Henry George on the grounds that the latter believed in a radical solution to the problem of land ownership whereas he was willing to take a slower and less drastic approach.

For specific evaluations of Walras, see Milton Friedman, "Léon Walras and His Economic System," *The American Economic Review,* vol. XLV (December 1955), pp. 900–

909; John R. Hicks, "Léon Walras," *Econometrica,* vol. 2 (October 1934), pp. 338–348. For a description of Walras's theory of distribution, see George J. Stigler, *Production and Distribution Theories: The Formative Period* (New York, Agathon Press, 1968). This study was first published in 1941. For a history of the general development of marginal-utility theory during this period, see R. S. Howey, *The Rise of the Marginal Utility School, 1870–1889* (Lawrence, University of Kansas Press, 1960). For a discussion of Walras's theory of "groping," see William Jaffé, "Walras' Theory of Tâtonnement: A Critique of Recent Interpretations," *The Journal of Political Economy,* vol. 75 (February 1967), pp. 1–19.

II

Pareto's major works were *Cours d'économie politique,* 2 vols. (Lausanne, 1896–97) and *Manuele d'economia politica;* (1906), translated into French as *Manuel d'économie politique* by Alfred Bonnet in 1909. (The references in the text are to the Paris edition, Marcel Giard, 1927 and are translated by the author.) The French edition also contains his mathematical appendix. Pareto's 1911 article "Mathematical Economics" is found in *International Economic Papers,* No. 5, translated for the International Economic Association (London, Macmillan, 1955), pp. 58–102. Pareto's *Les systèmes socialistes* appeared in two volumes in 1902–03.

Pareto's major sociological work was *The Mind and Society* (Trattato di Sociologia generale), ed. by Arthur Livingston (New York, Harcourt, Brace, 1935, 4 vols. An earlier study of his, *The Rise and Fall of the Elites: an Application of Theoretical Sociology,* is available, with an introduction by Hans L. Zetterburg, from Bedminster Press (Totowa, N. J., 1968).

For biographical studies and general evaluations of Pareto, see Joseph A. Schumpeter, *Ten Great Economists* (*op. cit.*), pp. 110–142; Franz Borkenau, *Pareto* (New York, Wiley, 1936); and "Demaria on Pareto," in Henry W. Spiegel, ed., *The Development of Economic Thought* (New York, Wiley, 1952), pp. 628–651. Pareto's statement concerning the importance of Walras's theories is quoted by Demaria on p. 635.

In the United States, Pareto became widely known in the 1930s for his sociology. His influence was especially evident in the works of Talcott Parsons, although it was probably less decisive with respect to Parson's attempted development of a value-free sociology than the works of Max Weber, the German economist and socialist. (The same could be said of Pareto's influence on Lionel Robbins' work on method, *The Nature and Significance of Economic Science.*) For an analysis of Pareto's methods, see Vincent J. Tarascio, *Pareto's Methodological Approach to Economics: A Study in the History of Some Scientific Aspects of Economic Thought* (Chapel Hill, University of North Carolina Press, 1966).

For a biography of Edgeworth, see John Maynard Keynes, *Essays in Biography,* reprinted in *Essays, Sketches in Biography* (New York, Meridian Books, 1956), pp. 95–113. The quoted remark of Edgeworth is from p. 108.

For a recent critical appraisal of "Pareto's Law," see Paul A. Samuelson, "A Fallacy in the Introduction of Pareto's Law of Alleged Constancy of Income Distribution," *Rivista Internazionale di Scienzo Economiche e Commerciali,* vol. XII (March 1965), pp. 246–250.

Pareto's statement to Croce on economics is from Vilfredo Pareto "On the Economic Phenomenon: A Reply to Benedette Croce," *International Economic Papers,* No. 3 (London, Macmillan, 1953), p. 185; his description of the "fact of choice" occurs on p. 191.

For an analysis of Pareto's role in the development of demand theory, see George J. Stigler, "The Development of Utility Theory (1950)," in *Essays in the History of Economics* (*op. cit.*), pp. 66–155. For a description of his production theories, see Stigler, *Production and Distribution Theories* (*op. cit.*), pp. 364ff. Schumpeter examines the tangled history of the production function in his *History of Economic Analysis* (*op cit.*), pp. 1926–1053.

The basic proposition of Pareto's welfare theory was that questions of the distribution of income could be treated independently of pure economics. There are two problems, said Pareto, to be resolved if we are to maximize the welfare of a community:

> 1. We have a problem of distribution: how ought the goods which individuals or society produces be divided among its members? It is necessary to apply ethical and social considerations, and comparisons of ophélimité among different individuals. . . .
> 2. We have a problem of production: how to produce economic goods in the manner by which, fol-

lowing their distribution given by the rules obtained by the answer to the first problem, the members of society obtain a maximum of ophélimité. (*Manuel,* p. 362)

Pareto expressed this point of view as early as 1897. (See *Cours,* vol. II, pp. 90ff.) This proposition made it possible for him to assume that he could advocate economic policies objectively for a regime he personally found repugnant.

Enrico Barone, who was also a critic of socialism, developed the economic principles of socialist production on the same assumption in an article translated and published as "The Ministry of Production in the Collectivist State," in F. A. Hayek, ed., *Collectivist Economic Planning: Critical Studies in the Possibilities of Socialism* (London, Routledge & Kegan Paul, 1935). The article originally appeared under the title "Il ministro della produzione nello stato collettivista," in *Giornale degli Economisti e Rivista di Statistica,* ser. 2a (September-October 1908), pp. 267–293, 391–414.

Controversy over the Pareto-Barone theory of welfare increased sharply during the 1930s. The issue of national pricing policies under socialism was analyzed by Abram Bergson in "A Reformulation of Certain Aspects of Welfare Economics," *Quarterly Journal of Economics,* vol. LII (February 1938), pp. 310–334; Benjamin E. Lippincott, ed., in *On The Economic Theory of Socialism* (Minneapolis, University of Minnesota Press, 1938); H. D. Dickinson in *Economics of Socialism* (London, Oxford University Press, 1939); and Maurice Dobb in *Political Economy and Capitalism*

(London, Routledge, 1937). The general import of these discussions was that the Austrian belief in the impossibility of a rational allocation of economic resources under socialism was erroneous.

The discussion of welfare economics ranged over a wider area. A central problem was whether the value judgments of the community concerning income distribution could be divorced from the determination of a maximum-welfare position. In general, the answer at that time was yes, but it was pointed out that some third party to private transactions would be necessary to arrange desired transfers of income. The following are some of the leading articles of the period on the subject: Harold Hotelling, "The General Welfare in Relation to Problems of Taxation and of Railway and Utility Rates," *Econometrica,* vol. VI (July 1938), pp. 242–269. Nicholas Kaldor, "Welfare Propositions of Economics and Interpersonal Comparisons of Utility," *Economic Journal,* vol. XLIX (September 1939), pp. 549–552. J. R. Hicks, "Foundations of Welfare Economics," *ibid.,* vol. XLIX (December 1939), pp. 696–712; Tibor Scitovsky, "A Note on Welfare Propositions in Economics," *Review of Economic Studies,* vol. IX (November 1941), pp. 77–88; Oscar Lange, "The Foundations of Welfare Economics," *Econometrica,* vol. X (July-October 1942), pp. 215–228; and G. J. Stigler, "The New Welfare Economics," *American Economic Review,* vol. XXXIII (June 1943), pp. 355–359. See also Paul A. Samuelson, *Foundations of Economic Analysis* (Cambridge, Mass., Harvard University Press, 1947).

Postscript:

THE SIGNIFICANCE
OF CONTROVERSY

Economics cannot escape the value judgments that characterize the society it analyzes. Although economic principles may be laid down with due regard to testing hypotheses derived from them through experience in accordance with objective scientific standards, the social perspectives of economists furnish the valuation framework that guides the initial development of theories as well as their interpretation and application.

All the economists described here brought great ability, scholarship, and insight to bear on the development of their theoretical systems. Yet each had a viewpoint concerning what was important and unimportant in social relationships that gave consistency to the ideas he advanced. Social judgments were clearly not sufficient conditions for the development of theory, but they were probably necessary ones.

New visions, or perspectives, are relevant even in the development of physical sciences. The innovator, however well he understands the science of the period, is always one who is able to reach beyond current ideas and interpret the world differently. Thomas S. Kuhn in *The Structure of Scientific Revolutions* uses the term "normal science" to indicate a prevailing interpretation of past scientific theories that a "particular scientific community acknowledges for a time as supplying the foundation for its further practice." (p. 10) Such theories, which he calls "paradigms," attract a group of adherents who find them "sufficiently open-ended to leave all sorts of problems for the redefined group of practitioners to resolve." (*ibid.*)

Kuhn's theory of scientific revolutions attempted to explain why the normal science of one period was displaced in another by a new normal science. The rise of new paradigms, according to Kuhn, was the result not of a greater and greater store of knowledge, but rather of the recog-

281

nition of facts not adequately explained by the old theories. Normal science, says Kuhn perceptively, "does not aim at novelties of fact or theory." (p. 52) In fact, practitioners of a science governed by a particular paradigm, having enough to do to work out the implications of their own theorems, tend to resist new points of view. Yet anomalies, awareness of unexplained phenomena, and problems in interpretation do arise; and at this point a different theoretical approach may attract adherents who vigorously proclaim its success in resolving incongruities. In order to supplant the old normal science, however, the new view must open up previously unrecognized areas for research as well as shed new light on the interpretation of old problems. The new paradigm must be a theory capable of development, not simply a critique of the present way of thinking.

In many respects, Kuhn's theory of scientific revolution describes the history of economic theory. The major economists reviewed in these chapters, from the Physiocrats to Pareto, introduced different ways of looking at economic phenomena. Their new theoretical systems, or paradigms, attracted followers, stimulated new research, led to the investigation of subareas, and at the same time both excluded the old paradigms and frowned on later critics with new ones. Moreover, rarely does everyone at any given time adhere to a single paradigm; a cross-sectional inspection of the intellectual community generally reveals supporters of different paradigms, each competing for greater recognition. In the post-World-War-II era, there have been conflicts between the followers of Keynes and the older Marshallians, between the cardinalists and Pareto ordinalists, and between advocates of other theoretical positions that have not been reviewed.

Our purpose here is not to identify the components of the present normal science of economics and their historical roots; rather it is to indicate some of the features of the process by which new theoretical systems have been formed in the past. In that process there is a fundametal difference between the natural sciences discussed by Kuhn and economics. Value judgments affect all social-science categories; concepts such as income, wealth, and well-being are open to different interpretations. These interpretations are not "given," but arise out of different viewpoints concerning social objectives. Nor can we assume, as Pareto sometimes did, that society is free to "choose" its ethical standards. On the contrary, controversies over social values will remain so long as there are classes, groups, and nations with conflicting interests.

The distinction typically made by economists between positive and normative economics in an attempt to disentangle social valuations from a hard core of pure theory does not resolve the controversy. The positive approach, it is said, yields relationships on which all economists can agree. It is true, as John Stuart Mill and others have pointed out, that pure theory, with its rigorous and mathematical logic, is technically correct if it meets the test of internal consistency. If it can pass the test of empirical verification (or at least cannot be proven false by data), then so much the better. But, as Mill knew, the question still remains whether the explanation of any one set of "facts" is relevant or if there are other "facts" and problems more in need of explanation. New social perspectives that provoke controversy help economists find this out.

References

Thomas S. Kuhn, *The Structure of Scientific Revolutions* (Chicago and London, University of Chicago Press, 1962), originally issued as vol. II, no. 2, of the International Encyclopedia of Unified Science, University of Chicago Press.

Sherman Roy Krupp, ed., *The Structure of Economic Science: Essays on Methodology* (Englewood Cliffs, N. J., Prentice-Hall, 1966), especially Part I, "Theory and Dispute in Economics," and the articles by Martin Bronfenbrenner, Henry Margenau, Fritz Machlup, and Lawrence Nabers.

Robert V. Eagly, *Events, Ideology, and Economic Theory: The Determinants of Progress in the Development of Economic Analysis* (Detroit, Wayne State University Press, 1968).

INDEX

1 2 3 4 5 6 7 8 9 10 11 12 13 14 15   88 87 86 85 84 83 82 81 80 79 78 77 76 75 74 73 72